The Writings of Richard Stern

The Writings of Richard Stern

The Education of an Intellectual Everyman

DAVID GARRETT IZZO

McFarland & Company, Inc., Publishers
Jefferson, North Carolina, and London

Frontispiece: Richard Stern in Costa Rica, 1996. (Photograph by Alane Rollings.)

Library of Congress Cataloguing-in-Publication Data

Izzo, David Garrett.
    The writings of Richard Stern : the education of an intellectual
Everyman / David Garrett Izzo.
       p.   cm.
    Includes bibliographical references and index.
    "Richard Stern bibliography": p.
    ISBN 0-7864-1182-1 (softcover : 50# alkaline paper) ∞
    1. Stern, Richard G., 1928– — Criticism and interpretation.
    2. Stern, Richard G., 1928– — Knowledge and learning.
    3. United States—Intellectual life—20th century.   I. Title.
PS3569.T39Z72   2002
813'.54 — dc21   2001044073

British Library cataloguing data are available

On the cover: Richard Stern in California circa 1975. Photograph by
Elyse Lewin

Manufactured in the United States of America

McFarland & Company, Inc., Publishers
  Box 611, Jefferson, North Carolina 28640
    www.mcfarlandpub.com

To RGS for the night he read;
To Carol Ann Corrody, who loved what she heard.
To Melvin Smith, who kept Springfield Station
smiling and now rides with the angels.

Contents

Preface

In January 1999 I was seeking contributors for an essay collection I would be editing on W. H. Auden. I looked up the faculty at University of Chicago, and Richard Stern sounded like a possibility. For ten years I had been reading and writing about authors who began writing in the 1920s and 1930s— Aldous Huxley, W. H. Auden, Christopher Isherwood, Stephen Spender, Thornton Wilder, Stephen Vincent Benet, Archibald MacLeish, et al.— and my contemporary reading was nil.

Richard Stern agreed to write "With Auden," and it was quite wonderful. I thought the least I could do was to become acquainted with his other work. I started with his collected stories in *Noble Rot* and found them astoundingly good. I moved on to his other stories, novels, and essays with no less admiration. I was inspired to correspond with Stern again, this time on a personal level. To my delight, a lively e-mail exchange ensued, and our correspondence grew voluminous and wide-ranging over time.

We met in person when he was a visiting professor at Stanford and I was living in Chico, California. He is a gentleman and a "mensch"— a Yiddish word for a kind and nurturing soul.

I confess that my admiration for Stern's work and his being are very high. I am confident, however, that this admiration has had no undue influence on the critical evaluation that follows. Stern has never asked for, nor have I wanted to send him, any of this study to read before publication. We agreed that he would not see it until it was in print.

Richard Stern has been compared to Bellow and Roth, and both Bellow and Roth say he is a writer's writer whom people should make sure to read. Stern has not had their commercial success; yet he has been one of the most critically praised and award-winning writers of the last 50 years. And he writes still. More or less concurrent with this book, Stern, at age 73, has published another novel, *Pacific Tremors*, and another collection of essays, *What Is What Was*.

1

I wrote this book as a labor of love for a man that I feel privileged to know. I also wrote it as a service to intelligent readers who seek intelligent writers. This study is about the education of an intellectual Everyman. It is also about the education I gained as a reader of Stern's work.

Special thanks to Matthew Cowherd who assisted in the compilation of the bibliography.

— David Garrett Izzo

Abbreviations for Works Quoted in Text

G	Golk
E	Europe, or Up and Down with Schreiber and Baggish
IC	In Any Case
T	Teeth, Dying and Other Matters
ST	Stitch
HW	Honey and Wax
68	1968
FH	The Books in Fred Hampton's Apartment
OM	Other Men's Daughters
NS	Natural Shocks
IR	Invention of the Real
P	Packages
PB	Position of the Body
FW	A Father's Words
NR	Noble Rot
ON	One Person and Another
SH	Shares and Other Fictions
SIS	A Sistermony
Antioch	Antioch Review (Fall 2000)
PT	Pacific Tremors
TLS	Times Literary Supplement

Introduction

If we analogize the writer to an assassin, the reader is the corpse, the critic the coroner-detective. The feelings of the assassin and the victim are notably different, but at least for our purposes they can be called powerful ones. In the former's case, they are organized by purposiveness, in the latter's by force (scarcely conceived and rapidly terminated). The coroner-critic is the rationalist, the reconstructionist; he cannot alter the responses of the reader-victim, but he can, in a sense, alter those of future readers in such fashion that their reactions will be affected by his notions.
— Richard Stern (*FH* 249)

One of America's best kept literary secrets is that for nearly three decades [now four decades], Richard Stern has been writing some of the country's most wryly intelligent, entertainingly various ... fiction.... Mr. Stern has done as much to pry open the possibilities of the short story and the long story as any of his more illustrious contemporaries.... Stern's novels are robustly intelligent, very funny, and beguilingly humane. He knows as much as anyone writing American prose about family mischief, intellectual shenanigans, love blunders — and about writing American prose.
— Philip Roth

Richard Stern is one of America's most acclaimed writers of fiction, and his novels and short stories have been critically praised by critics and peers for 50 years. His collected stories in *Noble Rot 1949–1989* earned Stern a Book of the Year Award from the *Chicago Sun-Times,* which called him, in effect, a writer other writers want to read and an accomplished man of letters whose academic career and essays added to his depth as an intellectual Everyman. His fiction challenges his readers by assuming that they will comprehend *and* appreciate a sensibility, vocabulary, and allusions that require a degree of erudition that is not limited to degrees of formal education but include the post–World War II *Sturm and Drang* indicative of an era that in 1947 was suitably named by W. H. Auden as *The Age of Anxiety*. While Stern's fiction and essays can be appreciated by any generation, his readers will be acutely aware that they could only have been written by a man who is consumed by the compulsion to write about, or rather mirror, the *Zeitgeist* of *his* generation, *his* era, *his* age, *his* life. One of his characters, a Stern surrogate, is described thus: "So Edward's new essay ends. It is something for him, and he holds the typed sheets in fingers so sensitively agitated by the fatigue of typing and the excitement of release that he can feel the prickle of the black letters under his fingertips" (*ST* 138). Stern says of another Stern surrogate in *Natural Shocks*, "His real existence is at his Smith-Corona" (*NS* 49). Stern writes because he must, and he will write, as he says, for an audience of one: "Tales are told, narratives are narrated to someone, even if the someone be but the narrator's own shadow, that inner doubter in quest of reassurance, charity, or remembrance" (*HW* 9).

Stern's inner journey as an intellectual Everyman by no means implies a style measured in abstract introspection. This acutely sensitive man makes his self-estimations as an emotional antihero that is, in fact, the dominant hero of Stern's generation. He makes his quest with a great expenditure of sweat and blood that is made symptomatically as the by-product of living in his anxious environment, which is also our anxious environment. To write is a means of escape. To read is also a means of escape.

W. H. Auden — a hero of Stern's — wrote that "The identification of fantasy is always an attempt to avoid one's own suffering: the identification of art is a *sharing* in the suffering of another."[1] With Stern, readers identify with the tears and fears of his characters because they are palpably and accessibly identifiable. Readers recognize, through Stern's characters, the author's suffering because as an Everyman he is one of them. Auden then said, borrowing from Yeats, that the writer should convey the thoughts of the wise man in the speech of the common people. Stern's content may be intellectual but his prose style is also palpably accessible in a manner that could be called street-smart colloquialism for intelligent grown-ups. Embedded in Stern's ear-tuned way with words are explicit and tacit references to names, places, and ideas that an intellectual Everyman would muse about. For the reader a certain amount of cultural literacy is very helpful, if not strictly required, in enhancing the overall effect of Stern's work. There is explicit erudition. In his work *Natural Shocks*, Stern relates the story of a writer in New York City who is to write about dying; his subject, Francesca Buell, is a 22-year-old woman with cancer. After the first interview session,

Wursup walked out of the angled streets of the Upper Village, up Seventh Avenue into the small-business world of candy stores, diners, bars, novelty shops. He wanted to buy something for Francesca. Some terrific necklace of fur, or a picture.... What kind? Some Pollock calligraph, indecipherably beautiful, a gorgeous tangle into which she could dip into whatever she needed. Or maybe some confident Renaissance beauty, A Titian portrait of a doge, or a Piero della Francesca encounter — the Queen of Sheba and Solomon (souvenir of their own meeting). Or woods, isolated, empty, the lights fuzzy. He'd give her his postcards; at least he'd pick a hundred beautiful ones from all over, make her a little museum. Or would that make her see how much she'd never see? [*NS* 97]

Then there is tacit erudition. In the novel *Stitch*, the damaged protagonist, who has been left by his wife, reacts to the murder of President Kennedy:

From the first hours, after the first shock wave had passed, it was clear to Edward that what had happened in Texas had to do with everything that had happened to him. It really struck him when he heard the first surfers the next day. They made the same bird noises, their shark boards still zoomed in over the waters; nothing had changed for them. The water was here, the sun was out, the tide was in. What did they have to do with what happened? With what ever happened? Their stock of the past was like the birds' corralled into a few instincts plus a few syllables, automobiles, cans. Their memory was yesterday's waves. Reality was what was in your sights. The past was what you desired right now [*ST* 200].

In this passage, Stern gives homage to W. H. Auden, who was one of his earliest influences, by referring to the same theme Auden put forth in one of his most well-known poems, "Musée des Beaux Arts." Auden wrote it prompted by his seeing a particular painting, Brueghel's *Icarus*, which galvanized his emotions about life in general. Auden writes that the world goes on performing its daily, utilitarian tasks regardless of the disasters that occur simultaneously. Witnesses may notice the fall of Icarus into the ocean because of the boy's hubris that took him to close to the sun, but the farm work still needs to be done and this takes precedence. And the ship one sees in the painting may have also seen the falling boy, but it "Had somewhere to get to and calmly sailed on."[2]

In real life, in Wholly Truthful art, and in Stern, the exigencies of daily existence continue; tragedies are interruptions, but the world, if not necessarily particular individuals, goes on just as always.

Stern can also be very funny. The early short stories of the 1950s to 1962 along with his first two novels, *Golk*, 1960, and *Europe, Or Up and Down with Baggish and Schreiber*, 1961, are essentially comic while having

serious intimations; some of his later work is essentially serious with
moments of comic relief. Most often the serious and comic intertwine
with each work choosing to tip the scale slightly one way or the other
depending on the author's inclination. The often deadpan humor may be
in the form of bemusedly sardonic asides:

> Nothing of course came from the two boys of Harvey Mendel, though
> they had lived in the Winthrop [hotel] for fifteen years. [Miss Swindleman]
> was the only person in the hotel — probably including Mendel — who
> remembered their mother. Ina Mendel, a name like a sigh, a nice Jewish
> woman who talked to her in a flutey little voice. No traveler, but nonethe-
> less had once bought her a postcard of the Roman Forum before being told
> only mailed postcards were posted up [on the hotel bulletin board]. Ina
> took plenty from the two nut sons. Sonny, who at age fourteen, was nearly
> arrested for lowering an armchair out of the eleventh story to an accom-
> plice on the ground in full view of eighty-sixth street. He'd been hauled in
> ... by Lester, the cabbie, who looked up from examining one of the pigeons
> he liked to grab at the throat and pick at with his pen knife. Just last year,
> Sonny, now known as Harvey, had proved his early promise by being jailed
> for three months in Phoenix, Arizona, on a charge of taking pornographic
> pictures. The second nut was Burton, the railroad buff, who spent hours in
> the lobby memorizing the time-tables, but couldn't figure out change for a
> quarter. Ina lasted six-years, then went on the operating table to be knifed
> to death by some Lester of a surgeon ["Wanderers," *T* 49].

There is also sharply sarcastic repartee such as between two "friends"
in Paris where one is a perpetual moocher on the other:

> Higgins visits to Rue Verneuil usually revolved around borrowing money;
> he was on the GI Bill, while I was "on" the somewhat more luxurious pro-
> visions of the Fulbright Act. He paid for the loans, I suppose, by attending
> to my musical insights and two-fingered performances. That first winter I
> was analysing Beethoven's Opus 2, Number 2.
> "Listen to this figure," I'd say, hacking out a few measures from the stretto
> in the first movement. "Hear what's it doing?"
> "I need three thousand francs," he'd reply.
> "In the wallet. Listen again," and I bent to the figure. "Pure quartet writ-
> ing. The Dutchman was no more at home in the pianoforte than you were
> in Minneapolis."
> "Manitoba," said Higgins, fingering the franc notes.
> "Did you ever hear Backhaus play it? He doesn't even suspect what's going
> on."
> "Maybe he sees it another way."
> "Exactly."
> "What a loss to music when you took up the electoral college, Bucky."

"Bucky" is a fond idiocy of my family; the proper reduction of my name is Fred.

"I guess you're just a mechanic Higgins. A fish with gills, but can't tell sea from Siam."

"Come buy me a drink," he'd finish, and we'd go down to the corner bistro where I had an account.

Practically, the only entertainments we went to in Paris were concerts. Indeed, the day [his wife] Elizabeth went to the hospital to produce Danielle, Higgins called to see if I wouldn't buy her ticket to the Gieseking recital that night. Since I had loaned him the money for both tickets, I said I'd resume possession of one of them.

"Usurer," said Higgins.

"All right. I'll buy it at half price," I said, the thought of Higgins' new hostage to fortune tugging at my bachelor heart.

"I'd rather give it away," said Higgins, whose principles were of iron.

"Done," said I.

"But I paid all..." ["Assessment of an Amateur," *T* 32–33].

Within Stern's humor one sees the implications of characterization. Higgins's mooching might not seem such a fatal flaw if it were not attached to a more serious selfishness. He is a man who would rather go out than be with his wife on the night when she has given birth to their daughter during the day. Stern does not hammer readers with narrative by telling them what to think, but lets actions speak for themselves.

Auden also said, borrowing from Frost, that the two questions a writer should subconsciously ask of himself and prompt readers to ask themselves are: "Who am I? Whom ought I to become?" The reader learns by juxtaposing his or her own life with the lives of an author's creations. One learns (hopefully) that one does not want to become like Higgins. Richard Stern, lifelong teacher that he has been, and realistic Everyman that he always is, is smart enough to ask the two questions, but has enough sense to leave possible answers to his audience.

Richard Gustave Stern was born on Manhattan's Upper West Side on 25 February 1928. Stern remains the quintessential New Yorker of liberal democratic inclinations even though he has not had permanent residence there since 1944. His art and essays, no matter where they take place, sound like New York City. His father, Henry George Stern, was a dentist; his mother, Marion (Veit) Stern, enjoyed being a dentist's wife, seeking no other identity than that of Mrs. Stern. Richard was a privileged child, precociously intelligent and a voracious reader. His parents' apartment on Central Park West had neighbors such as Joe Dimaggio, who kept to his enigmatic self. For child Stern, an interest in larger-than-life figures would emerge.

Stern moved quickly through public school two years ahead of his peers and was admitted on merit into prestigious Stuyvesant High School. He achieved distinction as a member of Arista, the elite of an elite school. (There, on a selection committee interviewing for new members, he would pose this question to a student hoping to join the inner circle: "Who are William James, Henry James, and Harry James?") He graduated in 1944 at age 16.

Stern's math and science acumen did not quite match his brilliance in the humanities, and he just missed entry into an Ivy League University. He "settled" for the University of North Carolina at Chapel Hill. There he met lifelong friends and future poets, Donald Justice and Edgar Bowers. He also encountered a certain amount of anti–Semitism. In New York, what Stern would later call his "impoverished Jewishness" ("The Novelist on his Work," *FH* 152) had gone mainly unobserved by himself and his family. Others would make him more aware of it than his parents did. "When I went to the University of North Carolina I was sixteen and ... I became both conscious of my Jewishness and afraid of it" ("The Novelist on His Work," *FH* 153). Stern graduated from Chapel Hill in 1947, only 19, and relatively inexperienced though he might have thought otherwise at the time. He returned to his parents' apartment:

> I have a new BA degree ... and a mother who doesn't like to see it going to waste. Six dawns a week, she rouses me with anti-inspirations; my comebacks are unspoken. "You won't find a job on your back" Michelangelo did the Sistine on his. "You know who catches the worm." Who's fishing? "Jobs go to go-getters." I don't want to go anywhere but Paris. She has never held a paying job. I am her non-paying one....
>
> Now and then I elevator up to advertising agencies and publishers.... I talk about my honors BA in English.... I've published poems, stories and essays in the Carolina Magazine, reported and written editorials for the Daily Tar Heel, am, in short, accomplished, worldly wise, hard-working and willing to improve their operations... ["With Auden," *Antioch* 389].

Stern's pitch didn't work. Youthful success did not prepare him to be wise enough for worldly rejection. The easy approval he had been used to was now no longer there, which caused a shock that most college graduates encounter. For Stern *Natural Shocks* became the basis of his art. That summer, he worked briefly in retail sales for a clothing store in Evansville, Indiana, light-years from Chapel Hill, let alone Manhattan. He hated it and retained an enduring antipathy to the business world:

> Sale days were a revelation. From the faces bunched behind the glass and then from the almost abstractly insane drive past me toward the garments

whose price reductions Cele had featured in her ads, I understood what a mob could do, what revolution might be like, what Goebbels and Hitler had manipulated, what the class Auden hated built their fortresses against. No, my days at the store weren't good ones ["With Auden," *Antioch* 393].

Being admitted to Harvard's M.A. program in the fall saved him. Stern now knew that the business world was out; writing and academia were in. His appreciation of the life of a man of letters began and was enhanced when he became one. After getting the M.A. in 1949, he went to France to teach at the College Jules Ferry at Versailles. He saw the enduring aftermath of the war and the contrast of prewar "classical" Europe with a Europe in decline and the contrast of both with America. Stern's attachment to Europe and its rise and fall (and the rise and fall of fictional characters in other contexts) would haunt him and his art, factoring in early short stories, and being the featured theme in his second novel, *Europe, or Up and Down with Baggish and Schreiber*, 1961.

In 1950, a 22-year-old Stern met and married Gay Clark in Paris. They had a son, Christopher, in 1951, a daughter, Kate in 1952. That year Stern's short story, "Cooley's Version" was published in the *Kenyon Review*, marking his debut as a professional writer. Stern received a Ph.D. in English (creative writing) from Iowa in 1954, and that same year "The Sorrows of Captain Schreiber" was selected for *Prize Stories of 1954: The O'Henry Collection*.

Stern began teaching at the University of Chicago in 1955, and in 1957, his son Andrew was born. He continued to publish short stories and in 1960 "Assessment of an Amateur" won the Longwood Foundation Award. The same year his first novel, *Golk*, appeared, which is a wry and dry comic satire of television's business side, a side that endures creativity only as long as it is a by-product of making money, and will kill creativity if profit is endangered. Stern's depiction of "business" types is parody with a poison pen. *Golk* anticipates today's attack TV and the media's relentless intrusions into privacy — a theme to be further developed in Stern's 1978 novel *Natural Shocks*. *Golk* was a "critical favorite," which is also a euphemism for its not being a best seller.

In 1961, son Nicholas was born, and *Europe* was published; it was also a "critical favorite." Stern was recognized as a comic writer of black humor and he had an "in" following that appreciated his quirky comedy and acerbic prose style. Stern attempted a more commercially appealing novel in 1962 with the publication of *In Any Case*, (later reprinted as *The Chaleur Network*), that fictionalized a World War II espionage case he'd read about. Previously, his work, wherever it took place, was based on his experiences concerning himself or people he knew or observed. Here, however, Sam Curry is an expatriate American living in France who lost his only son during the war. He is sent a book, anonymously, that asserts his son was a spy who betrayed his comrades to the Germans. Curry, who had not been a good father, seeks to clear his son's name and achieve redemption by doing so. He complicates matters by falling in love with his son's lover and befriending the real "traitor." The book's espionage elements are a device for Stern to explore a declining Europe, illusion and reality, and the different forms of betrayal that humans engage in. Apparent warfare is a collectively violent version of the various types of domestic warfare between the many configurations of human relationships that can exist. *In Any Case* is a departure from the first two novels. It was not parody first, tacit philosophy second; Stern's first-person protagonist and the people he meets muse mightily with explicit discourse on life and beyond life. The prose style here is more verbose than the terse "telegraphese" of previous work. Critics praised the novel, recognizing the new direction and it won the American Library Association Friends of Literature Award.

For the school year of 1962–63 Stern was a Fulbright Fellow in Italy. Here he had a near fatal — psychologically, that is — encounter with Ezra Pound. In 1964, on the strength of his growing reputation, Stern published *Teeth, Dying and Other Matters*, an anthology comprised of his short work published and unpublished going back to 1949. This included an essay, "The Pursuit of Washington," about his 1959 misadventures in attempting to interview — unsuccessfully — Kennedy and Nixon, and a play partially cowritten with Donald Justice at Chapel Hill. Hereafter, Stern became a respected and prolific writer of essays and reviews that would also be collected through the years. During 1963–64 Stern would turn the Pound contretemps into the basis for his novel *Stitch*, published in 1965. In that year he was also named a Rockefeller fellow.

In *Stitch* Stern goes back to his pre–*In Any Case* style as this novel is painfully contemporary and, for the first time, more overtly autobiographical. Whatever new direction *In Any Case* might have otherwise precipitated, *Stitch*, by necessity, reverts to Stern's more visceral — and personal — technique. Stern *had* to write this novel and the pain in it is catalyzed by Thaddeus Stitch, the Pound surrogate, who only adds to the already festering and bitter domestic warfare between Edward and Cressida Gunther. At the time those who knew Stern knew Stitch was Pound; fewer were aware that the marriage depicted was extrapolated from reality as well. After *Stitch* Stern's "fiction" would evolve, but never again depart, from the subject matter Stern knew best: himself.

In 1968, Stern won the National Institute of Arts and Letters Award for Fiction. He' taught in the summer of 1969 and one of his students was 19-year-old Alane Rollings, with whom he began an affair that would precipitate an acrimonious end to an already troubled marriage. During 1969–70, he was visiting professor at Harvard, and in 1970, published the collection *1968: A Short Novel, an Urban Idyll, Five Stories, and Two Trade Notes* (the latter are musings on the craft of writing). Here, Stern achieves a new level of excellence motivated by his personal life and the life of his country in the tumultuous year of 1968. The terrible tragedy of the Democratic National Convention took place in Chicago where Mayor Richard Daley called out the storm troopers to either incite or quell, depending on one's point of view, street protests. (Stern's is the former.) The short stories here became exemplars of the form of stories of private warfare that are just as violent as the street violence.

During 1970–71 Stern taught at the University of Nice. In 1972 he divorced his wife and continued his relationship with Rollings. His first essay collection, *The Books in Fred Hampton's Apartment*, was published in 1973. Here, one discerns that Stern's public essays correlate with many of his private concerns. Also in 1973 his private concerns indirectly become public record in the novelized account of his meeting Rollings and the ending of his marriage, *Other Men's Daughters*.

During 1973–74 Stern's stature as a man of letters earned him a Guggenheim Fellowship and he traveled around the world. In 1978, he continued his semiautobiographical fiction in the novel *Natural Shocks*. It is written with a rapid-fire glibness that belies the fact it is a meditation on sex and death while also being a prescient account — and indictment — of the early days of in-your-face media that now threatens to replace cultural literacy with cultural belligerency. *Natural Shocks* won the Carl Sandburg Award for Fiction. Stern's mother died in July. The story "Packages" resulted. (This story also became the title for his next short story collection in 1980.) Stern's father died in January 1979. His next essay collection, *The Invention of the Real*, was published in 1982 and featured the details of his meetings with Pound as fact, not fiction, which only pointed out how little the accounts differed. Also included, as if in response to the Pound fact/fiction issue, is "Inside Narcissus," a defense of, and almost an apologia for, the writer who replicates his life in his art. This essay begins with a meditation on the media's obliteration of personality by ubiquitousness in the late 20th century where the terms public and private have little meaning. "Inside Narcissus" precisely defines its time.

In 1985 Stern received the American Academy and Institute of Arts and Letters Medal of Merit for achievement in the Novel; it is given in six-

year intervals and recognizes a body of work. He also married Alane
Rollings. In 1986 he published the novel *A Father's Words*, about the domestic warfare between fathers and grown children, and the essay collection,
The Position of the Body. In 1989, Stern's collected stories, *Noble Rot*, and
his collected essays, *One Person and Another*, were published as companion anthologies. *Noble Rot* won the *Chicago Sun-Times* Book of the Year
Award. Stern was named Helen A. Regenstein Professor of English, University of Chicago, in 1991. His sister Ruth died in August. *Shares and
Other Fictions*, stories and a short novel, was published in 1992.

A *Sistermony*, a long essay about his sister's dying, appeared in 1995,
and won the Heartland Award for best nonfiction book of the year. In *A
Sistermony*, one sees that Stern the fiction writer and Stern the writer of
nonfiction are as little different as Christopher Isherwood is in his fiction
and nonfiction. That Stern and Isherwood derived their writing, "fiction"
or otherwise, in part from their diaries makes the comparison more apt
than one might imagine. The fact that they both admired E. M. Forster
also correlates. Forster "reported" his stories, understating tragedy as that
which interrupts the story rather than takes it over, making the tragic more
realistic and ultimately more effective. Isherwood and Stern do the same.

Since 1995 Stern has published nonfiction and earlier versions of sections of his novel in progress, *Pacific Tremors*, in periodicals such as the
Paris Review and the *Antioch Review*. Discarded chapters have appeared in
periodicals such as *Yale Review* and *Southwest Review*. The complete novel
was published in November 2001 by Triquarterly Books. For the academic
year of 1999-2000 he was a Fellow of the Center for Advanced Studies in
the Behavioral Sciences at Stanford. Alane Rollings has published four
books of poetry while married to Stern that have earned good reviews.
Edward Hirsch writes of her book, *The Struggle to Adore*, that "Alane
Rollings' large, inclusive, self-questioning poems meditate on the nature
of love and its accompanying mysteries. Here at last is a moving, completely contemporary record, a book of intimate attachments and love
poems." Collette Inez writes that "Rollings transforms us with the colors
and reach of her language." No doubt Stern and Rollings inspire each
other. Stern retired from the University of Chicago in 2001.

The Adventures of Everydog

In 1947 W. H. Auden's *Collected Poems* had a profound impact on
Richard Stern. Stern would meet Auden in the mid–1960s and in 2000
wrote about both occasions in his inimitable manner, which tells us as

much about Stern as it does Auden, or even more. In 1947 Stern has just graduated from college:

> September, 1947 ... Evansville [Indiana is not] my kind of town, this is not my kind of life [as a clothing salesman]. In the hotel room, on what is probably the loneliest, most unhappy night I'd spent since I was a little boy, I take out of my bag the one link I have to the life I want, *The Collected Poems of W. H. Auden*. It's the only book I've brought with me. I read it that night, as I will read it every single night of the six weeks I spend in Evansville, and as I've read few books since.... I still know several hundred lines I never tried to memorize ["With Auden," *Antioch* 393].

And then Stern writes out many of the lines, extracted, no doubt, from the mine of his memory.

This is how Richard Stern works: his life and art are inextricably linked, although he has been somewhat circumspect in admitting it. An appeal of Auden for Stern is that the poet cryptically depicted a great deal of personal meaning in his earlier work with a clipped and telegraphic diction. Stern's fiction also contains much of his person, sometimes in a prose that is also cryptically clipped and telegraphic. (He might also credit Stendhal and Hemingway.) Auden's code was deliberate, meant to be a lexicon understood by his gang, particularly Christopher Isherwood and Stephen Spender. (Isherwood and Stern are remarkably similar in *how* they write, if not in what they write about.) One can't say if Stern *knows* his work is coded, but there were certain readers who would recognize Stern's inner life. Sometimes, as earlier in his career (that is, pre–*Other Men's Daughters*, 1973), Stern's facts of (psychological) life were sublimated within stories that were contextual exercises to portray the persistent themes that dominated — and still dominate — his inner life. Later, starting with *Other Men's Daughters*, disguise was deemed somewhat superfluous and Stern began telling the story of *his* life without surrogates. (Except for the fictitious names, his characters were no longer strictly fictitious). Earlier, only Stern's closest friends and associates— the poets Donald Justice, and Edgar Bowers, the writers Flannery O' Connor, Philip Roth and Saul Bellow, and colleagues at the University of Chicago— knew that Stern's fictional conventions of plot and character were hung over certain Stern *bêtes noires* which he vented against through his compulsion to write and his manner of writing:

> *Stern:* The artistic "schemes" of the post mid-century writers have been — on the whole — more closely related to the incidents which will best describe the emotional curve of the central characters. This has meant broader excavations of the inner life and views of the world clearly distorted by the

ionized sensibilities of the characters. I would guess those of us writing now, whether conscious of it at the core of our work or not (and it will be mostly not), pour the stuff of such interior life over one traditional assumption after another. Whether we begin with a lust for novelty or just a desire to write about a person or situation as strongly as possible, the best results will deepen and reorder consciousness.... New energies, new scarcities, new gains, and new sorts of misery will be registered and worked out... [*FH* 283].

This overriding compulsion to write, in effect, congealed — as in the literal definition of to freeze or curdle — and preserved Stern's other compulsions for posterity. Later, anyone who knew Stern even a little knew he was writing about himself. Nonetheless, Stern will make the effort to not quite deny, but not quite affirm, that this is the case:

My novels and stories rarely deal directly with this life [academia] or with my own. [The inclusion of *directly* is key.] A few friends, fellow writers, occasional readers, and critics sometimes see in what for me are very different works certain recurrences, an absorption in great inventors and their hangers-on, the free women and the energetic, coreless men who are the source of so much disorder, the Europe-American Axis, and the use and abuse of narrative conventions. I grant but cannot imagine being governed by these or other recurrences. It is enough being governed by what more and more seems the noblest of habits ... [the act of writing] ["Statement," *FH* 141].

The "noblest of habits" includes both fiction and nonfiction, with Stern observing that the difference is, in modern terms, not really so great. (To emphasize this point, he would title an essay collection, *The Invention of the Real*):

The non-fiction novel is no novelty.... there is in our time the long endeavor ... to obliterate the bounds between fiction and non-fiction.... how many have written ... non-fiction using devices developed by the novel; the revision of the story's chronological and spatial lines, shifting viewpoints, the progression of effects, varied texture (letters, diaries, dialogue, expository summary).... God and literature fuse in Pascal's great maxim [*Tout comprendre, c'est tout pardonner* — To understand all is to pardon all] ["*In Cold Blood*," *FH* 89–91].

In order to understand all and pardon all, Stern writes about everything that takes place in his inner and outer life with the inner life having much more importance than the outer life. The outer life is, in fact, symptomatic of the inner life rather than the cause of the inner life. Events in his outer life are catalysts for galvanizing emotions already existing (or fermenting, or festering, or raging) consciously or unconsciously in his inner life. The more profound biography of the individual is not in the events that affect him externally, no matter how mundane or calamitous, but in the progress of the mind in reacting to these events in patterns that become inevitable, if not necessarily predictable. Another short story expert made his case for inevitability much earlier:

> And as for egotism a person who has been burrowing to his utmost ability, into the depths of our common nature for the purpose of psychological romance — and who pursues his researches into that dusky region as he needs must, as well as by tact of sympathy as by light of observation — will smile at incurring such an imputation in virtue of a little preliminary talk about his external habits, his abode, his casual associates, and of other matters entirely upon the surface. These things hide the man instead of displaying him. You must make quite another kind of inquest, and look through the whole range of his fictitious characters, good and evil, in order to detect any of his essential traits [Hawthorne, 1851, from his preface to *The Snow Image*].

Stern displays his "essential traits" as Hawthorne did and he carries on the Hawthorne tradition of psychological autobiography "metaphorized" as fictional narratives. Stern's narratives, while depicting "external habits" and "matters entirely upon the surface" are an architectural framework for Stern's much more important psychological foundation. His narratives and their "outsides" may change names and places, but the psychological "insides" remain that of the author. Hawthorne's Biographer Arlin Turner wrote of his subject: "he is the most autobiographical of our writers — in his particular way."[3] The dash implies volumes and applies to Stern as well. Critic Harry Levin (whom Stern knew at Harvard) said of Hawthorne: "while Hawthorne creates a world of his own, it is *his own* that we should emphasize rather than a world. To consider his work as a whole is to watch the recurrence of certain thematic patterns so obsessive ... they might well be regarded as complexes."[4] Stern again.

Stern's work, early and late, is driven by the same recurrent themes: *Routine* as either a safe haven not to be disturbed and protected at all costs including violence, or, conversely, to be rebelled against at all costs, including violence; *Reversal* as that which turns routine upside down whether chosen or imposed; *Randomization* as arbitrary interjections of destiny for good or ill; *Revelation* as moments when characters *and* readers learn the difference between knowledge and understanding; *Redemption* as a form of grace that comes with the wisdom acquired from revelation. In addition are these groups of interrelated ancillary themes within the major themes:

1. *Men / Women / Domestic Warfare / Secret Wish*;
2. *Approval / Sex, Compulsion / Creativity / Peanut Butter*;
3. *Aesthetes vs. Hearties / Mind* (imagination) *over Matter* (politics and filthy lucre).

The elucidation and development of the themes listed will be a framework for following Stern's work in chronological order; however, in Chapter One, further definition of the themes with Sternian examples will precede the time trail.

Stern's inner life, and a compulsion to express this life in words, remains paramount for him, with or without surrogates. For Richard Stern writing is like breathing, with an emphasis on the expiatory. A Stern foil in his third novel, *In Any Case*, talks about learning a method of achieving inner control while coping with outer flux by adopting innocuous physical postures that remind one of the possibility of maintaining a calmer *inside* when confronted with a more volatile *outside*:

> ...the practitioner becomes his own guru. The dances [postures] are only clues. He's not after the mastery or extinction of the body, only utilisation of it as a calendar of the interior, an ordered reminder by seven postures [such as crossing the right ankle over the left], one for each day of the week, that the interior must be attended to. You can assume the postures any time. They're inconspicuous; only people who have studied such things will notice them. The point is that you can do this without isolating yourself from ordinary life. But the interior is always there, and the postures are available, like breathing [*IC* 178].

Stern postures through the physical act of writing, which deals with his interior therapeutically. His confessionals are good for his soul and for the souls of his readers. Auden said that the literary artist is a "mixture of spy and gossip,"[5] and that he didn't believe "an artist is any good who is not a bit of a reporting journalist."[6] Stern, again. A Stern surrogate, a journalist named Fred Wursup, confirms the nature of fiction and nonfiction as a two-sided coin and that nonfiction can also be literature. Fred thinks of himself, with a bit of self-admonition, as a "Windy journalist. Wasn't the journalism episode of Ulysses set in the cave of the winds? Unfair. Joyce had done good journalism himself. Plenty of other good writers, too. Dostoevski, Marx, Orwell — millions of them" (*NS* 245). The poet, Donald Justice, said of Stern, "that his vision comes from a very sharp satiric eye. What we get is a journalism of the imagination, at once highbrow and tabloid."[7] What we get is prose that is intellectual and earthy, erudite and primal, philosophical and confessional. Aldous Huxley, who also confessed about his life and the people in it in his early novels, believed that,

> Art is a therapy. They talk again and again about the power which art has to get rid of painful emotions and thoughts which torment the poet — to get rid of them simply by paying attention to them and expressing them. This cathartic, therapeutic side of art has been found in modern psychotherapy to be extremely important. Innumerable people with psychological problems have found they get relief in making artistic expression of their ideas; the painful pressure within them is let loose, and they are able to carry on much more effectively as a consequence.[8]

Therapy educates via revelation; artists are makers who choose to be self-educated and self-"revelated." *Stern:* "Regular self-scrutiny, particularly published self scrutiny, requires strength, and not merely the strength of vanity. Many writers have to wean themselves from the timidity natural to most of us; psychoanalysis or regular confession of some sort helps the weaning process" (*FH* 139). The sharing of the artist's art with others is more of a byproduct than an end in itself, a validation rather than a motivation. How much great art would have remained unmade if finding an audience was the sole goal? Stern writes "that the life [is] lived for the art, or at least that only in art [are] the intensity and meaning of the life felt...." He adds that, "this is the case even for those artists whose lives are in no small measure consciously arranged to provide material for their work" ("Events," *FH* 101). To a degree Stern is one of these arrangers. To a greater degree, Stern will make his reality-based art as a matter of need, not audience. *Stern:* "'realists' wish to assemble the world in order to control it" ("Events," *FH* 100).

Stern, while breathing, expiating, and therapeutically confessing, has been a critic's favorite, winning numerous awards for his fiction and becoming an increasingly sought after essayist, which, again, while illuminating a variety of externalities (current events, book reviews, so on) is still primarily about illuminating Stern's best understood subject: Stern. Yet, this is not a narcissistic venture whatsoever; rather, a relatively unconscious solipsism. One says "relatively," as Stern is too smart to hide behind a cloud of unknowing.

In 1944 Auden put his *Collected Poems* in alphabetical order (not even by title but by first line) so that any reader's attempt to find any autobiography that might have been implied by a chronological order was made moot. In 1989, for the preface of his collected stories in *Noble Rot Stories 1949–1989*, Stern wrote:

These stories, written over a 40-year writing life, aren't arranged in chronological order. (The collection isn't meant to display literary development or
decline.) The arranger thinks of the reader as a story lover looking forward
to his nightly story fix. Such a reader is comparatively disinterested in the
towns and times of composition, the recollected fusion of experience and
invention. Fascinating stuff that, but uncooked fiction more or less, cooked
fact. Actually, the chief point of this note is its own superfluity.

When a person proclaims that what he just said doesn't matter, a
critic — skeptical devil that he is and by his nature comparatively interested rather than disinterested —*knows* otherwise. For this critic, this preface — the first published words he read by Stern — set the investigative tone
for all of his reading that followed, whether fiction or essays. Indeed, in
Stern's collected essays, *One Person and Another*, also published in 1989,
Stern's preface states: "This book ... is intended as a companion volume
to *Noble Rot 1949–1989*. It is the critical shadow of the author's fiction. The
selections are not arranged in chronological order; the collection is not
meant to display critical development or decline." *Methinks he doth protest
too much.*

The two books, prefaced as they are, demand that the reader — and
by now even the "comparatively disinterested" reader, let alone the interested critic — inquire as to what Stern is up to. What puzzle does he wish
to obscure by such declarations? The self-effacement is a courtesy by an
author who actually *does* wish to be investigated; his "protests" represent
an obligatory modesty by a modest man who prefers not to incur even the
slightest possibility of saying that he wants to be discovered and it being
considered a presumption. Nonetheless, Stern himself wrote, in an essay
titled "Inside Narcissus," about the Audens and Eliots who offer up a
reverse (even perverse) vanity when they vociferously "forbid biographies.
The results of such injunctions are well known. No one is more observed,
more hungered after than the reluctant self-exhibitor.... There is one sort
of maker who is driven to narcissism by his occupation. This is the writer"
(*IR* 181–82). Consequently, the writer, habitual narcissist that he is, cannot break the habit so easily when his life is subject to inquiry in the public forum. Yet, one must, as Stern does, have the good manners to be proud
without self-promotion and wait for others to make the discoveries about
him.

This critic will presume, on Stern's behalf, to do some exploring and
review his work chronologically; but only after setting up works by estab-
lishing the ambience and atmospheres of — with a tip of the hat to his
German ancestors— Stern's *Weltansicht*, that is, his special view or interpretation of reality. The effort expended for this table setting will compensate

for the relative brevity needed to explain Stern's plots, which are minimal. The emphasis in his art is not on plot but on characterizations that are vehicles for depicting attitudes—Stern's attitudes, or the philosophical *Weltanschauung* implied by his *Weltansicht*. His fiction is fuguelike: themes are enunciated in the earliest work, and these themes are repeated with variations that add richness and complexity while referring always to their psychological origins in Stern's inner life. (As an epigraph for his second novel, *Europe, or Up and Down with Baggish and Schreiber*, 1961, Stern quotes Nietzsche: "Every man of character has a typical experience which recurs over and over again.") Stern's extended fugue is a 50-year odyssey of written recurrences.

In Auden's commonplace book *A Certain World*, 1962, he said that he would be loathe to write an official autobiography (or for anyone else to write a biography), and that his selections for the anthology were as close as anyone would get: "I realize this sort of compilation is a sort of autobiography.... Here then is a map of my planet. Certain features are, deliberately or necessarily, missing.... Then, much as we should all like to, none of us can preserve our personal planet as an unsullied Eden. According to our time and place, unpleasant facts from the world we all have in common keep intruding, matters about which either we are compelled, against our will, to think or we feel it is our duty to think...."[9]

While Stern has not done a commonplace book per se (although he has "assembled" (his word) an esoteric anthology, *Honey and Wax*, 1966, of mainly short stories with an international cast ranging from Casanova to Kierkegaard), he does offer his essay collections, calling them "orderly miscellanies" supplemented by his commentary, as clues as to who the "I" is that talks to the "you." He writes: "From fear, laziness, stupidity, decorum or prevision of boredom, I haven't spent much time getting to know myself. As for expressing myself, that's another matter. This section [in the collection *The Invention of the Real*, the title a clue in itself] explores that in essays, and delivers some oblique self presentations.... If it's not the de luxe tour of the dark interior, it's all I plan to offer. The company motto is By Indirection Find Direction out" (*IR* 134).

In one manner of "indirection," Stern often expresses himself in his fiction and essays by compulsively quoting others to both illustrate and reinforce the map of his planet — his own oblique form of commonplace anthology. There is a Stern essay concerning the publishing, in facsimile, of T. S. Eliot's manuscript version of *The Waste Land*. The second Mrs. Eliot annotated this version with the assistance of Ezra Pound who had originally edited the manuscript into the landmark it became. Pound had a profound impact on Eliot as he would later have on Stern.

Stern quotes Eliot and the passage he chooses is a key to both of them:

> Various critics have done me the honour to interpret the poem [*The Waste Land*] in terms of criticism of the contemporary world, have considered it, indeed, as an important bit of social criticism. To me it was only the relief of a personal and wholly insignificant grouse against life; it is just a piece of rhythmical grumbling ["Stumbling," *FH* 301].

Stern, again!

CHAPTER ONE

Setting the Tea-Table for Wholly Truthful Art — Sweating the Details

> *If I'm anything, it's a story writer, somebody who gets at the truth in a roundabout way, by inventing people who feel intensely about something or other. Sometimes these people feel and act, as I might, sometimes not. At any rate, the interest is in the coherence and amusement, the power of the story. Often the story can only live because lots of big things are left out, things that would crush the little things stories love to feed on.*
> — Richard Stern — ["Storm," *FH* 172]

Realistic stories that readers can commiserate with are built on the "little things," which sustain everyday life through the ups and down that are interruptions of every day life. How one reacts to the peaks and valleys is predetermined by all of those little things that precede these momentous events. If one reads to escape only, then one can enter a fantasy world where melodrama dominates page after page with the anticipatory ebb and flow of a roller coaster ride. If one wishes for a more enlightened escape that teaches as well as provides a psychic holiday, then one would wish to eschew continuous peaks of tragedy for the more realistic fiction of what Aldous Huxley described as Wholly Truthful art: "Artists are eminently teachable and eminently teachers. They receive from events much more than most men receive, and they can transmit what they have received with particular penetrative force, which drives their communication deep into the reader's mind. One of our most ordinary reactions to a good piece of literary art is expressed in the formula: 'This is what I have always felt and thought, but have never been able to put clearly into words, even for myself.'"[10] For this reaction to take place, readers must be able to identify

with realistic characters; they must be able to imagine reacting similarly
if placed in similar situations. Fantasy may be fun, but one learns more
from reality. Reality requires art that tells the whole truth:

> *Huxley:* What are the values of Wholly Truthful art? Wholly Truthful art
> overflows the limits of tragedy and shows us, if only by hints and implica-
> tions, what happened before the tragic story began, what will happen when
> it is over, what is happening simultaneously elsewhere (and "elsewhere"
> includes all those parts of the minds and bodies of the protagonists not
> immediately engaged in the tragic struggle). Tragedy is an arbitrarily iso-
> lated eddy on the surface of a vast river that flows majestically, irresistibly,
> around, beneath, and to either side of it. Wholly Truthful art contrives to
> imply the existence of the entire river as well as the eddy…. Consequently,
> Wholly Truthful art produces in us an effect quite different from that pro-
> duced by tragedy. Our mood when we have read a Wholly Truthful book is
> never one of heroic exultation; it is one of recognition, of acceptance.
> (Acceptance can also be heroic.) The catharsis of tragedy is violent and
> apocalyptic; the milder catharsis of Wholly Truthful literature is more last-
> ing. There is no reason … why the two kinds of literature should not exist
> simultaneously…. The human spirit has need of both.[11]

Auden agreed with Huxley: "Memorable speech then. About what?
Birth, death, the Beatific vision, the abysses of hatred and fear, the awards
and miseries of desire…. yes, all of these, but not these only. Everything
that we remember no matter how trivial: the mark on the wall, the joke
at luncheon, word games, these, like the dance of a stoat or the raven's gam-
ble, are equally the subject of [literature]." Auden added that, "a moment
in which the characters are emotionally relaxed may be just as significant
as one in which they are emotionally stirred."[12]

Both Auden and his best friend Isherwood took lessons from one of
their role models, E. M. Forster, whom Stern would later write about meeting and describe him as "the Man of Sympathy who had invented unsentimental ways of conveying it" ("A Memory of Forster," *FH* 205). In his
1938 book *Lions and Shadows*, Isherwood — via his Cambridge classmate
Edward Upward — describes Forster's tea-table technique of understated
prose: "I saw it all suddenly while reading *Howard's End*…. Forster's the
only one who understands what the modern novel should be …. our fright-
ful mistake was that we believed in tragedy: the point is tragedy's quite
impossible nowadays…. We ought to essentially aim at being comic writers…. The whole of Forster's technique is based on the tea-table: instead
of trying to screw up all his scenes to the highest pitch, he tones them
down until they sound like mother's meeting gossip…. In fact, there's
actually *less* emphasis laid on big scenes than on unimportant ones: that's

what's so utterly terrific. It's the completely new kind of accentuation — like a person talking a different language."[13] In effect, as Stern said: "lots of big things are left out, things that would crush the little things stories love to feed on." In art as well as life, the little things add up to a great deal.

Stern emphasizes certain details and implies a greater context from these details that readers can surmise between the lines. He is a subtle crafter of subtext and gives his readers enough credit for brains that he lets scenes unfold in "real time" as they would appear to an observer; that is, he does not force an omniscient narration that insists on interpreting scenes instead of just letting them be. Indeed, Stern writes for the readers who are willing to engage the differences between observation and perception, and knowledge and understanding. One can observe without perceiving, and one can have knowledge without understanding if the implications of that knowledge are not understood: "Knowledge," Huxley wrote, "is acquired when we succeed in fitting a new experience into the system of concepts based upon our old experiences. Understanding comes when we liberate ourselves from the old and so make possible a direct, unmediated contact with the new, the mystery, moment by moment, of our existence."[14] Stern provides the knowledge in his "real-time" prose; the discerning reader, if so inclined, then observes the knowledge and provides the understanding. Stern supplies the effable text on the page, and readers perceive, intuit, and understand the ineffable subtext that lives between the lines of his text. Another Stern surrogate, writing in the first person in his novel, *A Father's Words*, says of this distinction: "For more than thirty years, since I started a science newsletter, I've watched some of the world's best minds use the most refined techniques to understand the tiniest facts. It makes me skeptical about understanding anything complicated. Knowing isn't understanding" (FW 12). It isn't! For example, much can be intuitively understood from having knowledge of "peanut butter":

> In her entire life, there were very few times she'd gone out with half-decent men. She'd come to think that perhaps it didn't matter, that she could make it without a man. If only people would stop pressuring her. Thousands of small pressures: salesgirls calling her Mrs. when she bought her father's birthday shirts; people being introduced to her at parties; being the extra girl and getting tied up with the extra miserable man, more miserable when he saw her; the hundreds and hundreds of self-pitying hours in her two rooms, Jack Paar jabbering maniacally on the twelve-inch screen while she shared him with Middlemarch, its pages stained with the peanut butter she sometimes supposed was more faithful to her than any person on earth ["Teeth," T 16].

Then there is Edward Gunther, the corpulent 37-year-old father in *Stitch*, who is nicknamed "hippodad" by his young son. Early in the novel, Edward's domestic warfare with his wife concerning dwindling funds is punctuated thus:

> That night they slept poorly, separately, and, the next morning the mail complicated their animosity. The Talman Federal Savings passbook arrived showing a balance of $4,830. Edward, in pajamas and sweater, came into the kitchen to join Cressida for his morning's coffee with the soggy English peanut butter he made do in Venice. The passbook lay open with a knife whose point was at the figure [ST 32].

Later, Hippodad has been left by his wife and children due to an infidelity with Nina, an aspiring poet:

> Every once in a while he wrote a letter to one of the children, ending with "Give everyone a big hug from and kiss from your daddy," but for two weeks he received no mail at all except for "Free Gift Coupon Inside" envelopes addressed to occupant, 502 Miramar Beach. He ate almost nothing, lived off bread, peanut butter, and cans of apple and pineapple juice [ST 193].

For Stern peanut butter "metaphorizes" anxiety, loneliness, and sexual frustration. Tactility, particularly oral, with a great deal of eating and drinking, is symptomatic of Stern's world. In this world little details aggregate into a cumulatively purposeful whole whose parts sum up much more integrally than they do separately. These progressions of seemingly (only seemingly) unrelated details are strewn about as clues for the unsuspecting reader, and these clues lead to turns of events, often reversals, that retrospectively prove that the details were purposeful, rather than random embellishments.

Edward's corpulence, with the allusions to his girth humorously scattered throughout the novel, becomes the sudden focal point near the end of the novel. Shortly after his wife leaves him, Nina dumps him also. Months later, he receives a letter from his cousin Walli:

> My dear Edward,
>   I came back from a short trip to Venice and found a letter … which has shaken me terribly. I can't believe that the separation of two people such as yourself and Cressida — not even thinking of the darling children — can endure. I can hardly endure to think of it…. I will do anything you ask me in the way of intervention or help….
>   I can hardly intrude my own news at this point, but I will, because it will interest and perhaps please you. The news is that I am, in a way, engaged.

"In a way," because there are certain conditions laid down by my almost-fiancée, who I'm proud to say, is Nina. [Walli does not know that Edward and Nina were more than friends.] Perhaps you did not know that it was Mr. Stitch himself [Edward's Poundian nemesis] who introduced us. I have gone down to Venice every other weekend since you left and I offered my hand this weekend. To my delighted surprise, I was not refused. I will tell you the odd but completely understandable conditions which this brilliant, beautiful, gifted girl laid down, although I am of course not anxious to have them generally known.

She says that she has a sort of aversion to corpulence.... I agreed to take off thirty-five pounds... [ST 194–5].

In sum: Edward is made to realize that he was physically repulsive to Nina and that the only time she conceded to sleep with him, after many rebuffs— which he thought were because he was married — was because she was blind drunk. The broke poet took Edward's money while fending him off until she was too drunk to notice. The novel's previous jests concerning food and girth are now retrospectively tinged with more malice and less humor. Now completely abandoned, Edward's fleeting pride over his ephemeral "conquest" of Nina has been turned into a reversal of complete humiliation. In Stern, reversals are either climaxes of revelation that close a story, or revelatory catalysts that begin a story. Sometimes one story has both.

Stern's dominant themes exist in both of Stern's lives: his public life as writer and academic, and his life as "metaphorized" in fiction. While Stern's inner life is replicated in his art, the emphasis is on Stern's life of the mind rather than his outward history. There are, however, two crucial events (scenes) in Stern's public record that say much about the writer's art that followed these scenes. The first is a non bar mitzvah with an identity crisis involving getting approval from his adolescent peers; the second is a premidlife crisis (age 37) after a meeting with Ezra Pound where instead of a hoped-for approval of Stern by Pound, a nonapproving Pound derided Stern. The rebuff was deadly enough to Stern that he based an entire novel, *Stitch*, on its "fictional" replication, one that emphasizes the Stern surrogate's fragile psyche, an inner insecurity that the "Poundian" incident doesn't cause but compounds into high anxiety.

The non bar mitzvah is revealed by Stern in a 1961 essay concerning whether or not he considered himself a Jewish writer: "Twenty years ago, on the Saturday I should have been 'bar-mitzvahed' but was not, because one wasn't in our family, I hid out in the Paramount Theater ducking the [Jewish] friends to whom on Monday, I conjured up my ceremony" ("Statement," *FH* 143).

A bar mitzvah is a rite signifying the arrival of "manhood" or at least pubescence at age 13. This tender age of heightened identity seeking usually engenders an insecurity that requires a quest for approval from peers. (Of this insecurity Stern notes elsewhere that "Adolescence is not a pretty thing to look at...." (*IC* 66). Stern's faux bar mitzvah, his charade for his friends' benefit, indicates an early identity crisis and his penchant for storytelling as a response to the crisis. The quest for approval, the questions of identity, and the compulsion to write about both, remain in his work. The need for approval to bolster identity led up to the incident with Ezra Pound in 1962, an event so telling, Stern notes, that "the emotional aftermath led me to write the novel *Stitch*" ("Pound Sterling," *FH* 292). Even years after the "fictional" *Stitch*, Stern wrote a nonfiction essay about their first meeting: "the face lined like no one else's, not the terrible morbid furrows of Auden, not the haphazard crevices of so many benign elders.... these lines had the signatory look of individual engagements" ("A Memory...," *IR* 3). This first encounter described in the essay is civil enough to invite a second:

> ...we talked easily for a couple of hours, though I felt like an extractor. He asked me what was going on. I told him what I knew. We disagreed about Eliot's plays—he liked them a lot.... Nothing overwhelming, but every sentence clear, complete, and underwritten by thought. "This is exceptional sanity." Now and then, an odd remark fell out of silence: "Don't think pianos waited for the railroad." (Which may have had to do with cultural independence.)
>
> Mostly, one sensed his instinct for occasion. It was not the reverse of simplicity. I think the word is probably *courtesy*: he acted fittingly. Which did not exclude play with social formula. "How are you today?" "Senile." Or to a visitor who said that X and Y asked to be remembered: "They're in no danger of being forgotten."
>
> Memory, though, was the central worry of that year. My one emotional session with him turned on it.... There was some talk of Peggy Guggenheim, who lived down the way.... I repeated something she'd told me about Pound in Paris days. Pound frowned, fretted a while, then said I was testing his memory, he was relieved to know for sure that what I said was fiction. The words froze the room.... I told myself, "Well, he's shown his hand at last. I guess the other stuff I heard about him is so" ["Memory...," *IR* 5–6].

(The "other stuff" was Pound's reputed anti–Semitism and profascist World War II broadcasts that won him an enforced stay after the war as a psychiatric patient at the U. S. Government's St. Elizabeth's mental hospital.)

Although Pound then offered a rather oblique form of apology and

Stern continued to see him a few more times, the debit of the rebuke and the damage done by meeting a hero manqué far outlasted whatever profit Stern earned from the brief visits. In this case, sticks and stones would have been much preferred. Stern, at this time, already a critically praised fiction writer, deliberately sought out the previous generation of the honored and revered such as Pound. (He would shortly after meet Auden with a much better result.) Stern hoped both to learn from their aura *and* to achieve their peer approval of him as a fellow writer. The quest for approval is a staple in Stern's fiction that is replicated from his life.

Stern's fictions— up to meeting Pound —can be considered progressive variations on the inner motivations of his fictitious bar mitzvah story to which are added varying degrees of emotional disturbances. *Stitch*, written shortly after meeting Pound and published in 1965, is Stern's first blending of his prevalent psychological themes with a more overtly fact-based autobiographical novel. The fiction that follows *Stitch* retains the emotional upsets but becomes more violent psychologically and is often reinforced by physical violence, including deaths. The Pound incident, however, was not all negative: "In *Stitch*," James Schiffer writes, "the genius figure deliberately, even cruelly, destroys Gunther's sense of himself as well as his affair with Nina. Gunther is singed by his brush with genius; the experience transforms him, but the transformation is in some ways a positive one."[15] Indeed, Gunther, whose girth is a symbol of a baby-fat, womb-cocoon infantility replete with peanut butter pacifier, is forced to grow up. For Stern negative reversals can sometimes be parables of revelation and redemption that teach through the wisdom of pain.

The Invention of the Real: Major Themes

ROUTINE

> *Amid the seeming confusion of our mysterious world, individuals are so nicely adjusted to a system, and systems to one another, and to a whole, that by stepping aside for a moment, a man exposes himself to the fearful risk of losing himself forever.... he may become, as it were, the outcast of the universe.*
> — Hawthorne

> *The commonest, one might call it the natural, rhythm of human life is routine punctuated by orgies.*
> — Aldous Huxley

> *Unlike scientists who can collaborate on all but the highest levels because they are working toward the mastery of what's really*

out there, *novelists work alone because their best work means a dissociation from the familiar.*
—Stern [*FH* 221]

Essentially, there's no taking over another novelist's territory. It would mean taking over his mind.
—Stern [*FH* 204]

Life is a matter of the routine that comes with responsibility; time is an artificial construct created to assign responsibility and structure the routine. Many people require, even desire, routine as a fortress or womb that will be retained at all costs. (Stern says of a character: "Scharf was happy. He loved not only his routines but the idea of them. That fact was beyond or beneath Yntema's comprehension. He resented such vegetal contentment.... How could a human being who was neither prude nor dummy restrict himself in a world so rich with possibility" ("The Girl Who Loves Shubert," *P* 123).

Some people accept routine until some reversal or revelation forces them to change; some want alternations of routine with sporadic interruptions ranging from commonplace leisure activities to legal or illegal danger; lastly, are those for whom routine, even if reluctantly followed, is a jail with a cruel warden within which either tangible plans or fantasies of escape run concurrent with the incarceration. The difference between routine and escape is the difference between *work* and *play*, particularly the play of the artist who wishes to achieve, as Stern said, "dissociation with the familiar":

Auden: "The writing of art is gratuitous, i.e. play.... Natural man hates nature, and the only act which can really satisfy him is the *acte gratuite*. His ego resents every desire of his natural self for food, sex, pleasure, logical coherence, because desires are given, not chosen, and his ego seeks constantly to assert its autonomy by doing something of which the requiredness is not given. In addition in to wanting to feel free man wants to feel important.... The rules of a game give it importance by making it difficult to play, a test of skill."[16] Auden talks about art as one example of *play* but *play* means any manner of escapism that temporarily breaks free from *work*; i.e., resented responsibility. The audience enjoys the artist's art and also gets to play the artist's game by escaping vicariously through the art. Stern concurs with Auden by quoting Freud's remark that, "the imaginative artist does the same as the child at play; he creates a world of fantasy, which he takes very seriously: that is, he invests it with a great deal of effect, while departing it sharply from reality'" ("Events," *FH* 100). The readers of a novelist's art appreciate and temporarily enter the autonomy of a writer's mind that, as Stern said, can't be taken over, only visited. The reader also enjoys brief autonomy from responsibility and the novel temporarily provides it. Not everyone who *plays* at escaping responsibility, however, is considered a benefactor by a majority of outsiders looking in on the person's attempts at autonomous independence.

Outsiders may see the person who seeks to escape routine as *the outcast of the universe*. The person will be reviled by them because a repudiation of *that* person's routine is a rebuke of *their* routine as well, a repudiation that strikes at their individual and collective egos. On the matter of conformity Stern quotes Konrad Lorenz: "The instinctive need to be the member of a closely knit group fighting for common ideals may grow so strong that it becomes inessential what these ideals are and whether they possess any intrinsic value" ("Coach Lombardi," *FH* 86). Stern, via Lorenz, is concerned with the herd mentality of collective subjectivity that is formed by societal pressures and spread by the propaganda machine of mass media.

In emergent totalitarian societies, artists and intellectuals are early targets for removal because they will be the first to see through propaganda and try to tell others about the truth. To conform to routine or not to conform is a major issue in Stern's art. Truth and betrayal, both public and private, are also core elements in Stern, along with the angst-ridden guilt that is the postwar antihero's de rigueur calling card. Guilt, however, while it became a more formidable and ubiquitous literary raison d'être after World War II, began, in fact, as a Puritanical American literary tradition detailed by the original outcast of the universe, Hawthorne. "Of course," Hawthorne expert, Hyatt Waggoner writes, "if [Hawthorne] had not known what it was to feel alienated and guilty, he could not have written so unforgettably about isolation and secret guilt."[17] Stern also knows about guilt; and guilt always plays a factor in making or breaking one's routine. For Hawthorne and Stern, many of their stories are about particular individuals who are metaphors for cyclical patterns or routines within the universe of man.

RANDOMIZATION

Randomization is the inverse of routine. The former defines the latter by its absence. In Stern, routine is established so that randomization can assert itself. In melodramatic fiction, interruptions of already tragic lives are not quite so abrupt and affecting to readers as the interruptions that disturb the commonplace of realistic, Wholly Truthful lives. In Stern's *Natural Shocks*, 1978, the writer-journalist Fred Wursup is assigned by an editor to write about "dying," after which his routine, one that includes spying on his ex-wife with binoculars, is randomly confronted by death and dying from all directions. While in Belgium on a story, his girlfriend in New York calls him at his hotel: He asks,

> …"What's wrong?"
> "It's your father," Sookie said. Her voice was clear; how he wished he were with her. "And Mona. They're dead."
> "My god. What do you mean? What happened?"
> "The janitor found them this morning. It looks as if they took sleeping pills last night. They were just lying in bed. Dressed. Dead. There's a note for you. I'm so sorry, sweetheart."
> His reservation for Antwerp was for that night. He went upstairs to the little room over the canal. Gretchen was undressed, naked, asleep, noisy. Inhaling, she snorted; exhaling, she whistled; nor was her rump soundless. Is this the food of love? Wondered Wursup. It had been a trying day for her. Gretchen reminded him of Mona. Though not as smart, as spirited, not nearly as *there* as Mona is. *Was.* Mona, a dear thing. What would poppa have done — how quickly the tenses of the past are — without her? But what could have happened? His father was vigorous, and as alive as he'd known, not sick, not gloomy. If anything, he was a nut of self-confidence, an old life booster. Maybe he or Mona had something, and they decided to go together. Mayerling. Did they both want to die? How else? Sookie said they were lying dressed on the bed. How did they decide? Over a month? A year? Overnight? What was the last night like? Did they talk while the pills took over? Watch Johnny Carson on *The Tonight Show*? Hold hands? Talk? What did they say? Did they change their minds?
> A rumble from Gretchen's rear. It was a beautiful, generous rear. The long legs spread at the groin; the protective tufts peered out. Magnetic. Wursup took off his clothes, and held her, front on rear. She woke up, annoyed, but feeling his interest, found her own. [Later Wursup thought] the little room thickened with absence. Gretchen grew noisier. A human bassoon. Under the sheet, skin to skin … if only one of her sounds could come from his father's body now, it would undo the universe [*NS* 198–99].

Randomization itself may be arbitrary but in Stern the implications and reverberations of randomization can be timeless and universal. If Fred's dead father made a noise, then the most profound meaning of routine would be turned upside down in a reversal that would up-end existence itself. In addition to being an example of Sternian randomization, the passage also signifies Sternian compulsions for writing about sex and food (as sex's tactile substitute).

Reversals

Randomization is most random when the interruptions are reversals so that they not only stem the tide of routine but permanently end or at least alter it. Reversals turn things around but do not always have negative connotations. Reversals can seem benign or malignant but are actually more like the whiteness of Melville's whale — neutral. The eye of the beholder measures their meanings so that the reversals act more as cues to self-evaluation and less as the causes of such evaluation. Things happen; people react. How they react is the difference between knowledge and understanding.

Thornton Wilder (also a writer and teacher at the University of Chicago 20 years before Stern) could not be more different in his style of writing than Stern but both serve the same end: self exploration. (All literary writers do.) Wilder and Stern see writing as a means of expression that teaches, with the most important learners being Wilder and Stern. In Wilder's art, reversals are object lessons from which readers may learn if they choose to learn. Wilder's 1967 novel *The Eighth Day* is considered in Russia (where Wilder is revered), one of the greatest novels of the 20th century. At the book's conclusion he writes:

> There is much talk of a design in the arras. Some are certain they see it. Some see what they have been told to see. Some remember they saw it once but have lost it. Some are strengthened by seeing a pattern where the oppressed and exploited of the earth are gradually emerging from their bondage. Some find strength in the conviction that there is nothing to see. Some[18]

The last "Some" trails off into the varieties of human possibility. Wilder's narratives philosophize overtly; the omniscient narrator is essential to his cause. Stern's narratives philosophize tacitly and the omniscient narrator is distinctly absent. Wilder's reversals are more explicit because they are aided by the narrator's voice. Stern's reversals are more tacit and happen to the reader just as they happen to his characters; both readers and characters are left to figure things out for themselves. Reversal only reverses those who have not found a calm center that withstands the spin and flux of life's hurricane. In real life the control of inner weather is hard to attain, making reversals more troublesome. The inventor of the real can't make it easier in fiction and Stern doesn't. A grown daughter says to her mother:

> "You don't know your own nature, momma."
> "Maybe I'd run away from myself if I did."
> "No. If you knew where you were, what you are, things wouldn't happen *to* you all the time. You'd happen to them" ["An Ideal Address," *P* 45–6].

One's degree of centripetal equanimity determines how much a reversal will have an effect on one's equilibrium. If one is in the world, yet not of it, one can retain a balance in the world's flux without being overcome by it. If one can affect the world more than the world affects one, then one can learn from the experience.

REVELATIONS

Stern on Joyce: "Joyce's concern is also with the apprehension of that 'vital power' which reveals itself to the artist with the sudden power he called epiphanic…. he seems interested not in a novel's craftsmanship but in its revelations of personality" ("Proust and Joyce," *FH* 229–30).

Randomization and reversals interrupt routine; sometimes people learn from the circumstances. Only in melodrama is enlightenment accompanied by drums and trumpets, choirs and cacophonies. Self-revelation comes in quieter moments more often than loud moments. Auden said of this, "a moment in which the characters are emotionally relaxed may be just as significant as one in which they are emotionally stirred."[19] Revelations can come to some of Stern's characters when they are "emotionally stirred." More often, however, Sternian revelations are his "residue of design"[20] to be found in the debris after turmoil is over, and discovered during quieter moments of self-awareness when knowledge becomes understanding. This education is not always reserved for characters; readers also benefit from personal revelations derived from their identification of a character's revelation so that the reader's knowledge becomes understanding as well. Sometimes, Stern provides revelatory evidence to readers that his characters aren't ready for; usually, however, characters and readers learn together as in Stern's story, "Packages."

> As I was staying in Aliber's place across from Campbell's, my sister asked me to pick up the package. "I guess it's the acknowledgement cards." Our mother had died five days before.
>
> Campbell's is a wonderful funeral factory. It does all for you, gets the notice into the *Times*, sends for the death certificates (needed by banks, lawyers, accountants), orders the printed acknowledgments of condolence, and of course works out the funeral; or, as in Mother's case, the cremation and memorial service.
>
> We'd held the service there in the large upstairs salon…. A black-gowned organist — the closest thing to a religious figure in attendance — played some of Dad's favorites, "Who," "Some Enchanted Evening" and "Smoke Gets in Your Eyes" (this one a bit much in view of Mother's chosen mode of disintegration).
>
> The package was wrapped in rough brown paper tied with a strand of hemp, which broke when I hoisted it. "Don't worry," I said to the shocked Mr. Hoffman. "I'm just across the street." I held it with one hand and shook

his with the other. Outside, Limousines and chauffeurs idled — it was a slow death day in New York.

Thursday, Garbage-collection day on East 81st. I left the package in a half-empty carton, then returned and covered it with yesterday's *Times*.... then back again to the package, which I unwrapped. It was a silvery can, the size of a half-gallon of paint; labeled. Curious about the contents, I tried to open it. No lid.... I stripped off the label, rewrapped the can, and covered it with the newspaper....

There are hours to kill before Doris picks me up. I activate air conditioners and sound system and pick out some correct music. A cello suite of Poppa Bach. Naked on the leather couch, I listen until it overflows my capacity. You need weeks for such a piece. It should take as long to listen to as it did to compose. Or is the idea to reduce vastness into something portable. A package.

I think I thought that then, though the notion may have come after I'd found *The Mind of Matter* in the wall behind my head. I read a chapter devoted to Planck's "famous lecture to the Berlin Academy in May of 1899," in which he described "that extraordinary quantity" which "for all times and cultures" made possible "the derivation of units for mass, length, time and temperature." Planck's constant. Not then called h. Only 6.625 ¥ 10^{-27} erg seconds, or by our author, "that stubby transmitter of universal radiance... Nature's own package," I felt some connection between it and Bach's and the one which held what was left of what once held me ["Packages," *P* 50–51].

The character's revelation that the package contains his mother was arrived at somewhere between leaving the *Times* on top of it and listening to Bach. The density of detail that follows the understanding of this knowledge by the character leads to the understanding of this knowledge by the reader. This is the residue of Stern's design. The wonders of natural mathematics that are contained in the packages of music and science correlate to the wonder of the package that contains the residue of the mother's life. This revelation is reinforced by the character's naked form that is "wombed" by the "leather couch," another package of a former life.

REDEMPTION

Revelation may be followed by redemption if a character redresses an actual or self-perceived transgression because he has come to understand himself and others better because of the revelation.

The previously mentioned moocher, Higgins, from the story "Assessment of an Amateur," has taken advantage of another expatriate's loneliness in Paris and has no shame in the degree of his exploitation. Higgins, who without portfolio claims himself to be the professional while his so-called "friend" Fred (Bucky) holds amateur status, plays the piano at all hours to the distress of elderly neighbors, Madame Souchay and her ailing brother. Silent warfare ensues. One day Madame is less silent:

> "I must wish, M. Higgins, that you desist in the pianoforte for some weeks. Reasons of crisis. My brother, I am afraid is yesterday dead."
> Whatever this meant, it might not have been true — we never heard — but Higgins answer overrode detail. "*La mort est triste, madame, mais la vie continue*" [Death is sad, Madame, but life continues] [*P* 37].

This incident and many others, particularly Higgins' egregious behavior towards his wife, for which Fred feels some complicity by omission, prompts Fred to consider solitude a better option. Finally, on a night when Higgins grubs another check from Fred and then proceeds to insult him for being an "amateur," Fred responds: "Enough, Higgins, or you'll grub from your own cheque tonight." Higgins, "artistic to the fingertips," grandly rips the check into shreds. Fred sees the light:

> "Well, Higgins," I said gently. "I'll see you in Carnegie Hall," and with that, which for months I regarded as the most felicitous sentence my voice had uttered, I moved on, leaving him — I imagined — crushed.
> I, on the contrary, was not crushed.... I walked away from him that evening ... feeling more elated than injured. Not only with my remark, of course, although that seemed impressive to me at the time, but with my release from the rigours of professionalism. Something like that. There were two ways of looking at the world and two ways of comporting oneself. One couldn't go both ways, and that was that. I had a marvelous dinner, got drunk, and slept fifteen hours....
> The money — all of it — I have of course looked upon as a fair price for an education [*T* 40].

In a journal entry of 12 March 1958 (prior to writing this story) Stern wrote, "Goodness consists in some proportion between kind feeling and useful action; it shows gracefully" (*IR* 143). This would seem to be the moral of the above passage.

So begins the education — and redemption — of an intellectual Everyman.

Subthemes Within Major Themes

MEN / WOMEN / DOMESTIC WARFARE / SECRET WISH

After the five dominant "Rs": Routine, Randomization, Reversals, Revelations, Redemption, there are persistent ancillary themes that run through Stern that are consistent aspects of human relations, and this is Stern's territory. Men and women appear in all of their roles: children, parents, workers, mates. Mating and "unmating" dominate Stern's work just as they dominate reality. Since Stern does not create from whole cloth, his characters are based on people he has been exposed to. He has known a lot of people and the variety lends itself to the creation of many different personas.

While there are no absolutes in Stern that are consistent from work to work and character to character, one can discern a general pattern that goes through many variations: men *need* women; women *put up* with men. Men resent this need while being compelled by it; women resent knowing that men resent them for this power they have over them. Both men and women resent the fear of being alone that drives many relationships beyond companionship into a desperate expediency often fueled with a mutual repulsion based on the hatred of the psychological dependency that has outworn affection. Repulsion in Stern mainly concerns mating but shows up in other forms as well, serving as a perverse magnet that repels and compels simultaneously. One can't keep away from real or imagined enemies or situations. The lure of the lurid seems irresistible even when accompanied by guilt or shame. One will run away not so much to avoid that which one fears, be it person or circumstance, but to avoid the *noir* emotions that the person or circumstance arouses. In effect one fears and loathes his reactions more than that which he is reacting to. Between men and women much of this resentment festers silently, even unconsciously. The resentment becomes sublimated anger revealed in bitter domestic warfare that skirts the real subject until the pot boils over into open acrimony.

In Stern's early short stories and first two novels, *Golk* and *Europe*, which were written in the 1950s, the influence of that white bread decade manifests itself in the relationships. Men are wimps posing otherwise as callous chauvinists; women are prefeminists whose resentment of male attitudes is an early stage of rebellion. Women counter the male chauvinism with a cold war by using the weapon of sexual allure that men can't resist. More overtly, the hot war fought by more assertive Stern women is waged with an "I-will-not-be-told" attitude; nonetheless, even these "independent" women have been shaped by a male world so that even in their rebellion they are shackled by the shape imposed on them, one which they are simultaneously fighting to break out of.

In the 1960s, women asserted their rights to fight collectively and The Pill—Stern's capitals as used repeatedly in *Other Men's Daughters*, 1973, to emphasize the enormous implications and changes inherent in The Pill's use — began to shift the balance of power that also gained momentum with the *Roe vs. Wade* decision. Men like Stern, who were born into the previous prefeminist world, became overwhelmed by these changes. From the late 1960s on, Stern's men want it both ways: to retain the old chauvinism with the double standard that women are to be chaste, yet men don't have to be, while also being compelled/repelled by the new reality that women no longer have to be either. Consequently, the title *Other Men's Daughters*, succinctly sums up a man's hypocritical dilemma: men want to bed the new women but they want their daughters (or wives, or girlfriends) to be the "old" women, demure and virginal. Very often the desire for the "new woman" is concurrent with living with the "old woman." This desire becomes a secret wish that is only, and very temporarily, assuaged by surreptitiously ogling these new women, fantasizing about them, flirting with them, but much less often, culminating with them. (In Stern there are also secret wishes for other forms of fulfillment that provide approval.)

In a later story of Stern's, "Troubles," in the collection *Packages*, 1980, he deftly (and densely) "packages" the complexities of domestic warfare in 17 pages that say more than some books on the same subject. Hanna and Jay, the latter a frustrated graduate student (frustration and graduate student are synonymous), are married and in their late twenty-somethings: "Trouble, Hanna knew, seldom came labeled. And her trouble was not simple sexual confusion.... She herself was one of the straightest of straight arrows.... The confusion was deeper.... Troubles were deep structures. Or structural defects.... She thought keeping a diary would help ... and began burrowing into herself, her life with Jay.... her first entry in the speckled, Rorscach-y book dealt with him:

Kafka's lodestone was his father. Is mine Jay? Or myself with Jay? I only know I'm bottled up. But is he the bottle or the bottler?" ("Troubles," *P* 61–2).

Jay's problem is emotional distance. With Hanna sitting across from him, it is noted that "Twenty miles away lived the polite, handsome boy she'd met [long before].... Hanna felt an extraordinary barrenness. If only she had a few plants, something alive to care for.... *He's not cruel. He just hates what he has to do so much; he armors himself against anything that would tempt him from it. As far as he can love anyone, he loves me. He needs insulation. I'm insulation. He's so fragile inside he doesn't want to know about it.... This turns out to be more selfish than selfishness. The egocentricity of damaged egos"* (*P* 63).

Sex is not the problem. Jay is an "extraordinary" and "generous lover.... Love-making was his release and attainment" (*P* 65). He gave sex intensely and believed this was sufficient to prove to Hanna that she needed nothing more. Hanna has female friends, all of whom are disparaged by

Jay in personal and vicious terms: "Wanda was 'Mount Fat,' Clover Callahan was 'mouse,' Vanessa was 'the Tongue,' and Nora, who had nothing on which he could fix, became his incapacity to fix her, 'the Slitherer.'" To which Hanna responds, "'And you're the Archimedes of Slander,' but under her breath," because she is afraid to confront him. "Still abuse was better than silence. Most nights silence piled around her.... Jay would not discuss their relationship. 'It works or it doesn't. Ours mostly works. Discussion kills'" (P 66–7).

Hanna compares herself to her four friends who have their own litany of troubles with men. Nora seems the most stable and Hanna confides in her that sometimes, even though Jay has never abused her physically, she is afraid of him, afraid of the seething beneath his surface. "It's the anger itself.... But to be squeezed is so awful. To feel your nature so reduced. I'd always hoped marriage would give me space, energy, desire. It hasn't" (P72).

Nora responds, "'Try getting out of it more. Don't bury yourself in him. He's become your tomb.' ... Nora told her to come over for supper. Jay could manage without her. 'It would be the first time.' Said Hanna" (P 72). What had been a relatively cold war now heats up:

> "She didn't invite *me*?"
> Jay was assembling the evening's fortress: apples, books, ballpoints, the vaseful of Sanka.
> "She thinks I ought to get out on my own once in a while."
> "Fine. Just don't come back on a broomstick."
> "Meaning?"
> "Witchery's contagious."
> "Nora's no witch.... You and I don't exactly keep a great salon."
> "All we're trying to do is get out of here quick as we can. We're not the Salvation Army."
> "I don't mean to criticize," she said.
> "I don't know what you mean."
> "It's been my fault too. Our life's too airless. The girls have been a fine thing for me. I feel human with them. You pick at them. I know it's a kind of game for you, your way of being social with me, but sometimes it's too hard.... "
> "OK. I won't say anything about them. If I have an opinion you don't share, I'll shut up. But Hanna, I can't have those psychotic shrews around here. Sorry" [P 73–4].

Despite Hanna's attempt to be conciliatory and shift undeserved blame to herself to assuage Jay who is stubbornly petty, his childish insecurity is obvious except to his oblivious self. Hanna goes to Nora and leaves him a note that he should read her diary so he might understand her deep pain. Nora and Hanna have a sexual encounter. This explains the "sexual confusion" that opens the story. Then Stern writes: "Jay read the diary, more and more infuriated by what he regarded as its insensitivity." He blames the "shrews" and proceeds to get drunk. Hanna returns. "He sat in liquorousness like a fish in an aquarium" (*P76*). Hanna is pleased as she sees in his binge an emotional reaction — his fear of her leaving him. She also sees an erection and they make love.

> Yet, Hanna told herself, half an hour later, awake while he snoozed off beyond troubles, she was in the jungle with Vanessa and Wanda and Clover. Energy, talent and hope warred with her life; no relationship and no institution could help. She had the isolation of a pioneer in the circumstance of a soap opera. The only ax she had was the knowledge she was in trouble, that she was down there with the others [*P* 77].

The trouble in "Troubles" reflects a domestic warfare that most readers will recognize from either personal or observed experience. Faces, places, and actual words may differ in the particulars, but the conflicts are universal. The dialogues in Stern sound as if the proverbial fly on the wall overheard them. His fictional conversations, like actual conversations, imply as much or more between the lines as in them. Readers can fill in the alternative names of the Hannas, Jays, and Noras they have known; readers can often fill in their own names.

APPROVAL / SEX, COMPULSION / PEANUT BUTTER

The educator William Heard Kilpatrick said, more or less, that the greatest need of human beings is the need to feel appreciated. Stern agrees. Approval and the concurrent neediness that the want of approval creates in his characters run through his work as they run though reality. Kilpatrick was referring to his experiences as a teacher, first of children, and later of undergraduate and graduate students. Stern is either a teacher who happens to write or a writer who happens to teach. He loves both. A teacher gives appreciation and also receives it. Auden believed that the artist was also a teacher — through parable. Wilder believed this as well and further said that the parables must be subtle; didacticism kills art and the artist's message if it is heavily applied. Auden and Wilder were teachers before they became successful writers, which may have influenced their visions of the writer's role. Writers, teachers, artists, all seek approval. Writers who also teach may be even more aware of the need to give and receive approval.

Stern is acutely aware of the need for approval and many of his protagonists are very, very needy. Sometimes the need is one of quiet desperation (Hanna and Jay); sometimes it is more flamboyantly narcissistic with much pomp and circumstance or silly shenanigans acted out by childish adults (Gunther, Wursup, Higgins). The need for approval can bring out the worst in those who want it and they will try all kinds of shameless manipulations in order to get it. Two people who are desperate for approval can drive each other crazy. The needy are also sign-bearers who attract connivers and stone cold manipulators who appear to feed the need while actually feeding themselves materially or emotionally. Higgins, Golk, from the novel bearing his name, and Baggish, part of the title that begins *Europe*, knowingly take advantage of their needy victims to serve personal ends.

A need for approval on an emotional level — and that simply constitutes some version of love — if not met, will seek subliminal alternatives. In Stern this means sex as first choice, then food when sex is not available. Sex circumscribes, subsumes, pervades, and invades the fiction of Richard Stern just as it has done in society since The Pill, the 1960s, and *Roe vs. Wade*. (Even in essays, Stern alludes to sex: "A girl named Rafferty came up to me, said sweetly that she had nearly 'had me' as an instructor at college" ("The Pursuit...," *FH* 31). Many of Stern's men are constantly aware of sex and are driven by a metaphorical divining rod between their legs that intuitively searches for erotic stimulation whether as fantasy or actuality. There is much imagining among Stern's men of being with women they know (if not yet in Biblical terms) who are friends, coworkers, students, mates of their male friends or total strangers seen only for an instant. Much of the banter by men about sex is casual and reflects a reality prevalent in the gender that is just as common as the fact that this sublimated reality is rarely admitted to their mates. Sometimes, however, the pursuit of mental or actual sex is compulsive to the point of sexual addiction and even sexual predation. The predators in Stern are few and not only men. Women also employ sex as a means to some end and know too well how men can be slaves to their "divining rods." There are other compulsions in Stern such as the need to create, or to become successful on a financial or intellectual level, or to overeat and drink. These are never the real need. They are substitutes for sex and approval. The quest for approval and sex always engenders the possible counterpoint of betrayal.

AESTHETES VS. HEARTIES / MIND (IMAGINATION) OVER MATTER (POLITICS AND FILTHY LUCRE)

Auden, Isherwood and dozens of their contemporaries had foul memories of their days in Britain's "public" schools (which are, in reality, the most exclusive private schools). There, they made a distinction between "aesthetes" and "hearties." The former included themselves—sensitive intellectuals who were much less interested in sports and war than they were in poetry. The latter were the athletes and future empire protectors who tormented the aesthetes and would later excel in business, politics, and class snobbery. As a reaction to the hearties the Auden Generation became 1930s iconoclastic antiheroes who wrote about antiheroes to inspire the next generations of realists including Richard Stern. Stern regards business and politics with perverse fascination.

According to Stern, "One of the great twentieth-century novels is Christina Stead's *House of All Nations* [1938].... Its world is international finance; its characters are dominated by markets, manipulations, making money from gesture, rumor, or even occasionally real goods.... [There is a] knowledge of the world such that no work known to me better reveals the relationship of money to personality and politics" ("Out of," *FH* 254). Writing about his friend Saul Bellow, Stern notes: "Investments, deals, arrangements, the mean grandeur and farce of business have been no small part of Bellow's fiction" ("Bellow," *IR* 16). It is no less a part of Stern's fiction. The politician fares no better: "As far as his [the politician's] national personality goes, that is an illusion; a kind of allegory, standing for this, stemming from that, aiming here, avoiding there" ("The Pursuit...," *FH* 33). Elsewhere, in another article about politics, Stern quotes Auden's famous remark about the duplicity of human nature: "Private faces in public places are wiser and nicer than public faces in private places" ("George McGovern," *FH* 38). Of this duplicity, Stern writes in an "imaginary interview" with a politician; "When I was in office, I swallowed ordure from breakfast to supper. Some of my colleagues not only adjust to such nourishment; they crave it. I ate in public, vomited in private" ("Aurelia...," *FH* 113). The businessman of the American Puritan ethic and the politician with no ethics are the U. S. versions of the hearties, and the intellectual artist and university academic are today's aesthetes. Stern's preference for the latter began in his ill-fated and limited exposure to the business world in 1947. Nonetheless, Stern will not claim that the university is a safe haven immune to the human frailties found elsewhere:

> Perhaps the artist who works more or less happily in the university should prod his ease as Kafka prodded his quiescent neurosis: "The deeper one's pit, the quieter it becomes." This furred burrow one inhabits, is it too remote from the green world of change?
> ... Or is it that the college teacher's burrow is at a double remove, a burrow within a burrow? After all, the university has its special precincts, carefully chosen personnel; its lawns are tended by polite retainers; its meeting

places command good behavior. Plus which the university artist is lapped in the institutional radiance of tenure and pension. What can he know of street wars, cutthroat trade, the reluctance of field and bone?

Yet.

In a university one can be lonely; one can cheat, love, be loved; one can even be heroic, villainous. One breathes, eats, works, plays, engenders. What the writer writes about — alteration, doubt, illusion, gain, loss, forgiveness — are not these in the university as in every human nutshell? ... what other twentieth-century institution is at once pulpit, seedbed, laboratory, marketplace, the crossroads of what's been and what's to be....

There is no paradise for the artist; and he can make whatever hell is necessary for him wherever he is ["The Writer...," (*FH* 162–3)].

Indeed, there is a lot of hell in Stern and much of it comes from his life either indirectly or very directly. Hence, this leads to the question of how much "auto" is in his fictional biographies.

CHAPTER TWO

"Inside Narcissus":
The Issue of
Fictional Autobiography

> *I haven't wanted to write an autobiography, so when I recently took stock and noticed how much of my work these last years was flecked and sometimes saturated with autobiographical matter, I asked myself, "What's going on? Why all this calling attention to a self at least one part of which has never thought the whole particularly interesting? Or has that been the point?"*
> — Stern, 2001

Stern's bailiwick concerns the invention of the real. He produces fiction that is about characters any of his readers could know, and, with human nature able to predict human behavior, readers recognize types they *do* know. Stern steals from reality. The question remains as to what degree he replicates, imitates, or derives. After fiction, Stern writes essays; many of his essays explain why and how he writes fiction. Parts of the essays concern how and why he writes about himself. As prelude, herein is a news item about another author:

> South Carolina writer Pat Conroy [*The Prince of Tides, Lords of Discipline*] says he initially began writing his 1976 book *The Great Santini* out of spite. "I did not like my father," Conroy said. "I did not like one single thing about him." The book details a teenager standing up for himself, his mother and sister against an intolerant father. "My first conscious memory is my mother trying to stab my father with a butcher knife."[21]

This critic will not say Stern writes for spite. He does, however, as did Eliot, sometimes "grouse against life."

Post-World War II writers are reputed to be the literary leaders in personal grousing as compared to previous generations. While that's a subject for another study, one can point out that even if autobiographical fiction has become more prevalent, it is far from unprecedented. Aldous Huxley's first novel, the satire *Crome Yellow*, 1920, is based on his days as a guest at Garsington Manor, the estate of Lady Ottoline Morrell who fed and housed numerous artists and intellectuals. Lady Ottoline did not speak to Huxley for a long time afterward. Huxley's 1928 breakthrough best seller, *Point Counterpoint*, featured, with fictitious names, D. H. Lawrence, the British fascist Oswald Mosley, and Huxley himself as Philip Quarles, the aloof, too intellectual author who drives his wife into the arms of the Mosley surrogate (which did *not* happen in real life). Philip's son, the same age, seven, as Huxley's son Matthew, becomes horribly ill and dies— punishment for the illicit affair. Huxley's wife Maria was not pleased. Huxley's *Eyeless in Gaza*, 1935, features another Huxley surrogate, Anthony Beavis, whose father does not come off very well. There is also a detailed account of Anthony's best friend who has a stammer and is very fragile as was Huxley's brother Trevenen. The character, as did Trevenen, kills himself. More woe among Huxley family members. This would be Huxley's last *roman à clef*.

Christopher Isherwood is unique among 20th century writers when it comes to writing about himself. Isherwood wrote fictional autobiography and actual autobiography, but in both cases, for the most part, used his real name even when the art was ostensibly fiction and he became a "character" in his own work. This was a blatant declaration by the author that one should be perpetually puzzled by the extent of his "invention of the real." Isherwood drew extensively, sometimes verbatim, from his diaries, which were written with a literary ear for future publication.

Richard Stern also keeps journals. He notes that they do not become wholesale transcriptions in his fiction but sometimes serve as prompts. In his "orderly miscellany," *The Invention of the Real*, a section titled, "Getting at oneself," includes journal entries. There are 27 pages of who knows how many originally, and one can see at least three future novels represented: *In Any Case*, 1962, *Stitch*, 1965, *Other Men's Daughters*, 1973. The first two *do* have brief near-verbatim transcriptions. The particulars will be noted in discussions of these works to follow in succeeding chapters. One cannot know the proportion of adaptation without the journals in total. In 1996, for example, Isherwood's diaries were published for the first time and this required major revisions in considering his art.

　　Stern, at the least, uses journals as prompts to memory and it is in memory as recalled subjectively that the artist, in moments of tranquility or otherwise, reconstitutes the essence of his life or the *Weltanschauung* of his *Weltansicht*. Stern, the compulsive writer, has written often about how and why he writes fiction. This record, like much of what Stern does, relates to his need for explaining himself. This is a benefit for a book such as this one and also for interested readers. More authors are revealing how they do what they do, with Stern noting, "the twentieth-century public has been intrigued as much by the process of creation as by its results" ("Working Out a Story," *FH* 149). This public gets more satisfaction than ever as the media and the internet provide venues for explanation and confession by writers who are more than willing to get "Inside Narcissus." Stern has been willing to explain himself in essays for more than 30 years so let his will be done.

　　He notes, "One can, I think subsume all distinctions between art and actuality..." ("Events...," *FH* 94). For Stern, life influences art regardless of how far removed the art becomes from the life creating it. Stern makes a distinction between two types of novelists: "Novels take off from any and everything, but novelists are mostly virtuosi or realists. That is, they either aim at the remarkable, or organize what they feel about more or less imagined *familiar* experience until, because of their narrative gift, it seems remarkable to others" ("Country...," *PB* 44). Moreover, he writes, "Many fine fiction writers would be wiped out if they were prevented from using their own experience for their books" ("Inside Narcissus," *IR* 186). Stern considers the movement from illusion to reality among modern writers a psychological necessity in which, as he said, "'realists' wish to assemble the world in order to control it" (*FH* 100). The added quotation marks around "realists" are Stern's; his reminder that even writing about the real is a matter of invention, not transcription. Stern comments on the evolution from past virtuosi to modern realists:

> Now for about two hundred years psychology, in the novel and in psychiatry has bored in ever closer to the actions and intentions of human beings. The great acts of heroism and sacrifice have been honeycombed with the analysis of *real motive*, of unconscious "intention." A man's great action may have more to do with his past than the demanding present; the hero may be a vicious brute, the saint a "pervert." Only the witness has not seriously suffered the onslaught. Why? Because he has not pretended to greatness, so he has not minded his alteration from heroic self-sacrificer to wounded subliminator. The hero and saint have been crowded out of their niches, but the artist has grown — as a figure — in interest, and he is frequently the example of the anti-heroic hero ["Working Out a Story," *FH* 159].

Stern the artist is also an antiheroic hero. His protagonists are neither heroes nor saints; they are Everyman with foibles and frailties easily recognized. Sometimes, let alone not being heroes and saints, they are not even likable, and are occasionally despicable; yet, they are not commented on as such through the author's narration. They exist in their actions, not in the author's imposed view. Readers give judgment on what they do; and what they do is not evil, to the actors, but is their self-absorbed versions of solipsist Kierkegaardian necessity. They (1) breathe, eat, sleep, excrete, and (2) cheat, lie, steal, connive with little sense of proportion of how the first group differs from the second. *Au fond*, the author lets the villains be identified by what they do. The narrator does not say who wears a black hat. The reader is a witness to the actions described and arrives at personal judgments by applying the Auden test of juxtaposed comparison, *Who am I? Whom ought I to become?* While readers compare their lives to Stern's characters', Stern requires that they conduct the process with a degree of sensitivity. He also knows that authors don't find readers, but that readers find authors who please them. For example, Auden, when asked if he thought about what kind of audience he was writing for, answered, "No, I just try to put the thing out there and hope somebody will read it. Someone says, 'whom do you write for?' I reply: 'Do you read me?' If they say, 'Yes,' I say, 'Do you like it?' If they say, 'No,' then I say, 'I don't write for you.'"[22] Auden's point was that if he tried to write what he thought people wanted to hear he wouldn't have been listening to himself and ultimately would have pleased no one. The extreme of the insincere writer is the propagandist.

Stern is deeply sensitive as to the ways in which insensitive people take advantage of the need for approval in others who are as sensitive as the author is. At times his fiction can seem to be attacks of unrelenting cynicism; but the other side of a cynical man is a fallen hero. To depict insensitivity realistically can only be described by one who has been its victim. The perpetrators of callousness don't give a damn and waste no time considering that others do give a damn. Among those others are writers such as Stern:

> As athletes use their bodies, writers use their feelings, their insights, their fantasies, and sometimes, the very events, the very shape and feel of their lives. Charged with revealing the world, the writer has learned that the world he reveals is conditioned by his way of observing it, and this by his feelings ... many writers, therefore, have devoted themselves to self-examination and the exhibition of what Augustine called "the abysses of human consciousness...." If his [the writer's] memory were distorted, the distortion itself didn't betray fiction. If anything, it stood for strong feelings—which

is what counts the most. And narrative operation on such memory is likely to rouse more powerful feeling than treatment of less intimate material… ["Inside Narcissus," *IR* 184].

Consequently, writers, who by their natures are conveyors of feelings, will often gravitate towards that most readily available fount of feelings—themselves. Then they will, as Stern said, "organize what they feel about more or less imagined *familiar* experience until, because of their narrative gift, it seems remarkable to others" ("Country…," *PB* 44).

> The *maker* of a work reflects not so much upon the thing he wishes to present as upon the ways of presenting it. Subjects usually "come." Especially if you're geared to watch for them by considering yourself an artist of a particular sort. Not being a sculptor, I don't look for the configuration of rocks, but for seventeen or eighteen years [now fifty] I have looked for stories, and so I frequently come upon story "material…." The real job begins with working the thing out: I felt like writing about an uncle of mine who spent many lonely years living in an uptown New York Hotel. His only diversion was a weekly poker game at the home of a man who, in Vienna decades before, had let rooms to Hitler…. But how to tell it, how to *mine* the story…. I needed something else…. I then thought of another character for a story. This was a woman who put up postcards sent by her employers and friends around the University [of Chicago]. I put "Miss Swindleman" and my uncle, now Harvey Mendel, into one story. Miss Swindleman was to be the tool to get gold out of the mine" ["Working Out a Story," *FH* 159–60].

Stern wrote this story and then his essay about *how* he wrote the story before he turned to more overtly autobiographical fiction. Later he would come to grips with his personal explicitness:

> All right then, granted some fine writers claim they can't make anything up, that they have to draw every wrinkle from an actual face, that their creativity consists largely in the filtration of what strikes them as inconsistencies in actuality, still, still, why do some of these writers have to draw on their own intimate lives, on the people they know best, those whom they love? Why do they write about their own love affairs, children, divorces, lives and deaths of their closest friends?
> The fiction writer who wants his work to be a source of truth as well as diversion, beauty, merriment, whatever, may be unable to cut himself off from those situations which have affected him most deeply, and those situations may be impossible to detach from those who figured in them ["Inside Narcissus," *IR* 187–188].

Stern goes on to say that the writer, while he may be "unable to cut himself off from those situations which have affected him most deeply," can, by altering particulars, "intensify and embellish, ... shrink the tall, change the sex of children.... The easiest thing to change is yourself ... give yourself a bad leg and a profession rich in technical vocabulary which will suggest certain habits of mind or send you to places it'll excite you to go in the narrative." An example is in *Other Men's Daughters*, 1973, where the Stern surrogate is a biophysicist ("Inside Narcissus," *IR* 189). Stern sees some therapy in this kind of writing:

> There is a kind of purgation in such indirect confession, a special plea-sure in this indirect honesty. Put in the time you stole Billy's pen, but let the ex-mailman get punished for it.
> So the book gets written ... ideas pouring in from actuality or from delighted invention ... it's published. Friends poke you in the ribs: "You sure showed Charley." Your ex-wife tells you to stay away from the children. A learned ex-friend quotes Lord Hervey: "He never remembered an obliga-tion nor forgot an injury."
> If there's no woe, there may be no song. The writer knows that some of his finest passages come after his heart has been rattled around and he's gone to a typewriter and put down more or less exactly what he's felt. He thinks he needs more rattling ["Inside Narcissus," *IR* 190–91].

Stern lives to rattle and get rattled. In an essay from his third collec-tion of "ordered miscellanies," *The Position of the Body*, 1986, he writes about trying new mechanical approaches to writing such as dictation and a word processor and their inherent snafus. He talks about the time spent in the wrong direction before he found the right track that became the novel *A Father's Words*, 1986:

> The point is that the core of the book was never Firetuck, Riemer, and the Farce Movement. The heart of it was— is— a transfiguration and projection of the author's relationships to two wives and four children. The miscalcu-lations, waste pages, skewered drafts, the four thousand pages in the archives of failure have more to do with failure to see that than with the misdirec-tions of dictation.
> I think I've finished now with family novels. I've hurt everyone I can hurt. Not — as far as I know — trying to hurt, but there it is, and I paid for it with the thousands of pages, the thousands of hours wasted, the typed excursions to Africa and Tulsa, the hearts and pockets of invention I'll never use. I was punished for failing to see my subject. I must get another. No amanuensis or word processor can do that for me... ["The Debris of a Novel," *PB* 180].

In an interview, James Schiffer asked Stern about a scene from *A Father's Words*. *Schiffer*: "After he sees the version of himself on television, Riemer says to his son Jack that he understands why Jack modeled his characters on people he knows and feels strongly about. But Riemer adds, 'I just wish you didn't feel about me the way it shows up.'"

Stern: "My oldest son, Christopher, and I have had a lot of discussions. He said after *A Father's Words*, 'I realized how little you understood me after I read that book.' Well, I said, 'It's not just you.' [to Schiffer] You know the process.... I still have to answer for writing about other people."[23]

Stern admits that he sometimes writes close to the bone. Some critics and other writers have inferred that Stern writes about himself *too* much. Of this Stern said in the same interview: "I can remember arguing with [John] Barth, who doesn't think I'm an artist at all. [He says]'Oh, you know a lot, and you've got energy,' he says. 'But where's the virtuosity? Where's the Art?' I can't answer that."[24]

This critic will answer that he sees the art in two areas:

1. All art emanates from the known; nothing is created from an ether of preknowledge. Kierkegaard said: "life can only be understood backwards; but it must be lived forwards." Or written about forwards. Language is a reactionary medium created to account for the "backwards" so one can communicate "forwards." Without experience there is no backward upon which to base a forward. Consequently, all literature, since it employs language, is derivative of a writer's experience even if what he writes seems to have been written from whole cloth, which, in fact, is impossible. (To read further on this perspective, see the philosophy of Michael Polanyi [*Personal Knowledge*, *The Tacit Dimension*], and this author's study, *Aldous Huxley and W. H. Auden: On Language*.)

2. Shakespeare borrowed everything and no one blames him because the art is in his virtuoso presentation. In addition, the only two Stern books clearly *at* the bone of his personal life are *Other Men's Daughters* and *A Father's Words*. The rest are subject to speculation as to how closely art resembles life, speculation which, as this study moves to individual works, will be kept at a minimum. The tea-table has been set. It's time to move the emphasis from the brewer to the tea.

CHAPTER THREE

From Chapel Hill to Chicago, Eisenhower to Kennedy — 1950–1965

Stern began getting his short stories published in the 1950s — the Eisenhower era, mythically noted for a (false) sense of tranquility. Problems were ignored until they exploded in the next decade. When Eisenhower left office he warned of the insidious and incestuous centripetal coupling of the military-industrial complex that sucked money away from the nation's other needs. Superimposed on these hidden machinations was the public's collective dulling blandness and twin beds for Lucy and Desi. Even married people did not admit to sex on television and, for the most part, in the public's purview either. Gay people didn't exist except in the most perversely pejorative terms. The actor Rock Hudson, a matinee idol and closet homosexual, endured a paper-only marriage.

For those born after 1960, it may be difficult to accept secondhand accounts of this blandness and the notion of "ignorance is bliss" which existed at the time. One cannot imagine how different the world was then. The blandness masked repression that would become rebellion in the 1960s.

The best this critic can do to suggest — obliquely — what it was like is to advise younger people to watch movies and TV shows from the 1950s and compare. All movies were G-rated by today's standards. Bikinis didn't exist; *Playboy* barely — pun intended.

The shift from the 1950s to the late 1960s was as profoundly dramatic as the cultural literacy mavens now claim it to be. Then, it was not until bland left out the "l" and rock 'n' roll arrived, that a shift towards the present future began. Nothing has been the same since. If one compares MTV to Lucy and Desi, and *sees* what could *not* be viewed then and how much can be seen now by comparison, one must try to fill in—*de profundis*—what the psychological impact was on men and women who grew up in the first era and became adults in the second. Richard Stern encountered both eras and has lived to write about it. In an essay about his years at Iowa while getting a Ph.D. (1952–1954), he gives his impressions of the era:

> These were the years of Ike's [Eisenshower's] great tranquility. We had babies by the carload. So it wasn't just getting up the rent (the few bachelors survived on a Calcutta beggar's income), it was getting bread, milk, jello, and diaper-service into the till. We went to the MLA [Modern Language Association] bazaar, the only road to the well-filled trough. No one went off to the Canadian woods, to Paris or Washington [to avoid the Vietnam war]....
>
> White paper sat in our typewriter carriages: our Ithacas ... no war, no Watergate.... We weren't much *in the world*. Though when the Army-McCarthy hearings brought public swinery into the new quasi-fictional intensity of the tube, we were in the front row ... booing, groaning. Overcome with the event. Ten years later, babies would devour more event with their pablum ["Two Iowan Baudelaires...," *IR* 136–37].

Indeed, the world would change from a relatively news-starved 1950s into the new news-and-gossip-inundated present. In the 1950s the TV program *Candid Camera* claimed to secretly film folks in folksy, innocuous gags and then yell: "Surprise, you're on *Candid Camera*." Years later it was uncovered that the gags were setups and the show was as phony as the game show *Twenty-One* that featured Charles Van Doren as the set-up winner. *Candid Camera* was the pseudo height of the decade's "invasion" of privacy.

Stern was fascinated by the show. (This was before the perfidy was discovered). He imagined what the same type of show might be like if "folksy" became "*Golk*-sy." The result was the deadpan, wry, darkly comic novel *Golk*, 1960. Norman Mailer said that *Golk* was "the first really good book I have read about television."[25] *Golk* is also a prescient look ahead to a time not far off when television and print media would go from twin beds, to one bed, to what happens in that bed, no holds barred, and no mercy on the private lives trivialized in Lewinskyesque detail. (The topic of Stern's essay "Inside Narcissus" has since been fully developed in Jeffrey Rosen's recently published *The Unwanted Gaze: The Destruction of Privacy in America*.)

1960: *Golk*

After a dozen or so short stories, Stern's first novel, *Golk*, is his first coherent fusion of themes that would become standards in his career. (The early short stories were first collected in the single volume, *Teeth, Dying, and Other Matters*, 1964, that was published after Stern's first three novels and will be examined in that order).

Golk's protagonist, Herbert Hondorp, is a 37-year-old insulated man-child absolved of all responsibility by his father the doctor. His mother is long dead. (Herbert is the protagonist but not the central figure; this is Golk.) Herbert, with his father's very willing support, does not work and has nothing but leisure time — as long as he doesn't leave dad. His daily routine is based on his self-delusion that he has no routine. Herbert wanders around Manhattan and Central Park. He sometimes reads the *Britannica* to obtain a superficial knowledge that will get him into a Persian rug shop where he piques the owner's interest by asking "whether the masterpiece at his feet was worked with the Sehna or Ghiordes knot" (*G* 7). These random *Britannica* interludes and play-acting break the routine that is not a routine. Herbert is a trickster about to be tricked. He enters a used bookstore to obey his father's dictum that "The unnourished mind withers," even though dad's mind-food is restricted to the obituary section of the *New York Times* and television. He browses in the bookstore and hears a voice ask him, "You looking or buying?" (*G* 9). The voice comes from the wall. From the voice's location Herbert pulls *The Conquest of Peru* and the voice asks him to read something from it:

> Drawing his sword, he traced a line with it on the sand from east to west. Then, turning towards the south, "Friends and comrades! On that side are toil, hunger, nakedness ... desertion and death; on this side ease and pleasure. There lies Peru with its riches; here, Panama and its poverty. Choose, each man, what best becomes a brave Castilian. For my part, I go to the south! So saying, he stepped across the line [*G* 10].

With this prompt, Herbert will step across the line into the world of Golk (formerly Sidney Pomeroy) to reverse the drift of his faux random, truly routine existence. Golk produces a TV show that tricks tricksters and innocents into being victims by setting up the unsuspecting. Golk — still a disembodied voice — asks Herbert why he likes used books. "They're cheaper." Golk chastises his remark. "'What's the matter with new books? The whole economy runs on what's new....' This remark took Herbert into the familiar country of his contempt for the world's business." Herbert retorts that "the economy can drop dead...." The voice then asks,

"'Now, tell me what your business is, pal.' Every man has a question which terrifies him, and to the avoidance of which he gives himself with energy that helps shape his life. This was the question that shoved Hondorp's diaphragm against his stomach, stiffened his throat muscles, hacked at his breath.... 'Whatever it is is none of yours, pal'" (*G* 10–11).

Herbert freezes at this question because the real answer shames him: to an outsider's eyes he lives off his father; he has no ambition, no life, nothing whatsoever to justify his existence. If Herbert *were* someone else and not so sensitive to what he thinks others might be thinking of him, his answer would suffice without his pride getting in the way. The manipulators— the Golks— don't care how they are perceived, but know that the Herberts of the world do care. Golk is insensitive to any needs but his own. This is not to say Golk is not smart; he is *too* clever, trapped in some precocity he has not outgrown and will preserve by whatever means necessary. Golk's needs are neurotically driven by his own demons and can never be satisfied. Stern gives Golk little back-story. One knows he was damaged in the past from how he acts in the present. Golk is boorishly selfish and arms himself with a good-offense-is-the-best-defense mentality that he acts out with infantile narcissism.

In the bookstore Herbert realizes he has been "Golked" by *the* Golk of local TV fame. Herbert warming up to this game, this *play* that breaks his routine, helps Golk "Golk" another gull. The question he had feared has now been answered. He is now in the business of Golking: "The confrontation with Golk was the one for which more than any other he had somehow been prepared. He'd watched the show a good many times ... and the promise Golk made to all New York at the end of every program.... 'Watch out. One of these days you'll be on camera too,' constituted for Hondorp one of the few contracts he felt might be fulfilled for him, one of the fewer he looked forward to fulfilling. 'For my part, I go to the south,' he said out loud. He had been discovered" (*G* 15).

A secret wish has been answered. This omen of stunning reversal cannot be ignored. Of all the people who could have been picked at random, Golk found a gull not only willing but also waiting to be gulled. Golk is a master at giving approval to fragile vanity and tells Herbert he is a natural for Golking. Herbert then meets Golk face to face and recognizes the "great bare dome" he and his father have seen on TV. Many of Stern's characters have bald or large heads or both, a seeming excess of brains signifying that too much knowledge without understanding can be a dangerous thing. Golk has the "chameleon knack" to be all things to all people. This is Stern's persiflage for "con artist." Golk's insincere praise and approval are tempting for Herbert; so is his fear of ending his routine: "He felt himself sinking into the huge blue bulges of Golk's eyes ... and they seemed to rot out the unformed but ruling notions of Hondorp's careerless life. 'I'm not fit. I'm not ready'" (*G* 22). Golk overcomes Herbert's fear by assuring him he is ready.

Herbert succumbs, but now on to a most onerous task: how to tell dad he has a job. "It was Hondorp's knowledge of what he meant to his father that led to the break which he announced at breakfast. Hondorp broke out of his cocoon for the sake of breaking the earthly peace it gave his father. He had no conscious desire other than this, no desire to do anything than what he had for years been doing, wandering over New York, regarding the products of the earth, the masterpieces of the ages. But through all the years, the break with his father had been waiting its occasion, and now it was with glee that he went to it, with fearsome glee, but with glee. It was the classic primal action: all else would stem from it" (*G* 24). Poppa protests, "you, my darling have had the rare opportunity of, in this life, studying. But no, what do you want to do? Push your nose into a lousy routine" (*G* 26). One man's routine is another man's temptation. Papa fails to persuade. His boy is now in television. "Today his walk was an occasion: he had a destination ... and destination was almost destiny ... other people's values were not his, need not be his ... he felt a corresponding thrust away from that hibernated self.... And an aspect of this thrust—as of nature's—was patricidal" (*G* 27–8).

Herbert's first reactions to the corporate structure in the immense Parlsak Building leave him cold: "These people seem unused to polite society." Nonetheless, Golk's lure is too strong. He knows exactly how to push the buttons that will tweak each particular individual to Golk's way. When Herbert intimates that he is a scholar in order to obscure his lack of practical experience, Golk feeds the approval meter: "'I'm a doer myself, but a man must fuel up with thought. That I know. Few know that like I know it. I'm glad to have scholar-types around me....' As if a coin had been pushed through a slot in his head, Hondorp found words tumbling out of him. 'It's wrong to think of scholars as idlers...'" (*G* 33). Herbert has crossed the line; he's joined the club; there's nowhere to go but across the line and south, that is, down. Further temptation comes from Golk's associate, Hendricks, a "lanky beauty in slacks and moccasins." This was not corporate attire in the staid 1950s when skirts and dresses were standard and is a hint of Jeanine's rebellious nature, which was also a novelty in the business world and one she honed after years of subjugation to men. Even though Jeanine is only 23—14 years younger than Herbert— she is years ahead of Herbert in education by bitterness. When Golk introduces *Hen*dricks to *H*ondorp, he tells them, "You alliterate" (*G* 34). Further bait

comes from "Elaine, the Negress, whose style had been modeled on ...
Lena Horne's." Neither Elaine nor Hendricks is demure. Elaine brushes
legs with Herbert under the corporate table (sex and power): "The leg was
as informative as a letter of intentions" (G 36). This tempts and terrifies
Herbert who is still inexperienced — completely.

In Stern, sex and death — both being horizontal — as well as sleep,
seem all of a piece. It is noted when Herbert first considered trying sex:
"He was eighteen and two days before had been at his mother's funeral.
It was there at his first experience of human mortality that he'd decided
to experience the other crucial human engagement" (G 37). He *decided* at
18 but has not yet acted on the decision. Elaine's leg almost overwhelms
him and pushes him into panic and toward escape, but he endures his anxiety and stays. The leg goes no further — for the moment.

The alliteratives have lunch. Hondorp tells Hendricks he thinks he
has seen her before:

> "You are different than people one passes in the street."
> "If not," she said seriously, "my life's been without point."
> "That makes you sound like a lot of others."
> "I don't mind sounding like them, just being like them" [G 40].

Hendricks tells him he has seen her on the show, the first time as a
victim, later as a victimizer. Long before Golk, she has been both, in ways
that make Golking seem like kindergarten. Hendricks finds Herbert amus-
ing, precisely because he does, in her estimation, a fair job of acting worldly
by trying to beat her actual worldly wisdom with droppings of self-learned
scholarship. Thinking he's rankled her with a learned remark, "Hondorp,
feeling his hook catch flesh, smiled coldly..." (G 43). His smug coldness
is a mask just as Jay's mask in "Troubles." Hendricks makes her assessment of Herbert as an amateur trying to act otherwise and finds him affect-
ingly humorous, like a high school calculus student arguing with Einstein.
"For Hendricks, Hondorp constituted a diversion from a routine which
... had come to smother her." A little later she thinks of him as "a natural
Victim" with an "amateur's face, a map of which exploiters could trace
with ease their devious routes. It was not her own ambition to exploit it.
If anything, it was to harden the face, or harden the man behind it so that
signs of worldly distress would be blurred into a worldly neutrality" (G
62). So begins their gender — if not yet domestic — warfare.

Hendricks' assessment of this amateur is also neutral; she considers
his education by her into worldliness as a matter of course. She spots Herbert ogling Elaine's overt sexuality. Jeanine chooses the slacks and moccasins

style as a degenderization that separates her public face from her private face; conversely, Elaine uses her sex appeal as a business tool. Jeanine is surprised to find herself angry at Herbert's lust; but she is equally amused, thinking that Elaine "can get the kinks out, and it'll give him some assurance. Primitive, but, I suppose necessary" (G 65). Elaine gives Herbert his first experience and he, ingenuously racist, attributes her arousing wildness to being African. She laughs this off and when Herbert tells her she is the "white man's dream of savage passion. She answers. "That's my aim in life ... I never sleep with a jig," revealing her own ambition and reverse racism (G 66).

Stern's story of Jeanine Hendricks' previous life starts with her, at 15 "running a Kotex pad up the flagpole as a mark of farewell" to the girls school where her scandalous father (her mother died in childbirth) had dumped her and from which she was now fleeing. Found, she is sent to a school in Brussels, "...the theory being that she could exercise less influence over foreigners and might therefore be subject to some. She was. Her guide was a precocious Belgian lesbian, her room-mate a girl whose sexual hatred of men had turned philosophic and so helped forge independence" (G 45). From this "philosophy" Hendricks learned not to hate men but to consider how to use them. After two years of tutelage, she tells her father the school is a "lesbian brothel." He wires her money and she flees again, this time to Paris. From here, "her route was devious and brutal." After various and foolish missteps that squander her cash, she decided "to marry money, and Immanuel Kant's glacial definition of marriage became her guide, her image of the woman-crippling condition" (G 47). She returns to the U. S., tours the meeting places of affluence with no luck, returns to Paris, finds a "mark" in George Hendricks, marries him and learns that she, the marker, was marked by her new husband to be his victim, not hers:

> Jeanine's marriage was her rack. Hendricks' contempt and detestation were unbounded in extent and savagery, and she was for him little more than a laboratory in which he experimented with the odder aspects of his passions. He moved systematically to grind down every gesture of the independence whose existence represented the creative act of Jeanine's life. Far beyond her in strength and shrewdness, his typical strategy was to rouse an argument, and lead it on and on until he'd led her to see herself self-contradicted, exposed, ridiculous. He baited her to rage, and fed it until it became violence; then he counter punched her attacks, knocked her groggy, threw her into bed or on the floor, and then, often as not, assaulted her [G 48].

She flees again, back to her Belgian roommate who numbs her pain with drugs for 15 months. Addicted, she runs again, locks herself up, endures withdrawal—"My labor pains ... and I come out my own child" (*G* 48). She goes to Nevada for a divorce, which George agrees to in exchange for silence concerning his sadistic predilections, and extends to her a credit line. At a steep price she has finally gotten her independence; yet, at first she will not use the credit line and struggles to make a living without it. "She was twenty-two, and on the edge of change, either of something outside the world of what she thought of as 'experience for its own sake' or, if necessary, of that politic female submission she had long ago fought to a standstill" (*G* 49). Hendricks has reluctantly accepted that in a man's world she must judiciously choose when to give up some independence so that she will never again lose all of it. Then she is "Golked" and finds the "change" she needed.

She and Golk have a brief affair and he is very plain that it will lead nowhere: "When love gets to be important to someone, it means that he hasn't been able to manage something else. Falling in love seems to me an almost sure sign of failure" (*G* 50). This cynicism is followed by more when she informs Golk of her unused credit line. He is appalled at her reluctance, which he condemns by declaring: "There's almost nothing in the world I can't find a use for" (*G* 55). By implication, this remark includes Jeanine. This was her life before Hondorp. Hence, to her, Herbert is, indeed, an amateur by comparison.

What Golk uses most is people. There is a whole philosophy behind Golking that exploits the frailties of human nature and by doing so explores human nature. Herbert's ear is filled by Golk's ego. "There are two pivots to the Golks we are doing these days.... The hook in the worm is one. You dangle a prize before a victim, play him like a hooked carp, and while he watches, turn the prize to dust.... The other kind is the kind we played on you. Stepping in between a man and his legitimate pleasures. We thwart a man from the satisfaction of the appetites he's entitled to" (*G* 61). In effect, in Sternian terms, Golk interrupts one's routine with a reversal.

Papa Hondorp's routine is also disturbed by his son's new life, particularly after Herbert doesn't come home after a night with Elaine. When his 37-year-old son returns the following morning, Papa slaps him across the face, after which Herbert decides that in the future he would call if he would be staying out. Papa's internal havoc expands to an external lipoma on his neck: "I cease playing host to my son and receive in his place a worm" (*G* 69). The lipoma will grow, as does the proportion of worldliness in Herbert that Papa had tried to shield him from.

Golk gets cranky and Hendricks knows that it stems from an attack of new ambition to turn the Golk show from local to network. Golk precedes this larger ambition with a smaller one. He has Herbert view the film of his latest Golk. It is of Papa being made to look foolish. Herbert is mortified and Golk believes this is Herbert's true test: if he accepts this humiliation and stays with Golk, then Golk has achieved power over him. Hendricks tells Herbert: "You just trotted up and ate shit because he threw it on your table" (*G* 81). Herbert has graduated out of kindergarten. He goes home to Poppa, ashamed to face him. Instead, he finds that Poppa is ecstatic. He loves the chance to get on TV. This is another revelation for Herbert and they are coming almost too fast to deal with; he is being carried along by the spin of the hurricane without centering himself long enough to understand the ramifications.

Golk, Herbert, and Jeanine go to the Parisak executive, Lurcher, to negotiate a network deal. Hendricks wears a dress, submitting to the "female" role for the sake of the show, explaining, "These execs letch ten hours a day" (*G* 83). The trio are successful and get a 13-week network tryout. Golk explains the psychology of execu-speak and how to turn it around on them:

> Every request we make of these boys is a threat to their image of perfection — which is routine. Routine means control for them; the new they cannot contemplate with ease. Our old format is a habit for them, and so they feel they're on top of it. They *are* on top of it. They know what to expect, and they can wait us out. For out we'll go, like everyone else in this business, if we stay the same. And they want us out, even though it may look like a break in their routine. It isn't. They'll just come up with another program, a lukewarm version of our half-hour that'll be a comfortable habit for a while till it drops out. Alternation of the lukewarm: that's their formula for novelty.... Every move we make to fashion a change for ourselves annoys them [*G* 86].

Golk tells the alliteratives that he will start out the network run with old-style Golks, but later he has a grand surprise in the works, which for now will remain secret. His evaluation of network TV is a prescient view of the nature of mass entertainment in the modern world: simple-minded pacification with just enough intelligent stuff to quiet the intellectual sub-culture. In the American tradition, intellectuals have not been heroes to the public, and intellectual artists only rarely. Intellectual art is here distinguished from the mind candy of pop culture art. Stern elsewhere has quoted Kierkegaard's estimation of public taste as the "great drum of triviality," where the mass, with much pomp and circumstance, exalts the mundane. Stern here begins his career-long consideration of the meaning of media in shaping the collective subjectivity of the anonymous public to whom the media appeals while the faceless public is absolved of any responsibility for its subsequent reactions.

Stern, via Golk, explains the reach and impact of TV, which was still fumbling its way out of relative infancy in the late 1950s. Golk's "progress," in TV, even while working in a vaudevillelike medium, "was almost always guided by principles...." What follows are the "four major and numerous subordinate classes of Golks." In Stern's work, there are often well-thought-out, preconceived "set pieces." Stern challenges himself and his readers to understand more than meets the eye. The first stage of Golks "just *were*"— the filming of people at random with the hope of capturing something worth seeing (*G* 94). Golk was looking at the world through the camera as if with the novice eyes of a child. In this first stage Golk took in knowledge passively because he was not yet ready to understand it. At this point "Golk had the habit of not yielding to a scene but of soaking it up ... with the effort to retain the scene's detail" (*G* 95).

The second stage came after a random happenstance led to a more lasting revelation. One night while soaking up a view of the Hudson River a man asked him for a match and blocked his view, thus interrupting his muse. This "led Golk to grab the little man's lapels and to whisper to him, mob-style, to move out of his way before he got blasted into the Hudson. Into the fair little head was a look of such terror that Golk brought it up to his own to study it. His study caused the expression to alter first to amazement, then to curiosity and finally to the dispersed truculence which was the face's habitual set ... with [this] flash which he had already come to recognize as the sort which really counted for him, he saw that the arousal of such pure looks was what he wanted for his Golks" (*G* 95).

With this revelation Golk learned that a person does not just have to observe his environment passively but can learn to make the environment react to stimuli. The *play* aspect of this discovery was in how to devise and set up the stimuli. New Golks "centered on such situations as people opening letters informing them that they'd been fired ... women noticing suicidal types balanced on their living room ledges...." Golk writes in his journal that, "The names of emotions— love, hate, pity, etc.— are just hideaways for the thousand feelings which creep under those labels, or rather, which language tries to bundle away in them. Even the simplest feelings— emotions— wonder what the difference is?— are impure compared to the purity of words" (*G* 95). By adding stimuli Golk realized that he could cause reactions and also study what the reactions mean. Subsequently, he could theorize about these meanings in order to devise stimuli that would anticipate certain types of reactions.

From Golk's theorizing the third stage followed: "This stage revolved around scenes, which somersaulted victims 'inside and out and back again, from laughs to weeps to laughs,' as the journal entry had it, through a whole cycle of discoveries ... and editing became the crucial part ... for only the emotional crests of the cycles were chosen and these had to be ingeniously juxtaposed for dramatic power. The Golks centered about such situations as people dispatched on endless errands, errands which were not completed until the victim realized that his own reactions were the object of the errand, that, as he played shuttlecock to two or more Golkmen, he was registering the varying forces which they applied to him" (G 96).

These Golks were more elaborate, with more cameras and locations. In the first stage, the environment was merely observed, no judgments; in the second, the environment was made to react to a single stimulus in order to study the reactions; in the third, with the study of reactions forming a pattern, one could create multiple stimuli to influence the number and probability of reactions and exert some control over their ebb and flow. This added more data for devising new and more complex experiments. The accumulated data gave rise to philosophical conclusions about human nature that Golk believed worth sharing. Consequently, stage three was followed by a brief interlude called "quickies" where Golk returned to filming, as he had in stage one, single subjects at random without devised stimuli. Now, however, the philosopher wove together his selected randomization and did a voice-over commentary on the natural — that is, nonstaged actions — in order to share his wisdom of how he could predict behaviors based on his studies. Instead of prodding nature through artificial stimuli, which had allowed Golk to theorize on the reactions, he let nature be natural and anticipated behaviors based on his previous experiments.

The fourth, or penultimate, stage of Golkism was concerned with what Golk called "beat'":

> Every decent show, every worthwhile thing anywhere for that matter, has its own recognizable beat. Music, people's talk, poems, love, meals, the stars.... To discover the rhythm, the BEAT of real-life situations, and yet to put one's own beat on top of them, that's what we've got to do now. Kind of a round, beat over beat.... The Stage Four golks were assembled into patterns composed of reversals, discoveries, double-takes, and these were timed, combined with narrative and musical themes, and blended with special camera effects. The results fell into a small number of recognizable categories, so that after a while, Golk could announce at the beginning of a show that the next golk would be a 'fast and looser' or a 'slow shifter' and thus anticipate the rhythmic patterns against which the Golk could play minor variations.... And the accomplishments seemed more and more important to him ... he was thinking of his work as a matter of public concern, and he discussed it with the respectful distance usually reserved for older and more conspicuous monuments of culture and civilization [G 97–98].

The four stages equate to four stages of human learning, with knowledge becoming understanding in steps that progress from utilitarian to scientific to philosophical to epistemological to the edge of metaphysical. Finally, there is the intuitive and often unconscious synthesis of all the steps, which leads to that transcendent purview of what is called art.

Stern's set piece conveys the most serious intentions while satirizing both the intentions and the world of television that takes itself too seriously. The four stages remind one of two other famous set pieces on how people learn: Bacon's essay, "The Idols," and William Golding's essay, "Thinking as a Hobby," both frequently anthologized as tour de forces of succinct and compact epistemologies. On one hand Golk's four stages would sound impressive if one could set them apart from their source — Golk; yet, since the philosophy is derived from the inane world of local television that beats "the great drum of triviality," and the perpetrator is a conniving megalomaniac, Stern's satire in this set piece takes on a tone as serious as the seriousness of the epistemology. Golk invokes the self-importance of self-believed messianic dictators who control the media to propagandize a willing audience if, as did a Hitler or Mussolini, they find the nerve in a not too discerning public willing to believe what placates their egos. Golk's consideration of his work as a "matter of public concern" sounds like the "concern" seen in the Committee for Public Safety of the French Revolution or the McCarthy-led House Un-American Activities Committee. The layers of satire and seriousness work on multiple levels. Golk as Messiah is ready for stage five.

After Elaine breaks in Herbert, Hendricks takes over, attracted to his amateur's innocence. Despite her scarred-over shell and her attack mentality that requires verbal barbs to disarm potential enemies real or imagined, she is still only 23 and still wishes for some tenderness to come into her life. She hopes Herbert's innocence is a partial antidote to her experiences with her husband, Golk, and unnamed others who have mistreated her. Concurrently, Herbert is trying to thicken his own skin in the aftermath of his shame at Poppa being Golked. He is moving towards what Jeanine *doesn't* want — another insensitive male.

Golk informs Hendricks and Herbert that his new stage will "vault the barrier…. We're going to instruct, reform. We're going to be the education of the audience … demonstrators, dramatizers, the portrayors of corruption, connivance, of the tone and temper of the world they live in and don't understand. Golk looked Hondorp deep in the eye, digging for approval" (G 101). Herbert is interested in this new stage because he feels he can contribute to the creation of something new after months of absorbing the old. He wants to move from stage one, observation of the environment, to the next stage of stimulating the environment. The student seeks approval from his master and now wants to teach as well as learn.

Golk will go after people in power, "for its own sake first of all, and secondly because in my nose abuse and bad power and dumbness and harsh force itch and smell, and I think that displaying them in our little Golks would be a great blow to them. I'm thinking this is the sort of thing we—the medium and us—may have been intended to do" (*G* 104). The itch and smell is also in Hendricks' nose from the fact that Golk is the pot calling the kettle black and that he is likely envious of real power rather than sincere in exposing it. She tells him, "What do you think you are, *The Dirty Drawers Digest*? Disguised as Political Science 31?" (*G* 106).

She is overruled and the games begin. Golk gets over on politicos and a mobster and puts them in situations where they act like their ridiculous selves and the results end up on TV. His gulls are, in fact, creeps who deserve their shame. The ratings are high but the backlash is higher. Golk has violated his own lesson about disturbing the Network's placid routine. The powerful, fearing that their day may come, intercede in the Parisak penthouse, and the more discerning media critics, while having no empathy for the deserving victims, see the greater threat of attack television. One critic's assessment is Stern in journalistic disguise with a description in 1960 that has turned out to be true today:

> What was a fictional nightmare in the pages of *Nineteen-Eighty-Four* has become a reality. A reality that proves, however, to be more garish a nightmare than ever George Orwell described. Orwell pictured a world in which men are constantly spied upon by the secret police of a super-state. On the Parisak Network, a New York comedian with the improbable name of Golk displayed not to the secret police but to the entire nation — or, at least, that large portion of it which is watching his sensationalist program — the private behavior of individuals who are sometimes men of international importance. Their behavior is under none of the constraints which awareness of being spied upon put upon the behavior of people in the Orwell state, and thus what the world sees reeks of the jungle.... Our reaction to this is one of rage. So serious an invasion of private life has probably never before been held over the heads of Americans. Golk appears before us as a comedian. It seems to us high time that we took him very seriously indeed [*G* 132].

Gossip travels fast and Herbert bemoans his possible forced exit. "'And just as I was beginning to like it all.' It was true. Hondorp had eaten it up, publicity, flashbulbs, and all. The total reversal of his obscurity, the grotesque extrapolation of his choice tickled him no end" (*G* 137). The network, however, instead tells Hendricks and Hondorp that Golk will be gone, but since ratings are good, the alliteratives will take over the show.

Lurcher summons Golk and tells him he is over. Golk, the pseudotough guy, throws up on Lurcher's rug, quickly going from Messiah to mess. This sets up the confrontation between usurped and usurpers: Golk vs. Hendricks and Hondorp. Stern loads this five-page set piece with dialogue that is dense with the three distinct personalities of the characters, and full of psychological implications about them in particular and human nature in general. The bitterness and vitriol is disturbingly vicious. Golk and Hendricks are in a verbal cat fight replete with metaphorical hissing and spitting. Herbert tries to pacify both while being caught in his own conflicting emotions: empathy for his mentor, allegiance to his lover, ambition for himself. Defeated, Golk drinks something and keels over — suicide. Panic ensues. Then Golk reveals he set up and filmed the whole episode — his last Golk.

Herbert and Jeanine move into a swank apartment on Sutton Place and throw a party. Golk is invited. "Some of the inner group [of Golk's staff] were affected by the occasion, and reacted by being especially solicitous of Golk. What the precise nature of this reversal was, they didn't know…" (G 186). After this incident, Golk vanishes. Hendricks and Herbert take over. They struggle to come up with ideas and the pressure makes Herbert colder and more aloof, not the man who was to soften Jeanine's own hardness. Herbert begins to see, or imagine he sees, Golk popping up for split seconds like a ghost. The tension in him causes more friction for the alliteratives. Hondorp tries something "new" for the show. He films and records a crowd watching a Chicago Cubs game, no prompts or set ups, just themselves. Herbert is re-enacting Golk's stage one of the learning curve as all human beings do; this is passive observation. Poppa and his second-head lipoma die suddenly. Herbert neglects to tell Jeanine until she asks Herbert how Poppa is. She is appalled at his indifference. She realizes he has become one of *them* — a venomous man — and leaves him. The show is canceled; Herbert is fired and becomes persona non grata in TV. He goes to work for a small radio station in Chicago, "all trace of his ambition, all desire for change gone absolutely and forever" (G 207).

Golk is a sure-handed first novel. Stern has a clear structure and focus with a prose style that measures every sentence without seeming deliberate just as an actor learns lines until they sound spontaneous. Yet, there is a cold heat in Golk, fire behind glass. Other than an eccentric but likable Poppa and the very first glimpses of an eccentric and likable Herbert, the characters become unlikable neurotics with off-putting defense mechanisms. Stern himself considers that this emotional distancing might have been caused by, what he called at the time, his "impoverished Jewishness."

Here is a book which unlike many of the works of writers I've mentioned [Bellow, Roth, Malamud, Salinger] does not deal with a Jewish scene or background, yet it may well be that there is much in it that can be thought Jewish in quality, in tone, in things which the author — less than anyone can see.

A reader may caution me at this point about the subject matter of this novel, *Golk*. Aren't two of the leading characters, Hondorp and his father, Jewish? It is here that I have to give a peculiar answer, namely, "probably." I say "probably" because on looking over the novel, not while I was writing it but after, it occurred to me that Poppa Hondorp is associated in my mind with people who are Jews.... There are Jews who accept and Jews who deny. Marx, Freud, and Trotsky are famous examples of denying Jews. In literature Mailer is one whose coldness may stand in part for a rejection of Jewish schmaltz. Much as I consciously deny this denial in my own work or life, something tells me this is my case. [Herbert] Hondorp is a conscientious denial of that notorious warmth and marvelous tradition of ethical accountability, which I think of as Jewish. For me, there is perhaps a ray of hope: at the end of *Golk* Hondorp renounces his chilly ways. Perhaps I too, in my way, am renouncing my denial ["The Novelist...," *FH* 152–56].

The chill, however, will last into Stern's second novel.

1961: EUROPE, OR UP AND DOWN WITH BAGGISH AND SCHREIBER

This novel was formed from distinct sketches, one of which, "The Sorrows of Sgt. Schreiber," was originally published in 1954. Stern wished to link two characters, Schreiber and Baggish, and each begins the book by ending his routine with a chosen reversal of his circumstances. Schreiber ends a stultifying marriage; Baggish, much younger, ends his mundane existence living with his dull parents and working a duller job. He will do anything and use anyone to get ahead. Baggish is a pre–Golk in the making; Schreiber is already what Herbert becomes after his disillusion with the real world. Since this book was in the works before Stern began *Golk*, although published a year after *Golk*, Schreiber and Baggish are antecedents to Golk and Herbert rather than successors.

The dual protagonists are featured in alternating sequences until their lives intertwine. Schreiber is a truly sensitive man among philistines; Baggish is a philistine feigning sensitivity in order to deceive people who will become the means to his self-serving ends. In chapter one the antipathy towards Schreiber as displayed by his wife and daughter sets the tone for his portrayal as perpetual victim: the daughter, Valerie, and her mother, Florence, are narrated as ceaselessly seeking ways to scorn the "patriarch." One subject, the Penniman house, is "one of those rare, really valuable subjects which never failed to arouse her [Valerie's] mother, to attack, that is, the fat slob who had one day invaded their lives in his captain's uniform, and then, doffing it, had played that other oh-so-cute game of being her father" (E 3). The novel takes place shortly after the end of World War II. Schreiber purposely returned in his uniform as it represented an authority and respect he'd enjoyed in the army that would not be replicated in his home. The allusion to the uniform implies the contrast between his wartime and postwar lives and also gives a clue to the pivotal reversal in Schreiber's life during the war. In Schreiber's present after the real war, the domestic warfare has deteriorated to sniping and ruthless sarcasm with little pretense at civility.

Max Schreiber comes home from work, and home is as much or more work than his job as a lackluster lawyer with minimal ambition other than survival:

> "I'll be right down," said Florence, but she didn't move from bed, only turned the pillow over for the fiftieth time in two hours to get some coolness from the other side. This time her arms wrapped it around her ears as if she were squashing a beetle. She listened. She listened for the noises her husband made in the kitchen as he drew out ice, trays, cracked the ice, and spooned it into Old-Fashioned glasses, probably before he'd dissolved the sugar and bitters in them. Or he forget the bitters. His coat would be off, his collar dirtier than a miner's and his tie would sport a gob of thousand-island dressing above his tie-pin; as if any civilized man under sixty wore one of those anymore. Most and worst of all she saw his fatness, saw, felt, smelled it so sharply that she could detach it from his form and measure the vices it accumulated about itself. Every day he seemed fatter to her; it was as if each pound were trying to bury whatever little they had together. He ate like a beast, his head sinking into the plates, grunting and sighing like a lover, himself with the thickest, ugliest components of every dish.... She held the pillow to drive out all his noises, real and imagined... [E 4].

By implication Max's lust for food is a substitute for sex and whatever other passions—known or unknown—that are missing in his life. Only his mother-in-law, who seems to like him better than her daughter, understands the change in Max since returning from Europe. "'You were away too long in the war, Max....' and she smiled, seeing that this casual remark had hooked her son-in-law, drawn red to his face" (E 12). In chapter two—originally published separately in 1954—a flashback reveals the reversal that haunts Max. Her name is Micheline.

During World War II, Captain Schreiber was in a noncombat role in rural France. While there he indulged in a pseudoscholarship as he had a secret wish to be an aesthete. He worked on:

a study of the villagers based in part on the letters he read as local censor. It had begun with his first administrative report, but he'd found a peculiar charm in the refined snooping and decided to pursue it on his own in a scholarly fashion. He had never before done anything so thorough, not even preparing for his bar exams. He felt he had a natural bent for research; its techniques brought him more pleasures than its potential results, or his Pisgah view of himself surrounded by other amateur scholars, bearded, sherry-drinking, international, the master of his fragment of the world. The books piled on his desk ... were like fortress ramparts behind which he scouted his empire.... In the evenings, he typed out his discoveries of the day [E 16].

This avocation, along with being in France and a captain commanding respect from the villagers, gave him "the feeling that for the first time in his life he was really alive" (E 17). Consequently, even before l'affaire Micheline, Schreiber enjoyed a world that would prove too great a contrast when he returned to his American domestic warfare after the European warfare. Schreiber met the very young and beautiful Micheline and gave her a job in his office. He also, at the urging of her parents, tutored a reluctant Micheline in English. He was hopelessly smitten. When he subtly put his hand on her shoulder, she subtly reminded him he had a wife, and he removed it. When the announcement came that the European war was over, the joy overcame Micheline and she allowed Max an embrace and perhaps a little more, but Stern is unclear if there was consummation. Schreiber was called away for a few months to Germany but fully intended to return to Micheline and run off with her. He had overestimated the meaning of their brief embrace. When he returned to France, she herself had run off with his driver, an African-American corporal named Tiberius Fitch. "'I'm thinking of suicide,'" he told himself. "'Over love.' In his pain, he was almost proud. 'Un peu ridicule,' he said aloud ... he started to cry" (E 27–8). Despite his pain, Max had felt passion for the first time in his life. The reality of his stultifying home life could only be more painful by comparison.

Returning to the postwar present, he has had enough of his domestic ridicule, which, though bitter, is trivial compared to his other peu ridicule. He tells Florence that it would be better if he left: " We shouldn't live together. I should go away.... Separation, divorce, whatever you want. I haven't thought of details. Only that together, we're worse than animals" (E 32). In 1947, divorce was a drastic, almost unheard of defiance of convention. With this knowledge, Florence has acted with impunity. Max's declaration for freedom leaves her shocked and unable to rebut him. Max ends his dead routine and heads back to Europe to find redemption for his heretofore wasted life.

Part two introduces Theodore Baggish who is in his early twenties (and Flannery O'Connor's favorite character). He is on a ship bound for Europe — a planned escape from years of routine endured for this moment. The reader and Baggish briefly meet Robert Ward, a preppie before that term was coined to define people like him. He has the aura that Theodore wishes to emulate. They part but will meet again later in the book. Baggish has little regard for the parents he is leaving. "In the three weeks between the arrival of his passport and his sailing, his mother said three or four times that it was hard when boys grew up and left their parents to age by themselves, but after the first utterance, it was said without particular feeling or meaning and it was accepted as another one of the formulas which protected them from life" (*E* 38–9). The parents insulated themselves within a routine to deflect emotion. Consequently, their son has none. Baggish writes a letter to his parents describing his voyage, more for personal conceit than consideration. "When he went to the post to mail the letter and saw the stamps with the picture of George the Sixth on them, the blissful fact of his departure really came to him. He never again wrote to his parents" (*E* 39). The reversal from his old life, the break from routine, has begun.

Baggish discovered that the etymology for Europe was "'wide prospect,' which pleased Baggish, for he *knew* that the coastline of his own future was congruent with Europe's, and he scouted like a bird of prey. Baggish also *knew* that there were certain preliminary steps to be taken before his real career could start ... one reason for coming to France first was that he shared the American Folklore view that one sort of experience was most readily acquired there. This was the experience of women, one which Baggish lacked entirely" (*E* 43). As had Herbert. Yet, while younger than Herbert, Baggish already understands and denounces the danger of sex compulsion. "That knowledge of women could be the pursuit of a whole life, a whole race of lives, seemed an absurdity to him. In his view, women were functions rather than ends, objects instead of subjects, essential to his own prospects but potential compromises of them" (*E* 43). Still, he knows he must pursue this "function" in order to alleviate sex as a source of distraction from his more serious work — achieving success. He also believes the knowledge of sex will give his countenance an aura of conquest that other men will respect. Regarding sex, the reference to "Europa" as "wide prospect" is one definition. There is another, more allegorical meaning

In classical mythology, the woman named Europa is a symbol for ravishment. Europa is famed for her beauty and, depending on the variation, either Zeus or Jupiter turns into a white bull that carries her off. In the

Jupiter version as described by Ovid in his *Metamorphoses*, the bull seems benign enough to Europa that, as he reclines peacefully, she follows suit and stretches on his back, all the easier for the god-bull to suddenly reveal his true intentions. Moreover, Ovid's purpose in his 15 books of verse was to start with the creation of the world and lead to the deification of Caesar and the reign of Augustus. One can argue for an American parallel after World War II. The term Europa (and its use by the erudite Stern) implies much more than wide prospect. There is an equation of sex and power, power and sex—the order subject to much debatable speculation. Stern's men, whether as complete novices or near novices, whether seeking sex as an end in itself or as a means to greater ends, want more sex than they are getting. In later work, even males who married young regret their lack of diverse experience despite their courtship and married experience. Stern married very young.

Baggish is a user and for him the world is a utilitarian opportunity. In Stern's world, a Baggish type is destined for business, politics or both. Previous shyness and failures have caused Baggish to think he is unattractive to women "but here he was wrong…. His chief distinction was that his impassivity was, at least, partially, the effect of his will, and there were certain women, women for whom the observation of men was a serious study, who sensed the play behind the impassivity, deduced the passion behind the play, and sometimes plotted to make themselves its object" (*E* 44–5). Female versions of Baggish will recognize a male counterpart and seek to merge forces.

Even playing a game of ping-pong has utilitarian value. "For Baggish, the interest stemmed from his ability to control Chad's mood, almost from shot to shot…" (*E* 53–4). An intellectual education takes all forms. Baggish, while an unschooled intellectual, is one nonetheless and will seek to educate himself in the forms of manipulation. He is bloodless. His ploys and smooth talk are a game; he practices on the useless so he can prepare himself to deceive the useful. He has no qualms about his utilitarian outlook. People are tools to be used; it does not occur to Baggish that they might mind. Baggish will consort with anyone, even if he can't stand the person if a gain is possible; he will just as quickly dump a person he likes to move on to one he doesn't if the latter can provide something that the former can't. Some of his inspiration comes from reading Stendhal's *Napoleon*. When he takes out Monique (while preferring the less accessible Birgitta), Baggish hopes that "he would get what he was paying for … [and that] for the first time in his life he wanted to drink." In other circumstances, he would not drink and chance a dulling of his mercenary alertness. When his goal of self devirginizing is reached, he says drunkenly, in English, "Birgitta darling." Monique doesn't understand English and asks what this means. Even drunk, he has enough con to answer, "It means 'I love you' in Swedish" (E 66). Thereafter, his letters to her would be signed, "Birgitta, Birgitta, Teddy" (E 68).

Schreiber's ex-military status lands him a job in Germany where he carries on his pseudoaestheticism and his efforts to blend into a Europe he thinks will form him in the manner of a Henry James, Edith Wharton, or the 1920s expatriates who thought one must go back to Europe's long tradition of history and culture to make up for the imagined lack of it in America. He recalls that in that land of the Philistines his "divorce had been much harder than he'd imagined; each paper they'd signed in the lawyer's office had hacked at the splitting wood, the final cut leaving them free but gashed, lighter but deformed" (E 74). Max observes that as long as he lives in the American quarter "his national identity was isolated and exaggerated, and that he was thus precluded from entering into that European life of the spirit for which he came" (E 75). Max then moves into a more endemic enclave where he meets a woman, Traudis Bretzka. One evening they sit in an empty amphitheatre and listen to their echoes. This prompts Max's memory and he tells her that "At Harvard there is a sound-proof room."

> "Not without interest," said Traudis.
> "You can scream as loudly as you want, and you can't even hear your own voice."
> "Sufficiently horrible. What is the association?"
> "I don't know," said Schreiber. "This reminded me of it. Both make you feel shut off."
> "Where?"
> "Nowhere."
> "Do you feel shut off?"
> "Naturally not," he said. "It's the sensation" [E 83].

It is more than a sensation. It sums up the displaced vacuity of Max's betwixt and between existence of running away from America but not finding peace in Europe. With Traudis he feels a hint of renewed equilibrium. His precarious balance is short-lived as he discerns a timetable for Traudis's attention to him. "Traudis' eccentric behavior assumed a pattern — for each month she stayed with him twice and borrowed the rent money once — he came to be less and less attached to her and to the life he so happily associated with her" (E 88). Schreiber, desperately needing approval, can't reconcile that, in effect, he was paying for her favors, and that, in his perception, her approval was bought rather than sincerely given.

To Max's psyche, one begging for appreciation, paying is a shame rather than a pragmatic consideration. This is an American nouveau Puritan attitude instead of a tacit understanding based on mutual need. A Baggish would see the pragmatism.

Baggish makes his way to Germany and at first has trouble finding a gainful situation. Frustrated, he stands on a bridge and throws a rock in the river, "wishing that it contained every man and woman he had seen that day" (E 96). In contrast to Schreiber who has romanticized Europe, Baggish sees it only as a postwar opportunity for serious carpetbagging. He is less than impressed when he sees a famous German university, thinking, "Yale wouldn't use this place for garbage disposal" (E 96). Yale is also where, emulating Ward, Baggish pretends he attended. He gets a room that has a rent-control ceiling but usually goes for more under the table. He verbally agrees to pay the landlord extra but once he gets the contract, refuses what had been a gentleman's agreement. Dr. Stempel, the Old European, tells Baggish, the Ugly American, he is no gentleman. Stempel is absolutely correct.

Baggish dates Joan because she works in the U. S. Personnel Placement Office and helps him get a job. He sticks with her for the moment so he will always know what better opportunities might come up. When he catches two men, one an American named Parsons, in passionate embrace, he promptly blackmails Parsons in exchange for silence. Parsons tells him he is with army intelligence and Baggish responds, "Useful" (E 107).

Schreiber sees a Gladys Culley whose main feature is an enormous nose that discourages amorousness. Instead, they had "evenings centered about food; the hesitations, jockeyings, and mindless springs reserved, and, perhaps, biologically developed for generic passion, were employed here around cuisine. Conversation about any other matter was tributary, stuttering, suspenseful; fulfillment was the wordless—though not soundless—immolation in meat and vegetable, sauce, fish, fruit, and wine.... It continued this way for a couple of months. Then the strain of unverbalized *gourmandisme* began to tell on them both.... Gladys decided to vary the program by inviting friends, or rather people who would come, her subordinates in the personnel office" (E 113). Her subordinates hate her guts but are afraid to say no. Hence, Gladys invites Joan who brings Baggish so that the down-bound Schreiber and social-climbing Baggish finally intersect on their up and down staircases.

Baggish accompanies Joan only because he thinks Culley may be of use to him. One of the other guests is an Italian, Signor Bosco, the husband of a Culley subordinate, Annamarie. Bosco observes that it is Friday and there is no fish; he takes great offense and makes a caustic remark to alert Culley to her "faux pas." (This novel was written in the late 1950s and is pre–Vatican II when fish on Friday was still mandatory among practicing Catholics.) Getting the hint Culley asks, "You Catholics?"

> "We are," said Signor Bosco. "I take it that you are not or you have lapsed. Don't let our medievalism distress you. Eat away and rejoice yourselves."
>
> "You could have let me know about this Annamarie," said Gladys, wheeling her head like a gun turret and pointing the cannon at her subordinate's forehead.
>
> "Perhaps," said Signor Bosco, "but I assumed that my spouse thought that the knowledge that Italians and Catholics are one and the same was traditional, a matter of common knowledge to all the heirs of Western culture. You are a Westerner, are you not...."
>
> "I most certainly am not," said Gladys precisely. "I'm a Midwesterner from Chicago."
>
> "Ah so," said Signor Bosco. "I was not certain of your provenence. There are certain aspects of your physiognomy which might pass, I think...."
>
> Here, while Gladys Culley gripped the table to brace for the rare insult direct, while Schreiber held up his knife and fork in horrific silence, while Annamarie and Joan trembled on the edge of an awful scene, Baggish leaned across for the roast and spilled Signor Bosco's glass of wine into his lap.
>
> "Ah, my dear Bosco," he boomed. "Will you forgive me?" He sprang from his chair and rushed to Bosco, dipped his handkerchief into the tureen of gravy and began rubbing at the streaks in Bosco's trousers.... Bosco exploded. Baggish recoiled, hit the table and bounced back knocking Bosco against the wall.
>
> In the subsequent fracas, Bosco abandoned the international approach for a series of unmusical imprecations in his native tongue. "*A casa*," he yelled to his wife, and gripping her wrist, he dragged her out of the apartment. "Chicago thugs," they heard him yelling from the Street [*E* 115–16].

Schreiber believes Baggish saved Gladys in a gentlemanly example of medieval — and very European —*chivalry*; Baggish *did* know what he was doing but his motive is to ingratiate himself with Gladys and Max. His "chivalry" was guided by utilitarianism. For Baggish, a second fount of fortune ensues as Schreiber befriends him. "With that pure instinct for opportunity which, in the eyes of those who lack it, is usually called luck, Baggish saw, or rather, at this stage, felt, that Schreiber was a strait through which he would pass to his wide prospect." For Baggish, the ever-aware mercenary, luck is the residue of design. Baggish chose to be at the dinner to seek opportunity; it just happened to come in a different form than he expected. Max is a new mark, an even better gull than Gladys whom Baggish recognizes as nobody's fool. Schreiber appears otherwise. "The evidence

... consisted of Schreiber's position as Chief Analyst of an Intelligence Section, his apparent wealth ... and, most of all, an air about him, which for Baggish cried, 'Use me. Dupe me.' Without malice aforethought, though without charity, Baggish moved in" (E 117).

The psychological gamesmanship of the ping-pong table has found new prey, a gull waiting to be Golked. Baggish plays the novice willing to learn from the older Schreiber. Max relishes the role of mentor with remarks such as, "Europeans aren't as squeamish about life as we are" (E 124). Teddy is not squeamish at all. Baggish, claiming that he never learned how to drive because there had always been servants to take him around, gets Schreiber to buy a car and take him around. Max eventually tires of being chauffeur, teaches Baggish to drive, and just lets Teddy take the car on his own — just as Baggish planned. "His principle of action was based on a La Rochefoucauld maxim about people not forgiving you the favors you do them but being gratified by the favors they do you" (E137). Max enjoys the favors he does for his young friend for which he receives gushing, if faux approval and appreciation. Baggish recognizes only that "Schreiber was a bridge to the fortress he had to take" (E 128). On Max's side he suspects nothing, living up to Teddy's estimation of him as victim. To the gullible Max, Baggish "understood what real friendship was, a mixture of respect, mutual learning and general good will. Baggish was almost European in sensitivity." Baggish, the great intuitive con artist, gives Schreiber what Max seems to need (E 130). As for Teddy's "sensitivity," Baggish is sensitive enough to sneak into Schreiber's desk, steal classified documents, write articles based on them and sell them to an American periodical under a pseudonym. He thus establishes a reputation that begins to gain him entry into larger venues of opportunity.

Robert Ward reappears. Ostensibly presented initially as a role model for emulation by Baggish, he is, despite the surface sheen, an insecure young man who has to push himself to take the slightest initiative. He is a counterpoint to Baggish in that Ward is handcuffed by the complete lack of arrogance that his wealth might provoke in someone else, while Teddy's machinations — without any seeming basis for his arrogance — go beyond arrogance to sociopathic narcissism. There is a basis, however, as Baggish had nothing to begin with so he has nothing to lose; there is neither fear nor compunction in him whatsoever. Stern contrasts Ward and Baggish with the former being unexpectedly naive and sheltered and the latter being unexpectedly predatory.

Robert sets out on a motorcycle tour of the French countryside, an enormous bit of assertion for him that is motivated by wanting to have a "Henry Adams-like notion..." (E 143). That is, he seeks, like Adams, to enjoy an intellectual education. He visits a monastery and is surreally charmed by the mystical ambience: "He sat in the church five or six minutes ... and it was not until half an hour later as he roared down the main road south that he disengaged himself from the spell. 'They nearly had me,' he told himself. 'A week of that, and they'd have had me.' He was quite proud of his susceptibility" (E 145). He is proud that he can be aesthetically sensitive in inverse proportion to Baggish's pride that he isn't sensitive at all.

Ward and Baggish meet again. They double date, Ward with Juliette, Baggish with Monique. Juliette had a first novel at age 16, a second novel a year later with both regarded as worthy yet youthful enterprises that were good for an inexperienced novice, but critics wondered if she would mature into a real writer. Still only 19 she considers herself an aesthete among the philistines. After the four see a grotesque avant-garde short film at "the most advanced Cine club in France" (E 149), Stern follows with a set piece in the form of an intellectual debate between the precocious European Juliette and the ugly American, Baggish.

When Juliette argues with Monique over the merits of the film — Juliette calls it art; Monique thinks it cruelty disguised as art — Baggish defends Monique, not for her sake but for the game of it, which is also a challenge to Ward indirectly, by challenging his date. Juliette asserts, quoting Baudelaire, that curiosity — in the sense of trying the new even if it torments — is the justifiable motivation for avant-garde art. Baggish sarcastically rejoins that "Curiosity is a coward's substitute for accomplishment...." He pauses for this puncturing of her pretentious balloon to sink in, then continues his attack. "Like variety ... people who seek it out are incapable of doing any one thing" (E 150).

> Juliette's face took off like a mob for a palace. There was a riot of "*Non, non, non*" and then, "Idiot, cretin, horsehead, mousebrain. First, you didn't get within two miles of the lines. Baudelaire says it torments us; it's not we who seek it out. Two, curiosity generates everything that counts in the world and a lot, like your ugly mug that doesn't. Thirdly, your French is impossible. You have no right to speak it. Fourth, what do you know about art or anything else?
>
> Point four seemed the place to move from. "I know what I like...."
>
> "What you know is what you know. Zero equals zero. You should try to extend yourself. You're still young [but he is older than she is]. Try to find some new experiences, look for something different. Life will mean more to you."
>
> "Difference," said Baggish solemnly, "is not the criterion of anything but itself. Watch out for the man who sells you a pair of shoes, a new form of government, or a novel"— this with a polite nod to his opponent —"by telling

you that you'll be reconciled to its absurdities when it becomes familiar to you."

The word "novel" affected Juliette the way an insult does a professional duelist. "Don't even think the word 'novel' in my presence, Bageesh. When you've served one up, then talk about it. In your own stupid language, the word itself means difference, newness" [E 150].

Stern alludes to *Golk* when he refers to the "man selling shoes" as this was how Golk Golked Hendricks the first time they met; he was selling shoes and kept bringing her the wrong size, filming her increasingly agitated reactions. Stern uses his set pieces to express ideas but does so in the context of the scene. In effect, Stern is here filming the reactions of Juliette to another Golk perpetrated by Baggish. Stern uses this dialogue to have a discussion of the "novel." Juliette says,

"What do I think when I face the page? I say to myself, 'A novel traditionally develops a single situation, identifies you with a single person, and that one more or less sympathetic at the start. One either follows his chase of a girl, or his gradual enlightenment, or his rising fortunes.' I say, 'Juliette, sweetheart, write me something new, something different, something which displaces this single-situation tyranny'— I am speaking of the small novel now, you understand, not this monster English-Russian-Scandinavian hodgepodge—'something which knocks the reader on the head by bringing in characters who don't recur, situations which work only in the roundabout ways of contrast and comparison,' I never let the reader take hold. When he thinks he has me, I'm not there. Ha, ha, ha, ha, ha," and she slapped her forehead.

Baggish, warming to her excitement, felt like kissing the slapped head. But he went on. "That's a third-rate excuse for incompetence." Her dark eyes bulged in disbelief. He went on further. "A novel is a roller coaster of distress and sympathy, love and desire. Everything must count in it, or the car shoots off the coaster. Nothing is worse than commentary. Novels which talk about novels are worse than violinists who discuss the piece while playing it. Such talk breaks the artistic rhythm, the world of the art form. It gives the viewer an in to the real world which shatters the other. I know. I'm a real novel reader, and I know how to separate my two worlds."

"I could vomit.... Your traditionalism enervates me, kills me. You are trying to strangle the very scene I am writing now, one in which a character talks against the form of the book in which he plays a leading role, while another character, an obnoxious one, imported clearly for the purpose, defends its technique. All this in a brief, classical study of a zoology student's seduction, corruption, and annihilation by an old roué introduced to her for sheer *frisson* by his third wife who detests her because she designs her own clothes with more brilliance than the wife's own Paquins and Balenciagas. This is the function of art, to commingle the inversion of tradition

with both celebration and violation of it. I could scream for the pleasure of it." This is what she proceeded to do. They were forced to leave the café.
   "She isn't usually like this," said Ward to Baggish…. "You seem to bring out something bestial in her. For me she's a wonderful new experience."
   Baggish could not shake his pontifical tone. "Experience is never its own good. People who say it are disguising their lack of philosophy with a hand-me-down slogan" [*E* 151–52].

As in *Golk*, where Golk's philosophy is, on one hand serious, and on the other satiric because of its source, Baggish expounds and swells with his profundity while being bereft of real compassion. Nonetheless, his rebuttals of Juliette and her attacks that cause them are not without deeper intimations.

The set piece touches on the issues of what is or isn't avant-garde/experimental; what is or isn't memorable, what is or isn't important in art. The question of avant-garde/experimental was raised by Auden: "Sincerity in the proper sense of the word, meaning authenticity … ought to be a writer's chief occupation. Some writers confuse authenticity, which they ought always to aim at, with originality, which they never should bother about. There is a certain kind of person so dominated by the desire to be loved for himself alone that he has constantly to test those around him by tiresome behavior; what he says and does must be admired, not because it is intrinsically admirable, but because it is *his* remark, *his* act. Does this not explain a lot of avant-garde art."[26] It does.

Stern relates that an English editor "After [reading the short story collection] *1968* [1970] told me that a lot of English writers thought … that I was an experimental writer. I wonder. I shied away from the *outré* or sheer kicks."[27] Stern is not a metafictionist. He can be different, but not just for the sake of difference. He achieves authenticity with a singular voice, but a very real, very accessible voice. He can shock, but the shock value is from the rigors of an identifiable, if sometimes cruel reality. (*1968*, to be covered in Chapter Four, has a minimalist approach that spares words but is rich in metaphor. In it, Stern employs a form of violent prose poetry that is startling, but for its content, not for any radical departure in how the content is presented. His presentation is not the end in itself, but a means to deliver the end with devastating effect.)

The question of whether experience is its own good also comes up as a Platonic dialogue between a professor and his student in Christopher Isherwood's novel *A Single Man*, 1964. The pupil asks,

   "— it's about experience. They keep telling you, when you're older, you'll have experience — and that's supposed to be so great. What do you say about that, sir? Is it really any use would you say."

"What kind of experience?"

"Well — places you've been to, people you've met. Situations you've been through already, so you know how to handle them when they come up again. All that stuff that's supposed to make you wise, in your later years."

"Let me tell you something Kenny. For other people, I can't speak — but personally, I haven't gotten wise on anything. Certainly, I've been through this and that; and when it happens again, I say to myself, Here it is again. But that doesn't seem to help me. In my opinion, I, personally, have gotten steadily sillier and sillier and sillier — and that's a fact."

"...I'll be darned. Then experience is no use at all? You're saying it might just as well not have happened?"

"No. I'm not saying that. I mean, you can't *use* it. But if you don't try to — if you realize it's there and you've got it — then it can be kind of marvelous."[28]

The professor intuitively realizes that experience in and of itself is just passively acquired knowledge. When one gains revelatory education through an intuition that evolves from experience, then experience becomes understanding. Baggish in his precocious estimation of experience is not so far off the mark. Experience only matters if an intuitive understanding of the experience emerges in consciousness. The understanding is rarely concurrent with the experience, but follows through a process of incremental maturation.

Stern's satire includes a feint at the pretension that Baggish disparages. Teddy says, "Nothing is worse than commentary. Novels which talk about novels are worse than violinists who discuss the piece while playing it." However, with Baggish and Juliette as counterpoint mouthpieces, this is exactly what Stern does, comment on the novel while "playing it." It would seem that Stern agrees more with Baggish than with Juliette. He de-emphasizes narrative commentary *about* ideas. Rather, he emphasizes ideas, even dialectic disagreements, through cutting dialogue.

Other novelists have grappled with ideas in their books. Huxley was an advocate and forerunner of the "novelist of ideas." For Huxley, particularly in his later work, this seemed to be the end to his means with the ideas becoming more and more prominent. The early novels were more "novel-like" with ideas as by-products of relatively conventional narrative and dialogue. His later novels increasingly became vehicles for didactic philosophy, which worked for readers who were interested in the philosophy, particularly if they agreed with it. Huxley had his following and they anticipated and looked forward to his expositions. This critic does not argue with an author who chooses to work this way, although one can say that a purist of novel reading might not consider them pure novels and have a case. Stern has his ideas but they are adjunctive and never presumptive for the reader who wants a "novel" to take precedence. The reader can go with the flow or stop and think a little more about the ideas if one chooses to do so.

Readers can think about the fact that Parsons, the blackmailee, works in army intelligence internal affairs and visits Schreiber concerning articles containing classified information appearing in the U.S. Parsons confirms in his purview that Schreiber is too naïve to be directly responsible. He then visits his blackmailer, Baggish, and tells him it is circumstantially obvious that he is the thief of the classified documents. While he does so, Teddy, "from his armchair ... reached for a jar of peanut butter to make a sandwich ... 'a fig for you, Parsons. A fat fig for a fair fag.... What are you going to do about it?'" (E 163). Baggish thus cruelly reminds Parsons of his sway over him. Parsons says to Baggish that, at least, they are even and that this should end the blackmail. Baggish calls his bluff and refuses to concede because at this time being gay would have ended Parsons' career. Baggish's arrogance is just warming up.

This is followed with a speech from Schreiber to Teddy that heightens the ironic position that Baggish has connived himself into. "'I sometimes have a feeling about people, that they have a direction in them, some down, some up, some both. I feel yours is up, and it's right for you. Most of the people who have that direction show it vulgarly in everything they do that it makes you sick. You aren't in there grabbing and punching; you're just working solidly.' Baggish took a huge swallow of Piesporter. 'Poor dumb jerk,' he thought. 'What kind of crud can a man flop around in.'" Even Baggish, who feels sorry for no one, feels sorry for Max, and suggests that Schreiber take a long trip. Teddy does so "in a tone less adulterated by self-interest than any he had used since he was a boy" (E 166–167). This is compassion from your executioner.

Max reunites with Traudis for his trip. Traudis tells him Teddy is a friend. "Not as you were Max. An intimate and — well, part of an arrangement. I admit all. I understand what you felt. I've thought about it ten thousand times since. You don't understand me, don't even want to, despite all your interest in me. Baggish understands, and Baggish forgives. You always think you're being used. You don't understand the passion behind 'using' someone. He does" (E 171). Absolutely, Baggish understands the value of commodity and that Traudis has bartered by necessity the only commodity that she has to trade. Schreiber, a son of affluence, cannot understand this aspect of the world. Traudis is a metaphor for the new Europe, the Europe broken, depending on the kindness of strangers for survival.

Baggish ingratiates himself with a German business mogul, targets the daughter, wins her, and moves into high finance. The daughter is no fool; she sees Baggish as he sees her, a like mind who envisions the utilitarian value of the match with his magazine contacts in America and natural savvy for public relations fertilizer. In fact, Teddy does genuinely like her and convinces himself that, "a strong passion converts what it sees into what it needs" (E 193). Hence, he rationalizes his affection with a utilitarian application rather than concedes that any real emotion is also a factor. A family member observes of Baggish, "'And we thought Hitler had plans'" (E 194).

Schreiber, as fate would have it — an inevitable grotesque fate — meets Tiberius, the driver who ran off with Micheline. Tiberius is now a changed man, "redolent of wealth and confidence.... Schreiber was seeing in Tiberius Micheline's rust-colored face" (E 206). Neither mentions the war or Micheline. After the war, Tiberius remained in Europe and became one of the plunderers. History repeats itself and Traudis runs off with Tiberius, thus referring back to the novel's opening epigraph. *Every man of character has a typical experience which recurs over and over again.* This is another reversal for Schreiber, but not quite as deadly as the original reversal with Micheline. A victim becomes accustomed to victimization, just as a victimizer recognizes whom to victimize. Schreiber in his closing remarks sounds like Herbert at the end of Golk: "If he'd learned something in Europe, it was that every day brought enough to live for. You lived in what came up. That made you what you were.... He had the odd sensation that he wasn't returning to Europe but leaving it. 'Funny,' he thought.... So long, dear heart. So long, dear, dear heart'" (E 213). His curse, begun with Micheline, has lifted; he remains in the Americanized Europe of external reality but leaves the Europe of his aesthetic daydreaming. For Max this is a tempered revelation and a major or minor redemption that will depend on whether or not he transcends his pain and learns from it. It is a question without an answer as the novel ends.

Stern did spend postwar years in Europe and this novel was his evaluation of what he saw there. Like *Golk, Europe* is about the cold war — not the U.S.–Soviet Cold War, but the cold war of the emerging modern world with the businessman and politician manipulating people and media. After World War II, the crude, yet powerful media propaganda of the 1930s evolved and developed more finesse while being just as effective. The postwar amorphous Public, faceless, and facilely willing to succumb to media charms, is victimized by what the 1920s and 1930s radical theorist V. F. Calverton called *Cultural Compulsives.* The author of this study has, in previous work, employed a similar term, *Collective Subjectivity,* and found that the almost unknown Calverton — who was removed from consciousness by the 1950s evisceration of radical leftists— had taken off from

Kierkegaard's ideas about a malleable public while also anticipating the philosopher Michael Polanyi's similar rendering of the idea of cultural compulsives in his book *Personal Knowledge*, 1958.

Stern is also an astute observer of collective subjectivity (see his essay "Inside Narcissus"), and an analyst of the post–World War II era here and abroad. Born in 1928, he reached early adulthood during the period of transition to a Cold War era that shadowed the consciousness of intellectuals until the fall of the Soviet Bloc after 1989. In the 1950s, America was the savior of the world and the protector of Western Europe. Stern saw political campaigns become media-driven enterprises where style often replaced substance. His first two novels, while entertaining and teaching, seem to reflect the aloof distance that separates mass media from the public it serves—or disserves. The satire is very funny, but the heat, even in sharply written dialogue, seems to be withheld. There is a sense of specimens under glass. Passion is muted as if its presence would, as Stern conceded concerning *Golk*, be branded as an emotionalism that might have tagged him as a "Jewish writer." One must know that during the 1950s one of the most popular TV personas was Molly Goldberg who was the quintessential depiction of the Jewish matriarchal "Yenta." She was the maker of chicken soup who, with the utmost in sappy schmaltz, solved everyone's problems while yelling across to her Brooklyn tenement neighbor, "Yoo hoo, Mrs. Bloom." Goldberg helped to counter a long-prevailing anti–Semitism while another TV show, *Amos n' Andy*, did the same for African-Americans; yet, these shows made Jews and Blacks appear simpler than any reality known to anyone with reasonable intelligence. Stern countered the image of a schmaltzy Mrs. Goldberg with, as he said, antischmaltz. His next novel, *In Any Case*, would be a period piece, albeit a recent period, and Stern would move closer to the more overt emotional style that would take over his career.

1962: *In Any Case*

This period piece, written in 1962 about the postwar Europe of 1947–1952, is a "spy" novel of sorts. Stern was inspired by, as he writes in the novel's preface, "Miss Jean Fuller's account of the Prosper Network in *Double Webs* (London: Putnam, 1958). Since a few of the people about whom Miss Fuller wrote are alive, I want to make it very clear that this novel is not about them or about any real people alive or dead. Furthermore, it does not attempt to offer an interpretation of any actual events." Quite right! While the fact that it was reprinted with the title *The Chaleur*

Network indicates that it has maintained continued appeal in the spy genre, the intrigue does not really come from this aspect of the novel but from the other forms of guilt, betrayal and redemption that the espionage context provides an excuse for portraying. This book is a transition from Stern's short stories and first two novels. Here, Stern "metaphorizes" his own personal meditations on domestic warfare among spouses and their children. In addition, sex, seen as tributary before rather than central, is now the focal point and an obsession for the novel's protagonist, Samuel Curry. Freud would have recognized the pseudoincestuous Oedipal rivalries present in the flesh and more so in the psyches of the characters (and perhaps the author who vicariously exposes himself).

The crux of the story is that of a bad father who lost his son in World War II, a victim of Auschwitz. He receives a book anonymously that calls his son a double agent, a spy for the allies who had betrayed the Chaleur Network operatives to the Germans. This is a reversal and negative revelation that the father must redress, not just for his son's reputation but for his own redemption to make up for a fatherhood mostly spent chasing women with his son as a nuisance to his prowling. (The son's mother died when he was little after injuries from a skiing "accident" that her family considers to have been a reckless gesture caused by a fight with the boy's father, which is, in fact, true.) Left with his small son, he says of this responsibility, "Raising a child was quite a strain on a man, and for a free-wheeler like myself, it was sand in all my parts" (*IC* 1).

This is Stern's first full-length venture into first-person narrative. The first person, Samuel Curry, is not Stern per se, but he extrapolated from Stern's bêtes noires that shadow Stern's fictional surrogates relentlessly.

Stern has said that his journals have served as prompts for his writing rather than being sources of wholesale transcription. Here is Stern's preface to his journal entries in *Invention of the Real*: "These excerpts ... (kept erratically for more than thirty years [as of 1983]) roughly center about the middle-class Western notion of individuality. The individuals are people of artistic and scientific accomplishment. Center stage, though, is the *Pere de famille*— fantasist-observer-gossip-lover-note taker-instructor-fiction writer-closet narcissist" (*IR* 140).

As a closet narcissist, Stern — too clever for happenstance — chose what excerpts would appear in his orderly miscellany. The choices are clues to understanding his previous work and are left to be found by the critic-as-detective (Stern's analogy) who might wish to solve the crimes latent or otherwise in Stern's mind. It would seem that a few journal words might have provided the psychological underpinnings to prompt an entire novel such as *In Any Case*, which is dedicated to Stern's son Christopher:

Stern's Journal: October 1960
Katie [Stern's daughter, then eight] gave me violin lessons. I contrast her
sweet pedagogy with my harsh attempts to teach Christopher French [then
nine]. Penitent, I tell him I wish I brought him more happiness. Christopher: "Oh, you bring me happiness." I: "Well, I hope you'll remember with
me love." Christopher: "I don't know if I will remember you with love, but
I'll sure remember you" [*IR* 144].

This would be a telling entry in itself even if there were no subsequent
reverberations—but there are subsequent reverberations. From *In Any
Case* Sam recalls what a lousy father he was with a flashback to an incident when his son Bobbie was in a French elementary school run by nuns.
Bobbie speaks French more often than English. After one of Sam's typical late nights, he awakens hung over, surly, and not in the mood for Bobbie to come bounding down the stairs like a typical little boy:

"What in the name of God are you doing exploding down here at nine-
thirty?" Chin, nose, eyes, down, away from my look. "What's the matter?
Forgot your papa's native tongue? Dig down, brother, and get up with a
response."
"No school today."
"Why not?"
"Saint's day."
"Saint's day. No, it's Thursday. Thursday. Your grandfather ought to get
a load of 'Saintsday.' Nuns. On their fat knees sixty hours a week while
working parents of their charges suffer the ignorance they're paid to elimi-
nate. All right, laddie. Upstairs, and write me a five-page description of the
Chateau of Versailles. Without misspellings. And the next time you cavalry
down here like that, I'm going to bat the living-hell out of you as sure as
you're standing there picking your nose. Disgusting. Now get out till I am.
Debarrasse-moi le plancher," to hammer it home in his own language.
But late that night I couldn't get off to sleep thinking of the way I'd treated
him....
"I was awful this morning, Bobbie, I'm sorry."
"You were hung over."
"No excuse," I said. "I was awful. Please forgive me. You know you're the
only thing in the world I care about."
"I know."
I kissed his head. "I wish I brought more happiness into your life."
"You bring enough...."
"I hope you'll remember me with love."
"Well, I'll sure remember you," but with a smile unlike any I'd ever seen,
so sweet you'd pardon a mass murderer if he showed it [*IC* 2].

Stern's original journal entry has set the stage for a gamut of extrapolated emotions that are fiction in Stern's novel but fiction based on

dominating factors of Stern's inner life. The wrestling with male sex compulsion is the novel's primary problem followed by the coexisting derivatives of betrayal, guilt, and then anger at one's self or at others as a sublimated reaction to the guilt or as a denial of the guilt. Stern and Sam express guilt over how they have treated their children. Stern's case may have just been that isolated entry in his journal, but his imagination developed the inherent emotions of the father and son context of that entry by asking how a father would feel if elements *x*, *y*, and *z* are added to the equation. Stern, in his fashion, has added to Auden's two questions — *Who am I? Whom ought I to become* — with additional questions such as *What would I do if...? How would I feel if...?* He poses these questions after coming up with the situations that will engender the most provocative answers. Consequently, Stern's answers become much more important than the situations that provide them. Stern's guilt over his son was recorded as a journal entry. In general one derivation of guilt is that one may attack whatever or whomever one feels guilty about. Or, as an alternative, one can create a complex parable to express emotions that become a form of cathartic intellectual venting on paper. Stern has previously provided indications that writing serves this expiatory function and that the function is equally important as or even more important than the artistic impulse that goes along with the therapeutic confessing. Stern may not be the model for his Sam Curry in actuality, but as with Hawthorne, one can only write so well about secret guilt if one knows it intimately. Stern knows it intimately. Consequently, Sam's (and Stern's) search for the truth is a perilous one. Stern likes to employ set pieces to present some intellectual argument within the greater context of a work. For this novel, the set piece is the entire spy fabrication from beginning to end. The greater context of sex, betrayal, and guilt is embedded within the backdrop of the espionage novel suggested by Jean Fuller's book. The backdrop is a bit of trompe l'oeil. *In Any Case* is an odd duck; the whole spy scenario is an excuse for matters of an entirely different focus. Stern could have written about the inner life of this book — its real life — in any number of scenarios other than the spy context because the book is not about actual espionage at all. It could have been transferred to the business world, the political world, or even the MLA conference world with the same inner psychological themes. (There is, in fact, a mystery novel called *Murder at the MLA*.)

Stern's plot is the most complicated he will ever write, which is misleading because normally he is almost without plot. He has said that he just writes with a general idea in mind and that he lets this idea develop spontaneously until it finds its natural end. *In Any Case* features a great deal of Sam chasing after people he believes may prove his son's innocence.

These sections are not the novel's strong points. Closer to the novel's inner life are Sam's recollections of his marriage and his son's childhood. He was a failure as a husband to Helene and as a father to Bobbie, betraying both to his compulsion to have affairs. These recollections set up the psychological turmoil that constitutes his present life after he receives the news of his son's supposed treachery. What really matters within the overall plot is that while Sam, who is 57, tries to clear his son, he meets his son's former lover, Jacqueline, who was a very young French operative during the war and still is very young shortly after it. They begin an affair. Sam meets the "real" betrayer, Aristignac, (the quotation marks will be elucidated below) and befriends him while his son's old lover, who is now the father's lover, will also become the real traitor's lover who was responsible for Bobbie's betrayal and death. The previous sentence is an oedipal trilogy squared. There is a pseudoincest factor ripe enough to raise a jaded Freud's eyebrows and just as many twists of fate to fool even Tiresias. Sexual confusion, guilt rivalry, and betrayal become the inner life of the book; everything else is, while not actually superfluous, not nearly as interesting, including some unconvincing scenes with characters who aren't part of the Sam, Helene, Bobbie, Jacqueline, Aristignac pentacle.

Shortly after Sam's flashback contretemps with Bobbie, he remembers a book "by a Spanish doctor named Maranon that explained how tenderness increases in men as their sexual power wanes" (*IC* 3). Sam regrets that Bobbie didn't live long enough for this waning to take place so that Bobbie could have benefited from a father's love unclouded by sexual compulsion. Sam thinks this even though the wane has not yet taken place. He has a homely middle-aged live-in cook-maid, Mme. Zdonowycz, a war refugee about whom he thinks, "If she were twenty years younger, took a bath on Saturdays, and shaved twice a week, it would simplify my life no end." Sam would welcome a routine that didn't include perpetual prowling. Sam receives the anonymously sent book and "read the one sentence that would change his life. 'It is clear that the Chaleur Network was betrayed into the hands of the [Germans] by Gruyere, the young American, Robert Curry'" (*IC* 9). This negative revelation sets him off on a chase to clear his son's name and his own conscience.

Sam recalls that when he knew Bobbie was dead, his "first thought was, 'So at last I'm alone.' Fifty-two years old, I had no child, no wife, no parents. It was a condition for which I'd now and then wished. Every attachment weighs against every other one, and I had visions of weightlessness, of complete availability. Now that it seemed my condition, what was there to do" (*IC* 10). Herein is Stern's purpose. Everyone imagines what one would do if one were free — even when one is not necessarily unhappy with the terms of one's *unfreedom*. These wish-fulfillment fantasies may cross over to imagining what one would do if one could get away with it. Finally, one tries to get away with it.

The most notable example of late 20th century pop-culture wish-fulfillment fantasy was seen in the best-selling success of the insubstantial *The Bridges of Madison County*. A housewife with a bland life has a three-day window to cheat on her husband with a charming photographer. She does, with the overall effect that if no one knows, no harm, no foul. The moral seems to be that she will be a better wife and mother and more willing to accept routine when her family returns because her fantasy has been fulfilled. The fact that the book sold so much might signify that it became a vicarious source of wish fulfillment for the millions who read it. There is little depth, even less than can be found in that other wish-fulfillment venue of TV's daily soap operas. One could surmise from the book's appeal that one wants the vicarious carousing with the absolute minimum of thought-provoking sidebars that would remind one of the more realistic complications that affairs entail. Stern is a realist; consequently, he is complicated.

Sam tries to rationalize that routine has value simply because he must comply with a routine in order to make a living. Yet he knows there is this counterpoint: "Even painful ruts may be paths of evasion, insulation from decision, but there is the hard fact of a job done every day, a useful job in a useful industry. If this doesn't stake claims in pride, it doesn't need apology either. Except that beyond, underneath, within the cracks, I always knew that life held something else" (*IC* 24). He recalls his parents' very regular life and how he was surprised that before his birth their lives had been less regular. The reader, if not necessarily Sam, sees that he, by being their child, had become the cause of their regularity, which in fact was the consequence of the responsibility that having a child entails. He thinks, "I was conscious of them, how little there was beyond the commanding voice, the sufferance, the exhaust gases of routine. For years, I regarded my own life as an incendiary repudiation of theirs" (*IC* 25).

When Sam was married to Helene, they read and studied philosophies such as Gurdjieff. Sam sums up this study as fervent distractions to prevent temptation on his part; consequently, little of the substance stuck. In the present he travels to see those connected with the Chaleur network to clear Bobbie's name. While he travels he observes the postwar resurgence of churches and religious statues as having this implied message. "All over the European country sides, you come upon such monuments of redemptive misery" (*IC* 27). Sam is reminded of his own need for redemption. As far as his search goes he considers that, "Masochism may be as strong a motive as curiosity, or even self-interest, of which it is a perverse form" (*IC* 44). Sam also notes that his dead wife's brother-in-law, Armand, while "Two years my senior … looks fifteen younger. Habit keeps him young, habit and avoidance. What he's had to do he's mastered, and he ignores the rest" (*IC* 52). Armand is another advocate of routine; yet, who knows what he has excluded when he "ignores the rest." Later, it will be conjectured that he ignored his wife, and Sam was only too willing to fill the void.

Of domestic warfare Sam notes that during the real war, "Something happened to the relationships between Frenchmen and women in the occupation. Defeat, public defeat, had sunk into the people's hearts, men's hearts, for its men who lose wars. This is what I learned at night from the ten or twelve girls who found my tenderness and need more satisfying for them than the muscular bodies from which defeat had siphoned authority" (*IC* 54). Maybe so, but Sam is a sexual opportunist who may have rationalized that he was doing these women a favor. Their men would likely have thought otherwise and disagreed with Sam's assessment of their collective shame. Sam is a slave to his divining rod. He seeks rationalizations for the fact that his compulsion is selfish and thus his explanations are self-serving.

His search leads him to Jacqueline, Bobbie's lover, who was "only twenty-two when she'd tumbled out of the sky, this provincial duck had performed like an Arthurian knight. An explosions expert, she could pin a train to a hill or bank it into a gulley, count the bodies in the dark…." (*IC* 56). Sam's image of her as an "Arthurian Knight," while being a compliment, is nonetheless chauvinistic — knights are men. She is more of an Amazon in the Wonder Woman mode and Wonder Woman comics began during World War II. Stern knows this and knows what he is doing, and while he is not a chauvinist, Sam is, as well as being a hypocrite. He thinks that as far as his business life has gone he considers himself to have been basically a salesman. His principal consumer is himself. He spreads his own fertilizer and believes it: "if anything, my credo centers about that old line 'understanding all is forgiving all.' That's the big thing" (*IC* 66). For the moment this also means, "Do as I say, not as I do" as Sam falls short of "understanding all" and "forgiving all." To analyze this thought and emphasize it by contrast, he flashes back to when he once told Bobbie, "Every man needs to be a diplomat." That is, a clever liar who fools others as well as himself. Then Sam recalls Bobbie's adolescent years. "Adolescence is not a pretty thing to look at, or, probably, to undergo, though I can't remember experiencing anything uncomfortable in my own" (*IC* 66).

Not true. Sam will contradict himself in other flashbacks to his own childhood. He did feel uncomfortable as a child but has blocked these moments out. His search for the truth about Chaleur will also include truths about himself as child and man. (Stern had his own uncomfortable adolescent moment when he concealed to his childhood friends his non bar mitzvah.) Sam recalls that as Bobbie passed from adolescence into late teenager, he regarded his own son as a rival, particularly as another man around available women. Sam, prompted by a macho allegiance to his sexual compulsion, even ridicules his son in front of a woman they are both attracted to — or that Sam imagines that Bobbie might be attracted to. Sam recalls that he remembers Bobbie noticing an attractive woman and at the time thinking the look "must be one of the most common my face has worn. We were a couple of the wolves on the prowl.... Something dies in a father when he sees this" (*IC* 70). Likely because it reminds Sam of some of his own very bad behavior. Not only is Sam a slave to his divining rod, if one calls it by the more colloquial and five-letter pejorative slang, he is one.

Immediately following this sequence, Sam's distress at his wife's Catholicism is recalled. "When Helene would return from one of her sessions in the confessional, I would detest the cleansed and easy self I could almost smell parading around me. I'd try and provoke the 'true self,' the unlilylike, soiled self who dared to rebuke in purified repose what I had no way of purifying" (*IC* 74). He is referring to his guilt. Helene's trips to the confessional are the Catholic symbol of one's perpetual guilt. This reminds Sam of his own guilt, guilt which causes him to be in denial. Stern emphasizes that this "rebuke" provokes guilt because Sam immediately follows this thought by recalling another man who, "Like myself ... was a prowler, boulevardier, and sport; married, but available, and always ready for what we called excursions" (*IC* 79).

Men like Sam often think — or rather they foolishly convince themselves— that women don't know what they're up to. Sam thought Helene didn't know about his "excursions." He resented her for merely existing as a reminder of why he had good reason to feel guilty. Guilt becomes anger at the source that causes it, in this case Helene. During a bridge game, Helene is particularly contentious over game points (Sam will later reveal that her anger was really about Sam's one-night dalliance with Helene's best friend, Villette, who is the wife of Helene's brother, Armand, who is Sam's best friend.) Sam verbally attacks Helene in the most vicious terms. Helene throws coffee in his face, grabs her skis, flies off at reckless speed, crashes and is seriously injured. Her wounds turn gangrenous and she dies terribly. When Sam says he resents having to raise Bobbie alone, he also means he resents being reminded of his guilt over Bobbie's mother.

Sam later considers a difference between men and women. "There is a kind of history-consciousness in men that makes them isolate the events of their life more than I think women do, makes them aware of stages, triumphs, losses, defeats. Women are less finicky about time, it may be, 'the years I was having children,' 'the years before I married,' 'the years I worked' but life is generally more continuous for them. Also, women are used to accepting partial success, are trained to disappointment, withdrawal, regret. In a difficult love affair, a man is pressed to the constant possession he cannot have and tortured by its absence until it breaks him, or he breaks its hold" (*IC* 105–6). Sam's self-serving evaluation represents his era; women of today might not go along with his view but a woman's world in *his* day was very different.

Stern engages in meditations on the nature of guilt and the possibility of redemption. Ultimately, the macrocosm of actual warfare between nations and the multiple microcosms of domestic warfare between mates, parents, and children become one and the same. The former is just the ultimate extrapolation from the latter but the latter is Sterns' primary concern. (In 1986's *A Father's Words*, another Stern fictional surrogate will say; "Isn't it more likely that war is the social expression of our souls? My God, look how we argued in the family" (*FW* 27). Bottom line: while Stern had second-hand knowledge of war, he wasn't in one and his fictional counterpart cannot write about war guilt except by inference. However, domestic warfare is part of Stern's purview. Ultimately, for Stern, while there are different forms and degrees of betrayal — war, infidelity, parent-child rivalry, pseudoincest — the ensuing reverberations and guilt come from the same region of the human psyche.

While Sam interviews people he thinks can help him clear Bobbie, he hears war stories about how the exigencies of trying to survive during wartime transform individuals forever. The principal thought conveyed here is that survival has no principles. Concepts of good or evil give way to the more tangible needs of the many that force choices which will make some of the few expendable. The bottom line seems to be that the barber or the businessman or the farm girl of before the war became the spies, double agents, and killers of the war. Then after the war they attempted to return to some degree of normalcy. In Wholly Truthful reality and the art that mirrors that reality, the routine of life goes on no matter what horrible tragedies interrupt the routine. The overriding truth the survivors want to believe is that they should not be held accountable for their actions, which were the result of extraordinary strain on ordinary individuals. This does not mean that there is no guilt, but that the past actions causing the guilt will not be undone by subsequent persecution and punishment.

Stern emphasizes this idea when Sam confronts Phebe Delattre, one of his former casual affairs who also slept on both sides of the French occupation. He believes she learned information casually from a Frenchman that she then passed on just as casually to a German with the result of sinking the Chaleur network. Phebe responds.

> "So, you've been waiting, you've been lying in wait, holding your gun on me, waiting for me. You to whom I gave — life [sexual comfort after Helene died]. You're a traitor, a swine. I told him [the German], yes I told him. I told him as you'd tell a man it was Wednesday. I told, but not the way you tell. To hurt. The way you tell me, to kill. I didn't tell the way you look at me. Was I to kill Bobbie? Are you telling me I killed Bobbie? Look at yourself, you, famous all over Paris for your disregard of him. Your women — me, brought and flaunted in front of him. It's you who knocked him down. You couldn't stand anyone in your way. You were made to be alone. Lying with me, moaning over me, you were always by yourself, loving nothing but Sam. The American, Uncle Sam, free and alone. You sit there now, dead in your insides, and claim that I killed your boy…" [*IC* 145].

Stern follows this with a confirmation of the point. Sam remembers taking Bobbie to the circus where his son became ill and vomited while sitting among the audience. Sam, rather than being sympathetic, became enraged because Bobbie shamed him. On the next page after this flashback, Sam takes Jacqueline to a circus, his first since the Bobbie fiasco. Is this compensation for past guilt by his affection for Bobbie's lover or just affection turned again into a rivalry?

Sam meets Aristignac, also known as "Robert" during the war. This is the person that the author of the anonymously sent book confused with Bobbie Curry. He was the real "traitor." Or was he? He claims he was forced to make a choice to sacrifice the few in order to save the many and the decision came from the overall intelligence apparatus that supervised Chaleur. He was just following orders. The more Sam knows him, the more Sam likes him. Hate becomes difficult as they both share an interest in existential and metaphysical philosophies. Here, Stern ventures into his own philosophical territory. Are these men really seeking some form of mystical transcendence or are they looking for complex methods of rationalization as distractions from their guilt. Sam soon learns that Aristignac also shares Jacqueline. The betrayer betrays again. He caused Bobbie's death; yet, Bobbie's father and Bobbie's lover can't resist him. For Jacqueline, her guilt over sleeping with Bobbie's father and her guilt over sleeping with Bobbie's killer seem equal.

The shock to Sam is tempered by a bit of previous knowledge turning into true understanding: earlier he *knew* the expression to understand

all is to pardon all; now, he is beginning to *understand* it. As Sam evalu-
ates his learning process in the understanding and pardoning of others, he
is also learning how to pardon himself:

> Lastly, there was a general sense of the predicament of others. I was very
> weak; it felt as if I were at the bottom of great columns of hot air. Zdonowycz
> asked me how I was, and instead of saying, "Fine" or "lousy, how do you
> think?" I said, "How are *you*, Madame?" Tea slopped over saucer. She put
> both on the table and wiped the overflow with her apron. Incredible as it
> is, I had never asked her how she felt, not even conventionally. It was because
> I'd never cared.... I had no regard for her condition. "I'm a lot of trouble to
> you," I said.
> "Nothing, nothing...."
> "Thanks for everything."
> "You dying?" [*IC* 164].

Sam is not dying; he is trying to learn how to live for the first time.
His new understanding is both a revelation and a redemption, after which
he begins to consider a more inclusive view of the world instead of his previously excluding narcissism. This prompts some more aesthetic philoso-
phizing by Sam about human nature. "I wish I had scholarly talents. For
I'd like to do a study ... the deceptive by-blows of the war, the activities
of the undercover men on both sides ... and the blends that make up a
large spectrum of neutrality. It's my view that never before can so large a
part of war have been determined by men whose actions belied their
announced positions, that never before has there been so much deception,
camouflage, treason, betrayal, and lying" (*IC* 169). Sam's view seems true
to him because he has been put in the middle of the world he has just
described in both his public and private sphere. Human nature is constant;
Sam has changed, not the world. Later Sam thinks: "what if life were but
one aspect of something that counted more, that didn't need judgement,
decisions, traitors" (*IC* 184). Life *is* something more — or perhaps less —
than what human beings impose on it. Life, or nature, is the whiteness of
the whale — neutral; men disturb the neutrality by asserting their will. History is not the chronicle of how nature effects man but rather how man
has disturbed nature.

Sam and Jacqueline confront Aristignac over what he now calls a
choice of betrayal forced upon him. Jacqueline asks; "'Have you ever
thought about restitution? ... have you ever thought you could do something for those who were injured by you.'

'I've thought about a million things,' he said. 'Haven't we all. Didn't
you think about the families of the Germans on the dynamited trains? It

has to stop somewhere. For your own protection. What you do doesn't end with the doing of it, but the decision comes first, and I think you have to stick with it morally. Only God knows the consequences of his actions, and even he's supposed to let the bad things happen as they happen'" (*IC* 188). Aristignac then reveals that it was he who sent Sam the book, but with a note that Sam never found saying not to believe everything you read. Aristignac had tried to make some restitution in his own way.

Aristignac tells Sam about "some Gutamela Indians" who, after some long-ago teachings by Mayan Jesuits, have now confused the worship of Jesus with equal homage to Judas because the former could not have been God without the latter. If Judas hadn't betrayed Jesus, Jesus might not have fulfilled his role as a Messiah. Sam then asks Aristignac about this Jesus/Judas counterpoint, "Is it because they know that without him [Judas] there would have been no crucifixion, no redemption?" Aristignac answers with a transfer of Sam's metaphorical counterpoint concerning wartime betrayal and guilt to the real subject of the novel's inner life. "The Judas god was invented to take care of sexual guilt. Here's where all the real treason occurs, where the temptations are strong and the taboos also. The Indian world is harrowed by adultery and all kinds of license. The Judas god marks the end of passion, and he expiates their guilt" (*IC* 217–218).

The Irish poet AE (George Russell), whom Stern quotes preceding his collected essays, *One Person and Another*, also has a meditation-poem on the Christ/Judas duality. In his book, *Song and its Fountains*, 1932, AE describes how his inner life of visions and dreams inspires his outer life of art. He writes of his dreams and visions that they are a form of "meditation which discovers another being within us, unites us to it in some fashion; and in retrospect we seem to have lived two lives, a life of the outer and a life of the inner being."[29] The outer man's art is symptomatic of the inner man's vision. Art displays the true man, the inner man, symbolically. AE gives an example of art reflecting a meditation on the inner being. He recalls an early painting of his own with a man casting a giant shadow far larger in proportion to the body casting it. This indicated to AE that his intuition about the great psyche of the inner being's memory did, in fact, loom much larger than the mere physical man whose imposing shadow is the aggregate accumulation of multiple pasts—child, adolescent, young man — until in old age it seems to stretch infinitely. From this past the understanding of the present follows, but only if one chooses to find it. AE follows his explanation with a poem in which he reflects on how one's past sets up one's present and future and how childhood determines adult behavior: "In the lost boyhood of Judas/Christ was betrayed."[30]

AE's symbolism signifies that Christ, the hero, is the best part of Everyman and that he atoned for the sins of Everyman; Judas, the betrayer, is also Everyman. Within each Everyman, there is hero and betrayer. One cannot understand either until one uncovers the past that made them both. AE also writes, "One part of us is seer and another is creator"[31] Art comes when the seer part inspires the creator part. Stern's inner man orchestrates his outer art.

When Sam learns that Jacqueline has been seeing Aristignac, he also learns to accept that she has needed a break from him in order to decide if she can deal with her own guilt over Bobbie. In turn, Sam needed Jacqueline to make the break in order to learn about the nature of his own guilt. When he begins to understand himself, he is able to find redemption in taking her back despite Aristignac, thus expiating his guilt over Bobbie and Helene. They marry and she is four months pregnant with a child whose father is unknown. He accepts this and will raise the child as his own.

Sam's exclusive narcissism has matured into a more inclusive love for his present as well as his past. Stern comes to a resolution for Sam that he is far from finding for himself at the novel's writing in 1962. His inner turmoil gets a full hearing in his next novel *Stitch*, 1965. Before this more personal expiation in *Stitch*, however, Stern would publish his collected stories written from 1949 to 1962.

1964: *Teeth, Dying and Other Matters*

After the critical success of Stern's first three novels his short stories were collected in 1964's *Teeth, Dying, and Other Matters*. They were written from 1949 to 1962 and are formative exercises towards enunciating the prevalent themes that would dominate his subsequent work. Three of the stories were referred to as examples earlier: "Teeth," featuring the lonely Miss Wilmott and her loyal peanut butter; "Assessment of an Amateur" with the moocher, Higgins; and "Wanderers," the saga of the "two nut sons" and postcards. For the last story, Stern previously explained that the spur was an eccentric uncle who lived in a Manhattan hotel. The rest was invention by derivation. One imagines that all of these stories have a simple link to a Stern familiar that is turned literary by an aggrandizement via extrapolation.

The earliest, "Good Morrow Swine," is from 1949 when Stern was 21— two years removed from his B.A. at Chapel Hill. It is a snapshot of a charismatic French teacher who stimulates his students through a pseudodictator persona augmented by a severely exaggerated French accent.

He is the evil Foreign Legion commandant of bad black-and-white movies. The title is his room-entering salutation accented by slapping a yardstick hard on his desk. The students, well-trained in the routine, answer in unison: "Vun, two, tree, four, five, seeks, seven, hate, hate prime, ten." What follows is the call and answer of a drill instructor and his recruits. French and English phrases alternate with quotes from notables such as Emerson: "*Le coeur pleure quand les vices triomphent.... Nous repeterons la phrase mot a mot.* [The heart cries when vices triumph.... We will repeat the phrase word by word.] Mr. Perkins led the class through the sentence.... He assigned the English to the Conquerors and the translation to the Conquered" (*T*43). This interplay continues with English and French word play. When it is time, Perkins bids them adieu: "Pleasant dreams, swine" (*T*44). That's it. In four pages, one recalls every good or crazy teacher one has ever had. The credo of teachers of writers is, "Write about what you know." At age 21, Stern knew school and wrote about it. A formal education was now a partner with a writer's education.

In another four-page story from 1949, "A Short History of Love," a man and woman who work in the same office have a conversation, which reveals that she, who has not spoken to him before, and does not know his name, has eyed him silently. She summons up nerve to speak to him in a gush of rushed words that reflect the urgency of this chance opportunity and the opening to reveal her feelings. He is not overwhelmed with any sudden reciprocal feeling. He hasn't noticed her before this. She sounds a bit silly and he attempts to be polite. She attributes to him qualities created in her imagination that his behavior now refutes. He attempts to be kind, but it is clear that this is nothing more than a neutral kindness. Finally, her fervor dims. When he tells her his name, Charles Page, "She began to say, 'How inappropriate,'" that is, he was no longer a romanticized figure and, to her, his storybook name is a contradiction; "she seemed to see the name issuing from him like a fog, and she raised her hands as it moved towards her, grey, lethal" (*T* 117).

Stern here depicts that impenetrableness of the "I-You" dichotomy where the "I" speaking to the "You" and the "You" speaking to the "I" do so from an inherent mutual exclusion that bears on the age-old conflict of illusion and reality. Of this Huxley writes: "For in spite of language, in spite of intelligence and intuition and sympathy, one can never really communicate anything to anybody. The essential substance of every thought and feeling remains incommunicable, locked up in the impenetrable strong-room of the individual soul and body. Our life is a sentence of perpetual solitary confinement."[32] Language, as a reactionary medium that is derived from feeling, can never truly convey the feeling of those feelings to another. One can tell another "I love you," but the "You" can never feel what the other feels, only react with one's own emotions, which may accept, reject, or attempt to emulate, but can never duplicate, the other's feelings. Even at age 21, Stern understood that the words spoken by his characters may express knowledge, but not necessarily understanding, and that the gap between knowledge and understanding can result in bitter misunderstandings. This fundamental inability to transfer one's feelings and the misunderstandings derived from the futile attempts are standard operating procedure in the post–World War II Age of Anxiety. Stern emerged from adolescence into adulthood (he was 17 in 1945) at the beginning of this era.

"A Counterfactual Proposition," is from 1956 and the logical extension of "A Short History of Love" as it develops the same theme of the mind's ability to create scenarios about people one has never spoken to. Patchell, a college teacher, misses Europe, which he visited briefly and has now romanticized. When he is not daydreaming about Europe, he daydreams about women: "Almost every night Patchell lay down his book and took transport to Paris, to the streets and to the girls he'd found there three years before. [Then] he came back across the ocean to the girls whom he saw each day at school, the thousand careful bodies with whose minds alone he was entrusted, minds which he dreamed of easing out of the flesh towers they inhabited so that these towers could be taken without outcry" (*T* 59). Then he masturbates.

Twyla K. Digges is the particular object of his vicarious sex. She is beautiful and bright enough to intellectualize her own self-indulgence by loving herself in the mirror. This sexual solipsism also ends in masturbation. Patchell and Digges are two islands unaware of the other but unknowingly united by unrequited sex drives. "For Freddie Patchell, she became disease and mania" (*T* 61). Like many with this form of mania, he was oblivious that everyone knew about his infatuation that he thought he had cleverly hidden. When Twlya's roommate is in his class, he becomes inebriated by even this second-hand proximity and asks her questions that bring him closer to Twyla by some deluded refraction:

> "And what did you say yesterday about the nature of pleasure, Miss Druse?"
> "Either the conscious satisfaction of a need or the elimination of an obstacle to such satisfaction."
> "What is a counterfactual proposition, Miss Druse?"
> "As in Newton's System.... A proposition which though apparently valid is insufficient and is revealed to be so when it contradicts another proposition of the same system" [*T* 62].

After a year and a half, his obsessive routine is randomly interrupted by a chance meeting with Twyla; he dares to speak with her. Minutes later — revelation — they are in bed. Ten minutes more and they are discovered by the house mother for a reversal of cosmic bad timing. Mrs. Pitcher reports it to Miss Emory, the college president. Emory "is the prototype of the woman too good for marriage, the woman whose intelligence overpowered her attractions in the form of scorn for suitors" (*T* 65). And even more scorn for males who were her professional subordinates. Emory is an intellectual Gladys Culley. She awaits the foolish — to her — Patchell in her office knowing he has been the subject of general scorn for his recognized infatuation. He had succumbed where Emory had long refrained; thus, he is weak, as are all males. She expects crying and begging. What she gets is Golk and Baggish in training. She wants him to resign. He informs her he will sue. She counters that he has no chance of winning. He rebuts that he will blame it on a hysterical plot. (McCarthyism and Miller's *The Crucible* were still fresh memories.)

Emory has her own revelation: "She now understood him, and she cast the first respectful look at a person that she had in years. 'Well, what do you want?' she asked. Certainly not to remain here."

"I want ... a year's research grant in lieu of salary, so that I may work at the Bibliotheque Nationale, and a letter to Miss Digges' father persuading him to agree to her fervent desire to spend this year at the Sorbonne, claiming a heartfelt talk with her this first day as the reason for your sudden intervention" (*T* 67). Emory agrees. Patchell has posed his own irrefutable "Counterfactual Proposition." Sex and power are juxtaposed. Weakness for sex does not obviate the will to power if the object one uses the power against (Emory) is not also the object of the weakness (Twyla). Digges is the "conscious satisfaction" of a need; Emory is the "obstacle to such satisfaction" that must be eliminated. Emory learned that "a proposition which though apparently valid [that is, Patchell's lust] is insufficient and is revealed to be so when it contradicts another proposition of the same system." In the "system" of sexual attraction, the compulsion for sex is in inverse proportion to the power one summons to overcome any obstacle to getting sex. This is an early Stern "set piece." He posits an intellectual proposition and lets it loose through characterization.

Illusion and reality open the 1952 story "Cooley's Version." Calvin Cooley is a nondescript academic in New York City who feigns an indifferent nonchalance to a world that is quite indifferent to him. He pretends not to be aware of the world so that he can ignore that no one cares if he is aware or not. A little French translation work comes his way and he takes the package casually but can't wait to open it in private. He reads it and has a revelation; he believes the author is his intellectual kin and has brought "stylization and integration to his sensibility as well as extension and exegesis of it. The reading of Delphine Treves' novel had meant for Cooley no less than a marriage ceremony" (*T* 120). He sets to the task of translation with the passion of a dedicated midwife. Cooley and Treves begin a professional correspondence of strictly technical matters. The first three of her books that Cooley translates are not successful. The fourth — almost four years later — is and the earlier three are reappraised favorably. Cooley thinks of her as "his author" (*T* 120). He is told there is a picture of her, poster-sized, at a bookstore that is surrounded by his translations. Illusion and reality take a crooked turn as Delphine is unattractive and it seems impossible that she was the "physical instrument of the brilliant spirit he had let out into the American air" (*T* 112). "He walked up the Avenue reeling with terror" (*T* 113). Here is a serious reversal of his hoped-for revelation.

They meet. She is "plump." She tells him he is the only translator who truly understands her. They go to dinner with their American editor. Her appetite explains her size as she revels in food and drink — a substitute for the passion that otherwise only exists in her books. After her feast she (in a move that anticipates Baggish) spills coffee in the editor's lap so that he exits and leaves her alone with Calvin. Rowing in Central Park's lake, the effort of the oars arouses Calvin's interest in Delphine's large breasts that bob with the motion of the boat. "Something about them as they shifted under her blouse, as if in sympathy with his exertions, gave him the feeling that he could go through with what he had intended. His face bulged with the thought of it" (*T* 125).

They go to his apartment. But the reader does not go in with them. She goes on a book tour and he receives a letter two days later that remembers him fondly but is ambiguous in terms of what he should take from the one night. "...yet our relationship has become, swiftly and intensely, the one I have always felt to be the perfect social version of the delicate interactions of our work" (*T* 128). He chooses, as he has chosen to do with the translations, to interpret the letter in "Cooley's Version," one that allows some redemption for his otherwise bland life. "Cooley was at first unsure of the letter, yet as months passed and the memory of the day in New York faded, he came to regard it as the most stunning emblem of their relationship, one which never failed to reassure him amidst the difficulties of hammering out the ecstatic convolutions of the later texts" (*T* 128). He has willed his memory to conform to the needs of his imagination.

1953's "Arrangements at the Gulf" is the earliest story to emphasize the theme of routine. Eighty-six-year-old, wealthy, wheelchair bound Mr. Lomax is disaffected with his large family, which he has escaped from for the last 23 years by doing Florida in the winter. He is particularly disgusted with them this fall as he causally mentioned that he thought he was going to die in Florida — but he wasn't saying when. Hence, when he boards the train south, they see him off and "goggle" at him.

Lomax is very happy to leave them, and looks forward to Florida, as this is the "every-other-year" when his friend Granville will visit there instead of going to California. They have an affinity that is stronger than Lomax feels for his relatives. This idea that blood is *not* thicker than water will become a Stern staple. Granville is a writer who started writing and getting published after he retired. Lomax contrasts this with his own lack of late-year productivity, but not with any resentment. Both men are courtly tea drinkers from another era, which is the basis of their mutual appeal. Granville wheels his friend around graciously, and graciousness is the virtue that Lomax most treasures. They are men of routines to which they held fast. Granville is a lifelong bachelor and envies Lomax's legacy — his children. To this, Lomax responds, "The virtue of children is a fiction of bachelors" (*T* 134). Later, Lomax adds, "I miss you the odd years." So does Granville. Lomax tells him, "Old friends are true family" (*T* 135). Then Lomax, the man of routine, hints to Granville, another man of routine, that either this winter or no later than next will be his last. Granville understands. "I'll come down then, Fred, said Granville."

"They sat for a while looking out over the Gulf. Then Granville wheeled Mr. Lomax into his room, and, contrary to their custom, they shook hands as they bade each other 'Good night'" (*T* 136).

"Gardiner's Legacy" is from 1957 and defines the silent domestic warfare that remains another Stern feature. There is here an early bitterness on the subject of marriage that seems extreme from a 29-year-old Stern. If it is fantasy, it is nonetheless deadly close to a reality that many readers know or fear knowing, that of a devoted hate that was formed from a masochistic need. The Gardiners are dead. Elinor recently, her husband in obscurity 20 years before, after which the revelations came furiously. In life he was a writer of no success; in death, as resurrected by Elinor's assiduous research, his unknown art is compared to "James and Melville and Faulkner" (*T* 137). She devoted her life to him by working menial jobs so he could just write. "It's been reported that once in Rome she prostituted for him…" (*T* 138). She claimed a symbiotic harmony. "He created me." Perhaps, but how? Her devotion to his artistic exhumation — at whatever cost to her — is revealed in a three-volume posthumous opus named *Elinor* that is a 40-year record of his hate for her. She is described as "the hair shirt" or "the Adversary and the Primal Sin in one." She, who kept him in "Hell (he capitalized it, for he turned out to be a secular theologian of that mental place) ... she had taken the measure of his loathing, knew how he detested her spirit and her flesh, mocked at her with his women, put her remarks in the most disgusting mouths in modern letters" (*T* 139). He lists 86 women and "that he forced at least ten of the women to have abortions" (*T* 140). This when they were illegal and potentially dangerous. And yet, and yet ... Elinor was no fool. "Is it possible that she was the great mover all along, that she made him *living* as she later made his legend? ... the universe within which they were written, did she not provide that, shape that.... Was his work as much report as vision? This is the oddest mystery of the legacy" (*T* 141).

Not quite. The mystery is in the title. Which Gardiner is leaving the legacy? The capitalized "Hell" and the secular theology forecasts the capitalized "Pill" (as in Birth control) of *Other Men's Daughters* and the secular theology that the advent of the pill entails.

Also in this collection are four stories all written in 1962: the aforementioned "Wanderers," and "Teeth," as well as "Dying," and "Orvieto Dominos, Bolsena Eels." These were written after Stern's first three novels and display a more palpable, less distanced style than his previous work. By this time, he was a critical success and ran away less from his "impoverished Jewishness." Consequently, he works from an emotional base that is more secure about showing emotion in his work. Cynical humor is now balanced with a bit more warmth and pathos towards his characters. The pathos is never maudlin; indeed, it is portrayed in a rather dry absurdity that marks British humor. Stern's characters are still pathetic objects buffeted by life's shifting waters, but now they are also *subjects* who engender less scorn and more empathy.

"Teeth" features the lonely Miss Wilmott, with peanut butter as a substitute for affection or sex, and a "troglodyte" armchair for company. "The only arms that ever held her" (*T* 21). She is a put upon "low-grade instructor in the History department" (*T* 15) and in no danger of fending off scores of suitors. She needs a dentist and meets Dr. Hobbie; after which she *needs* Dr. Hobbie and invents toothaches to see him. He may or may not be oblivious to her interest, but he does not reciprocate although he is kind in his quiet rejection of her. She begins to read bicuspid esoterica to charm Hobbie with his only hobby — teeth. As in "A Short History of Love" and "A Counterfactual Proposition," there are the silent presumptions on Wilmott's part about a reality that doesn't exist. Hobbie has Wilmott meet Mr. Givens, "a short, good-looking Negro of forty, dressed in house-painter's stained overalls...." Givens is a Marxist, if hardly an intellectual, but he has read the "manifester" and is well meaning. "Dr. Hobbie's other book patient. After this, most of her appointments coincided with Mr. Givens ... while a beaming Dr. Hobbie stood by" (*T* 18). She didn't get it. Wilmott plans a dinner for Hobbie but neglects to inform him until the last possible moment, no doubt hoping he will not have a chance to say no. He says no. Coincidentally, she sees Givens and invites him instead. He asks her out; she declines. He apologizes if he has insulted her — this is 1962. She says he hasn't offended her but has no intentions of being so bold as to date a "Negro" even while imagining she might want to. Hobbie leaves town and Wilmott's last hope for real arms instead of an armchair is dashed. She has had a late middle-age fling that is solely of her imagination. Her destiny is to be alone. This is both Wilmott's routine and revelation. Stern's metaphor is that life for the Miss (or Mister) Wilmotts of the world is one of literally pulling teeth to get even the slightest reaction from anyone that they exist outside of their own minds.

In "Wanderers" there are the "two nut sons" and their father from whom the bent genes seem to have been taken. Mr. Mendel is one of Stern's most extreme cases of a man driven by a need for compulsive-obsessive routine, which, in 1962, was still hardly recognized as such and certainly there was no Prozac even if the disorder was diagnosed. In addition, a Mendel — a creature of the Great Depression — would not have allowed himself to be psychoanalyzed because he would not have any idea he needed to be. (This is a familiar scenario for children of depression-era parents.) Stern here, for the first time, rebuts his "impoverished Jewishness" by making his characters clearly Jewish. The story's first sentence is a declaration of intent to do so: "Those Jews sure did travel." Stern noted previously that Mendel is based on an uncle, which might suggest that he could not avoid the character's Jewishness. Perhaps, but Stern has also made clear that he can take an ounce of truth and extrapolate it into a pound of fiction by changing features, characteristics, professions. He could have done so with his uncle. Yet, he doesn't. This is a Jewish story without equivocation.

Miss Swindleman, the lobby clerk, recalls that "as the depression slid away, and the quiet goyim died, the Jews began moving in. They too were bachelors, spinsters, widows, and small families, but they had not been broken by hard times [as the goyim had]. Decades of finagling, deception, complaints and theft had hardened and renewed them. As the guardian of Hotel Winthrop, Swindleman took her new clientele very seriously. With the onset of the Jews, though, Miss Swindleman had conceived her life's mission: their assimilation. Assimilation of the ways and manners of the older stock which she represented.... Every cheque she eyed, every sum she re-added, contributed to their education, to the enforcement of the rules of western life, to which no amount of traveling could educate them" (*T* 45–6).

This is not their education; it is Stern's. The 12-year-old boy who lied about having his bar mitzvah is having his rite of passage vicariously in this story. Yes, the Jews in "Wanderers" travel, but Stern didn't until he went to college in North Carolina. There he became more aware and wary of his Jewishness, which he had not much considered on the surface of his life in New York — although he did lie to his friends in 1940 about his bar mitzvah. Yes, the Jews travel, as did Stern in the 1950s. Europe was nearly destroyed by Hitler's intent to find and kill Jews. No wonder Jews moved around. They were not wanted, so they traveled. But not Mendel. He never went anywhere and hardly left the hotel at all. This was obstinacy in reverse. No one would make him go anywhere. His recreations were sitting in the hotel lobby, people watching and, according to Swindleman, an egregious cheapness. "The number one Jew for cheapness. The Winthrop never collected a penny more from him than his rent" (*T* 50). Cheapness is also a form of obstinacy, a refusal to give ground or give in to anyone; it is Shakespeare's obstinacy as created for Shylock in *The Merchant of Venice*. Mendel doesn't want a pound of flesh; he demands to retain every bit of his own through his frugality. The anal retention of his money is his symbol, his metaphor, his resistance to conformity, and his refusal to be assimilated into anything other than his Jewishness. Mendel's Jewishness is not impoverished; yet one can't say it is enriching either. Rather, Mendel's Jewishness is his defiance toward a world that had allowed Hitler to exist. Mendel would now also exist, sitting in the lobby, defiantly immovable. "Miss Swindleman objected to more than Mendel's cheapness and third-rate vanity. She objected to his fixity. There he'd sit in the lobby, three sofas, six armchairs, stand-up lamps…. In the midst of this discipline sat that unsmiling, waiting, staring Mendel, isolated like a monk in a burlesque show. It wasn't until Lepidus went out the window that she understood all this about him" (*T* 51).

Lepidus was Mendel's business partner who visited once a week and they would work at their tailoring. Just before Lepidus enters this story, a story within the story is crucial. Mendel knows a Dr. Schlag who once rented rooms to Hitler before he was Hitler: "Miss Swindleman would say wickedly to whatever black Jew she passed it on to—'Adolf Hitler. Ha, ha, ha. Old Schlag could have saved you an ocean voyage…. A little arsenic in the chicken soup … and Schlag would have had a place in history.'" To which, she is told, "Wouldn't have been no history then…" (*T* 54).

Exactly! No history of scapegoating, hate, death, and Jews who sit defiantly in the lobby resenting Hitler's nearly final solution. Never again. No one would tell Mendel anything; no one would get a penny more than his resentment could stand parting with; no one would make him a victim, not even Lepidus, his partner. Lepidus asks Swindleman to change a $50 bill. She won't, as he is not a hotel resident, though she knows he knows Mendel. She says she is obeying rules, but the rule is shaped by her dislike of both men. Mendel comes down to change the 50. Swindleman thinks, "What was the world without rules ... not adding what was appropriate in this instance, that the trouble with Jews was that they fled rules, claiming that rules had rigged the world against them. That's why they'd had to wander since Christ's time, evading the rules.... The Jews had a history of taking it. Nevertheless, sometimes, they turned.... For humanity, for peace, for an end to persecution, they rose up" (*T* 53).

After Swindleman wouldn't change the 50, Lepidus took it out on Mendel: "Lepidus had started on Miss Schwindleman [note how Stern adds "ch" to the name]: 'piss cold anti-semitischer virgin-whore....' Lepidus wouldn't stop; he got hotter and hotter. He, Mendel, caught fire and gave him a push. One push. The window sidings were weak..." (*T* 55). Lepidus landed on 86th Street. The police called it accidental. Tacitly, in the context of the story, no one believed it. Tacitly, in the context of Stern, Mendel was the oppressed. Swindleman the oppressor wouldn't change the 50 for spite. Lepidus wouldn't let Mendel forget he had been insulted because they were Jews. Mendel's awareness of being Jewish in a world that had allowed Hitler to murder his people was not acceptable to him. He couldn't kill Hitler who was already dead; he couldn't kill Swindleman who had the temerity to believe she should teach these Jews how to behave. So in a rage fomented by the recent impotency of millions of kin, Lepidus took the fall for the silent Swindlemans among the faceless public in whose name ignorance was bliss while Jews were put in their place. Mendel's pugnacity was symptomatic of postwar Jews who were forced by the war to remember that Shakespeare created Shylock for a reason — to define a pervasive anti–Semitism, latent or blatant, that should never be allowed to happen again.

"Wanderers" is Stern's first "Jewish" story. The postwar consciousness of Jewishness is front and center. If there is ever an anthology of postwar short stories by Jewish American writers, "Wanderers" should be a priority for inclusion.

Yet, this is just two years after *Golk* in which Stern said he thought he might have shied away from the Jewishness of his characters. "Wanderers" is a complete about-face. Why?

In 1961 Stern's success with his first two novels became the impetus for him to be asked about his heritage in two forums. Each is reprinted in Stern's first orderly miscellany of essays from 1973, *The Books in Fred Hampton's Apartment*. The first was in response to a *Commentary* symposium of April 1961 where Stern was asked six pointed questions concerning Jews and Jewishness. The questions required Stern to reflect on the very concerns that he had heretofore avoided in his public life and his published work. The inferences of the questions are directly related to the altered postwar view of the world by Jews and of Jews by the world. The first question sets the tone.

"Do you feel that the situation of the Jew in America has altered in the past fifteen years? If so, has this had any influence on your present attitude toward your own Jewishness?"

Stern's answer (in part): "*The* situation. *The* Jew. One might collapse Mississippi Negroes or Algerian colons in useful singulars. The unembarrassed and unfearful chameleonizing of the Jew in America has given him nearly as much elbowroom as the white Anglo-Saxon. With of course the attendant loss which the American Jewish writers have been chronicling since the last war" ("In Response...," *FH* 143).

Stern then tells the story of his non bar mitzvah, and adds that, "Five years later, in college, I claimed to be half–Jewish, partly to avoid Hillel functions and partly to try my luck on the other side of the street. Today [1961], being a Jew is like being a Chicagoan.... I'm glad rather than not, but I don't spend thirty minutes a year congratulating myself, or indeed thinking of myself as a Jew" (*FH* 143).

Stern wouldn't congratulate himself in 1961 and would not now; however, this author believes the then 33-year-old Stern protested too much, and no doubt, believed himself assimilated, especially after getting through the homogenized 1950s. Yet, only 30 minutes a year on thinking about being a Jew? Shortly after saying this, Stern gives himself away by saying, "As for my children, they are half–Jews to the extent that I am Jewish, and they know about that, and what would have happened to them if they had lived in Munich in 1935" (FH 146).

One can conjecture that Stern, who was seven years old in 1935, also considered what might have happened if *he* had been in Munich.

The second forum in 1961 was "A talk for a synagogue series on Jewish writers."

The nonchalant Stern of assimilation seems to have broken the spell he held over himself. He talks at great length of contributions Jews have made to the 20th century, and that through meeting other Jewish writers, Bellow, Mailer, Malamud, and "my colleague at the University of Chicago, Philip Roth, I became conscious of my place, not as a Jewish writer but as a writer who was also a Jew even though his material has never been explicitly Jewish" ("The Novelist on his Work," *FH* 155). Then Stern refers to Hondorp, his anti–Jewish Jew as a denial "of that notorious warmth and marvelous tradition of ethical accountability, which I think of as Jewish. For me, there is perhaps a ray of hope: at the end of *Golk* Hondorp renounces his chilly way. Perhaps I too, in my way, am renouncing my denial. At least I am now writing a book [*In Any Case*], which is about a man who is trying to reclaim what has been thrown away; and I am having emotional trouble with the book. My agent says it doesn't sound like me. A colleague says that it is a sentimental book. I know something is wrong, but I have a feeling that I am both going to continue and going to pull myself to the tone I want without faking it.... I shall conclude by saying that this Stern feels there's some chance he could not have broken out of his literary borders if the glow of his Jewish past had not somehow been transferred into the body of his work" (*FH* 156).

After this, Stern wrote "Wanderers," which is as "explicitly Jewish" as anything the other Jewish fellows have written. *In Any Case* is a transition from denial to acceptance, from "chilly" to hot. Stern's next novel isn't overtly Jewish, but it is overtly emotional, edgy, and tumultuous. The focal point hangs on a brief and telling moment of anti–Semitism that becomes the catalyst for the Stern surrogate's calamitous aftermath.

1965: *Stitch*

Stitch is Stern's first overtly biographical novel and the narrative voice changes from a clinical and cold observation to hot involvement. One notes that the term "overtly" deserves an asterisk and the note for this asterisk might say what Stern says in his opening preface:

> It is important to emphasize that this is a work of fiction because occasionally the real names of people appear in it. The emphasis does not mean that there are not substantial obligations here to actual persons and facts; it means that these obligations are part of the author's gratitude even as he transforms them in the interest of whatever vividness, force, and beauty his art can obtain.

While Stern seems, once again, to obfuscate his intentions as he has done elsewhere, one can see here the summary argument before the court of readership that will decide if this is life or art. Stern's key word is "transforms." He hangs his hat on the peg of an incident with Ezra Pound and then extrapolates the emotions derived from that incident and transforms them into a chain of events. The Emotions are shock, anger, disappointment, rebuff, rejection, rebuke, attack on self-esteem, denial of approval as artist and man, and a re-emergence of personal insecurity that becomes the thumbs-up or thumbs-down pivot of success or failure. The events that become the outer and, particularly, inner narrative of *Stitch* will be found more *between* the lines than *in* the lines.

With *In Any Case* Stern tried a more effusive and discursive prose to match his philosophical musings. *Stitch* returns to a sparer narrative that lets actions speak louder than digressive words of explanation for these actions. (Stern also notes that in the wake of Pound he wrote in a very concise, emblematic prose.) Stern is concerned with the psychic violence that will lead him to his peak of inner and outer destruction in the work that follows *Stitch*, the short stories of *1968*. The aforementioned letter from Walli to corpulent Edward, explaining Nina's condition for marriage to Walli (that Walli not be fat like Edward) is absolutely devastating; yet, this is near the novel's end and is punctuation for the original impetus for destruction that begins to take place much earlier, which is Stitch's psychological cruelty. Edward reacts more acutely than someone else might because he lacks self-esteem. Subjectivity, however, is the crux of all human life (as well as the art that reflects life's subjectivity) and is more real to the individual than any other standard of objective reality that observers might otherwise think they see. Edward Gunther is a travesty of self-destructive compulsion. He is selfishly self-indulgent, narcissistic, vain, grasping, and a maker of his own myths, which, by their very narrowness, are in themselves pathetic in their lack of substance. Nonetheless, as depicted by Stern, Edward's solipsism is heart-rending because his selfishness is driven by a desperate need for approval that he feels compelled to look for outside of his immediate family. This need underlies even his compulsion for sex, which is as equally symptomatic of the need for approval as is his tactile knife-licking of peanut butter, and signifies some form of safety in an Oedipal womb. Sam Curry is a precursor to Edward, and Edward is a sequel to Sam. Gunther is the younger Sam; Edward, by *Stitch's* end, seems to have learned a little on a schedule that is ahead of Sam's more delayed enlightenment.

Edward's first meeting with the legendary sculptor (and court-convicted traitor), Thaddeus Stitch is not the deadly one, but Stern does not flinch in letting Edward — and readers — know where Stitch stands. Stitch is taciturn; each spare fragment of his speech is, according to Edward, "a stopping remark" (*ST* 6). Edward has met Stitch accidentally at Nina's, and after Stitch abruptly leaves, Edward chastises her for not telling him she knew Stitch. Edward becomes jealous of Stitch even though the old fellow is likely not a sexual rival. Gunther seeks to inject himself into this secret aspect of her life — knowledge of Stitch. He assumes he is an equal to Nina and entitled to such a benediction.

After Edward departs, Nina is grateful because "she thought tonight might be his pitch" for sexual favors. Nina, the aspiring poet, revels in knowing Stitch as one artist-intellect to another, and is not inclined to share him with Edward whom she considers less deserving. Stitch flatters her, praises her mind, and, to her delight, admires a *canzone* she's written and then reads to him, telling her, "'You have music in you Nina'" (*ST* 13). She is accepted by the great man; thus, she is in the same bailiwick for a touch of the ineffable. "She had been recognized by someone in the great tradition. It was the first indication that she belonged there herself" (*ST* 13).

Nina's existence depends on the "kindness of strangers" and she takes advantage of the European respect for the artist that is not so prevalent in America. She lives on handouts as unofficial grants for her artistic muse. "Of course she had debts in cities all over Europe and America, but oblivion and expectancy settled whatever pain they'd caused. If she ever got money she would repay everyone. She did not enjoy this way of making ends meet. Still her work was in the world's interest, despite the world's ignorance of it" (*ST* 15). Every artist anywhere has believed this. "There are," Huxley said, "no mute and inglorious Miltons."[33]

Edward has come to Europe as another Schreiber, seeking a culture and refinement he thought could not be found in America. (Later Stitch will recall one of the original America-rejecters, Henry James, whom Stitch-Pound would render relatively innocuous, compared to Stitch's own "America-hater" behavior during World War II.) The narration recalls that Edward's first meeting with Nina was over a lunch where he poured out his misery about which Nina thinks, "It had better be a good lunch" (*ST* 19). She barters her ears for food just as Traudis bartered sex for Schreiber's paying of her rent. Nina is not prepared for *that* step yet, if ever. She understands her sex appeal but hates sex. Nina, like Twyla Digges, realizes her attraction is a tool. "Hours she had stood naked in front of mirrors staring at what had so often been solicited, never given, never really given.... Only twice had it [her body] been called into service, and then in pity, not necessity" (*ST* 20).

Chapter one ends with Nina's ruminations; chapter two contains Stitch's ruminations. This is a Stern set piece considering the nature of the artist as the person who links past to present in a perpetual continuum governed by the hovering muses who inspire the re-creation of divinely-inspired Awe through artistic endeavor. Here Stitch remembers Henry

James. One thinks this is Stern's homage to art and life. Not for long. A page and a half later in this chapter, Stitch recalls that, "In jail, Perry the rapist called him Perfesser. Because of [Stitch's] beard" (*ST* 23). The magnificent and mundane in tandem. This is followed by a pettiness harshly juxtaposed with the glory of the artist. Stitch knows that he is now, despite much earlier adulation, just an old withering, unproductive man. "…he worked no longer. Slept and shoveled in food, and excreted, painfully.… He'd always known that ninety percent of what was known about anybody was baloney. Enemies wrote and bystanders. He could see an account forming in the fathead at Nina's. Dazzled by celebrity, a groveler, a witness of events, a newspaper reader with protective covering of names and tags. A Jew of course, in essence at any rate. A secondhand dealer. Not knowledge but opinion" (*ST* 24). Both Stitch and Nina see Edward as pathetic and grasping, and while they are unkind in seeing this, they are also correct.

The reader now sees what hand Stitch will deal Edward when the time comes. One also sees the hand Stern is dealing. The reconstituted Jewishness of Stern, now no longer impoverished, if not nearly rich as yet, is presented clearly. *Stitch* is the true sequel to "Wanderers" and Edward is a younger Mendel, the Mendel before bitterness who learned that Jews are different in the eyes of much of the world and must defend themselves accordingly. That said, Edward doesn't really defend himself but suffers a humiliation that triggers a sequence of events that will change his life and perhaps better arm him in the future. Is Edward, Stern? Yes and no. This writer doubts that Stern was as vulnerable as Edward, but one can also see that Stern's 1961 ruminations on Jewishness, which precipitated "Wanderers," are not a small factor in *Stitch*. Stern has confirmed that "Wanderers" was written before *l'affaire* Pound and thus was not an effect of Pound but a prelude to him.

Pound stung Stern, but did not disable him; Edward is crushed by Stitch. Stern was able to put Pound into a context sharpened by his own recent self-awareness as a late-blooming Jew; Edward had no context to put anything into. Stern already knew esteemed artists and intellectuals who considered him a peer; Edward had no such bolsters to his self-esteem. Yet, Stern knew that he *could* have been Edward, and extrapolates what he might have felt if he were Edward. This is the typical Sternian modus operandi: *what would I do in his shoes?* No matter whose shoes he tries on.

After Stitch's defamation of Edward, which followed much loftier thoughts of art and artists, he resumes the artistic musing. Now, however, he regrets not having fulfilled his promise, that *l'isola di Stitch* — his Venetian Island of sculptured tapestry, described as a tour de force of images in chapter four — has not been completed, or ever will be, as he is too old to continue.

> He no longer had strength to cut stone, memory to spell out what he would like others to cut. And what he left, his sixty years work, was so oblique, so dark. When he'd wanted above all ascent into light, enlighten-ment, order, spelled out as the Egyptians spelled it out, as did the Indians did against Hindu bunk, as Dante and Homer and old Bach and Kung and Francois Arouet had spelled it out, the human order which mirrored the cos-mos, the divine ordering. Years and years, what were they now if he'd left only disorder, hints, scattered notes? Waste. And self-inflicted as much as anything. Despite years of warning against the corrupters, the bedeviled innocents, the poisoned beetles who loved nothing but their own stink and death of those who didn't help them make it [ST 25].

Stitch is a bitter, bitter man. The greatness that Nina and Edward would wish to have rub off on them is their myth, not his. His myth is one of failure, which itself is overstated. Pound did not fail, nor did his Stern-ian alter ego. Stitch just thinks he has and the curse of subjectivity can-not see the evidence of success that others are glad to see and remind him of; yet, he is unable to see and give this to himself. This is his tragedy.

The acerbic, erudite acidity of tone reminds one of early Huxley — *Crome Yellow*, 1920, through *Point Counter Point*, 1928, which, at the time, critic Malcolm Cowley said was mandatory reading in the U.S. and U. K. Then, Huxley was still writing about his own life among England's upper class. Stern and Huxley revel in a crusty sharpness with the cuts less dan-gerous than the infection-by-thought that follows the initial wounds.

The American expatriates celebrate Thanksgiving. Nina is invited to join Edward, Cressida, and the children. The three adults are not thrilled. Edward is depressed because the turkey cutting reminds him of the old routine of which Venice is supposed to be the antiroutine. Cressida resents Nina's presence and Edward's recent dips into a finite bank account that conjoin with his friendship with Nina. Nina knows she is in the middle but wants the free meal. There seems little to be thankful for. After Nina leaves, Cressida berates Edward for his sloth and profligacy: "You and your self-examinations and reflections and studies or whatever other camouflage you're emitting these days. Why don't you get off your fattening rump and do something before you drag the whole lot of us with you" (ST 33). He doesn't answer but leaves to go to Nina.

He has been challenged. His motives attacked. What can he do to jus-tify his existence in Venice as an intellectual-in-waiting? He will seek val-idation by 1) trying, but failing to bed Nina; 2) seeing the great Stitch again. But not yet.

Chapter four is the visit to the island and Stitch's sculpture. Stern's description is a charm of word-inspired three-dimensional impressionism. The representation also considers if there is more than meets the eye in Stitch's world. Many critics didn't think so, referring to "Stitch's fraudulent folly." Hence, Stitch is pleased when Nina recognizes a horse in the "decorative chaos" (*ST* 38). Despite his critics, Stitch had and has given much thought about "divine ordering." Is there a hidden order in his metaphorical chaos? Is this what the artist tries to achieve — the metaphorical measuring and ordering of nature?

> *Auden:* Both in life and art the human task is to create a necessary order out of an arbitrary chaos. A necessary order implies that the process of creation is not itself arbitrary; one is not free to create *any* order one chooses. The order realized must, in fact, have been already latent in the chaos, so that successful creation is a process of discovery. As long as this remains latent and unconscious, conscious life must appear arbitrary; one grows up in the degree to which this unconscious order becomes conscious and its potentialities developed, to the degree that one's life ceases to be arbitrary, to the degree that one becomes conscious of and true to one's fate. An artist is someone who is able express human development in a public medium.[34]

By Auden's definition, Stitch tried for order, but believes he failed to achieve it because he was too willing to be distracted from his work particularly during his rant and cant years as a radio shrill for fascism. He has no guilt over his views, but he is guilty over the energy his views diverted from his art. His island is incomplete and misunderstood. Guilt leads either to remorse or, in Stitch's case, anger and bitterness. This is the creature who will torment Edward-the-pretender, Edward the purveyor of knowledge without understanding, Edward the symbol for those whom Stitch blames for his own failures by having distracted him with fawning attention and false praise. Yet, is Edward also a mirror in which Stitch sees himself? Both have excuses for sloth instead of work, which is avoidance of responsibility through distraction. Stitch recalls "The rant that consumed him for six years. *Stitch on Power. Stitch on State control. Stitch on the Perversion of American Politics...*" (*ST* 44). He also refers to his hated enemy, the "paralytic," meaning Franklin Roosevelt. Yet, he can be kind to those he likes (if only as a form of emotional bribery for future considerations). He gives Nina a small sculpture of a bronze centaur. "Nina felt a long warmth swell inside her body. For this old magician, who'd so finely gifted her, she felt great love" (*ST* 50).

Meanwhile, Edward is not feeling great love and is so starved for approval that he often competes with his son. In a description of Edward and his son, Sam Curry is revisited. "Brose and Edward were equally competitive, and though they had drawn closer in their European isolation than they'd ever been — for the first time Edward regarded the eleven-year-old as a friend to whom he sometimes spilled his latest insights into world affairs and doubts about his own — there was active baiting of each other which frequently culminated in arguments, shouting, accusation, and blows. After Brose's tears on such occasions, Edward could face his idiocy objectively, and then love for his sturdy little son would soften his fierce heart and he would offer apologies Brose was sometimes too proud to accept" (*ST* 52). "Idiocy" is the appropriate term. If Edward is too acutely insecure to not fight with his son, what reaction can one expect when a celebrity icon attacks him?

Stitch's daughter, Catherine, arrives for the Christmas holidays. Edward sees Stitch and Catherine walking in the square but is afraid to approach them for fear of more rebuffs. Conversely, he is delighted when Nina later tells him that she, Edward, and Cressida have been invited to visit Stitch on Christmas Day, and thinks: "To be included on Christmas Day in a Stitch family affair was an investiture of cultural nobility" (*ST* 55). Nina has dinner with Edward's family before they go to Stitch. Cressida declines to go and Nina tries her best to assuage Cressida's "tightness … she did everything possible to ease Cressida of discomfort, pumped her about the problems of shopping, heating, clothing, caring for the kids, made her tasks seem Herculean, her triumphs miracles…. Cressida's tension however, was not a reaction to Nina, but to her realization that she felt literally numb toward Edward. It was astonishing. Even when she'd been furious with him, she could feel love underneath the fury. Now there was nothing left…. That this filthy, shiftless, self-satisfied bum should be in charge of her children was outrageous…. I've got to leave him … now she didn't care about his whoring around. All the better; he'd leave her alone" (*ST* 56–7). If "whoring," by her definition, means getting sex, she is wrong. If it means trying to get sex, then she is correct.

Nina and Edward go to see Stitch. Edward is a nervous wreck. This anxiety is somewhat allayed by a pleasant greeting from Catherine: "I would know you both from the nice things said about you." They enter. Stitch is his aloof self. "Edward felt immense besides him. Indeed, he felt that the little room was stretched by his bulk" (*ST* 58).

"…then to recover a renewal of nervousness he poured out talk of Chicago, its museums, its crime, sports mania and beauty, and was advocating some Stitch sculpture to replace Mestrovic's Indians when Catherine came up the stairs sideways with a tray. He leaped up, took the tray, shoved some books off the table putting it there, stepped on her feet as he bent for them, apologized, straightened, just missed the chandelier, dashed in to take the first cup poured and brought it to Stitch, who, expressionless, waved it with a wrist snap over to Nina. He passed all the cups, then handed round the plate of cookies, again coming first to Stitch, who again waved him to Nina.... All sat back, Edward in a butterfly chair where he sank like a stranded whale" (*ST* 59).

Edward has been obsequiously fawning, and worse, from Stitch's view, gauche, by not following the protocol of serving the women first. Catherine makes small talk explaining she'd lived in Europe all of her life and it was not until two years previous that she visited America. Her passport nonetheless is American, to which Edward adds: "'Best to be American and live in Europe. The other way round and the baby goes out with the bath water'" (*ST* 60). Catherine asks her mother what this expression means.

> "You must ask Mr. Gunther."
> "Ahh," said Edward, "I pass," and he waved toward Stitch, who sat hunched in his sports jacket, staring at his daughter and Nina across the room.
> Catherine laughed and said, "I will never learn now." Edward explained it, and then wondered that English was not her first language, she spoke it so well.
> "How good of you. My range is very small. Isn't it?" She asked her mother.
> Stitch said, "You have lacked the opportunities of Mr. Gunther."
> Edward did not measure the time between this and Catherine von Goedlingen's reply, which was, "It's clear Mr. Gunther has merited all he enjoys," but he knew something unpleasant had happened.
> Stitch stared straight ahead. In the canvas depths of the great chair, Edward managed to say, "I have been lucky."
> Stitch did not look at him, but said, "The luck is part of a system. Mr. Gunther's talk is more schematic than haphazard. He ensures his success by inventing fifty-eight percent of what he says. He quickly takes over where others give way. He invents what he needs to fill gaps."
> Stranded in his own bulk below the level of everyone else, Edward felt the heat of their attention. His eyes were pressed by rising blood, his face ached. Above him, he saw but half of Stitch's face, which, oddly, wore an amused look. He croaked out a response. "I am sorry you feel this way. I guess much of what I say in company is—well, frivolous. Though I can't recall anything I said that's sheer fiction." And then, to accommodate whatever Stitch was feeling, for he didn't want an explosion, he added, "Perhaps my training hasn't prepared me to distinguish fiction from fact."
> Stitch nodded two or three times, his beard splayed on the sweater under his jacket. "An effective answer. I particularly admire the way the voice falls away. It's good to know we're watching theater. We don't have to confuse it with anything real."
> Edward realizing that the Stitch ladies were not going to come to his rescue

this time said, trembling, "I'm sorry my answers appear theatrical. I don't intend it for effect," and he shook his head, faded off, crumpled. Is this madness? Anti-semitism? Fascism? Or was the old fellow explaining his life to his daughter who must have had some mighty bad times when he was in prison? No, there was more. Chicago Semite *Venitian?* That was too easy.

Stitch had sunk back into silence, a signal for Catherine and her mother to speak at once, loudly. Was Nina getting enough heat in her apartment? Wasn't Venice terrible now? Where did she buy coal?

For ten minutes they went on, then Nina said she had to go. "Good-by," she said coldly to Stitch ... and went downstairs followed by Catherine and Miss Fry.

Edward wondered if he should even say good-by, decided it was his duty as a guest and gentleman. This would be the last he would see of Stitch. Yes, the reports were right. He was a broken Fascist. He turned to him — the old man was still staring at the floor — and said. "Good-by. I'm sorry I annoyed you. You're partly right about me," and held out his hand.

Stitch raised his old lion's head, looked into Edward's eyes, then brought both his hands over Edward's and drew him down. Edward bent over nearly double. The hands held him.

"Wrong, wrong, wrong," said Stitch. "Eighty-seven percent wrong. I've never been able to recognize benevolence...."

Edward, hand held tight, felt his back cracking. He went down on one knee before the old man's worn-out face. "Oh," he said. "No. Not so. If you've been wrong, how about others?" The raddled head shook back and forth. "Yes," said Edward with sudden authority. "There are probably mistakes. But what you leave is there, clear and right."

"Notes," from the barely moving lips. "Scattered notes."

"No," said Edward. He patted Stitch's hand with his free one. "No. The Tate bronzes. The Rememberer's Shelf. They're there. All the way." The head denied, the hands held tight. For help? For companionship? "You wrote the bigger the bite, the harder to—"

"How about once on the wrong road, it's too far to return. I can't remember. You don't know what not remembering means." Headshaking, trembling, hands tight. "Only sure thing is nothing's sure. I know nothing. I used to think there was something to know. This ... doesn't exist. No Europe any more. The idea of Europe's gone. The last rememberer crawling out of the wreckage...."

Edward felt tears coming, fought them, tried to speak, felt his voice break, could but shake his own head. "If, if, if only," and stopped. He drew his hand from Stitch's. The old man looked straight into his eyes. Appeal? Message? Edward touched the checked shoulder for good-by and went downstairs in a trance [*ST* 60–62].

This is rather poignant, but one wonders who is now doing the acting? Edward catches up with Nina who is furious at Stitch, whom Edward defends, still bidding for the icon's approval. He even blames himself for provoking Stitch.

One can see how Stern's nonfiction account is extrapolated into the fictional rendering. In terms of how much *auto* goes into Stern's fictional biographies, this is an acute example of how 10 percent fact graduates into 90 percent fiction.

Edward's psyche will not accept that he has been disapproved of and rejected by Stitch and gives more import to Stitch's whining at the end than the insults that came before the whining. Nina compounds the incident by telling someone else about it. "'Old Stitch just gave the business to poor Edward here....' Edward burned red as a yelling baby. 'Nonsense. Why in hell can't you get anything right, Nina?'" (*ST* 64). Edward lies to himself in the retelling; "he found it oddly blurred" (*ST* 64). Edward will be in a blur for another 140 some odd pages. A bad Christmas Day doesn't get better; the local prostitute, a crazed Adele, badgers Edward on the way home and curses him out when he tries to give her a few coins to leave him alone. He arrives home and Cressida has no use for him even though he is dying to tell her of his day. He hoped for some warmth and doesn't get it; he doesn't deserve it.

New Year's Eve arrives and the locals give a party that Edward and Nina attend sans Cressida and sans Stitch. Stern follows with Nina's frantic behaviors without explanations that are symptoms without diagnosis. Interpretations are left for readers who are witnesses as they would be in real life. Nina gets drunk and insults hosts and guests alike with cruel and blunt jabs, calling one a *cher mafioso*, another a greaseball, another a cheapskate. Her not-too-subtle wit signifies that she's at her wit's end. Her boozed attacks are prelude to a panic that will be explicated 20 pages later. For now, Edward carries her off to an empty bedroom to prevent her from doing the violence her temper seems headed for. He asks, "What in the hell has triggered this?" (65).

Her answer is to pull him down to give him what he has been chasing for over a month. Then she collapses into sleep. Edward dismounts and returns to the party, making apologies for her. When the party breaks up, he wakes her and Nina's first thought is not any kind of affection but the fear of pregnancy. "I'm almost at my period. I suppose there's little chance." Mr. Sensitive, who cried over Stitch's theatrics, answers, "'We were lucky in a lot of ways. That's the wildest that's ever happened to me, Nina. You may be a vestal three hundred sixty-four days a year, but, my God, what a New Year's Eve performer.' Her hands went to her head, and she tapped it, then pointed a finger at Edward. You, it meant. 'You piece of junk'" (*ST* 72–75). She dashes off without him. In a week, he has been dumped by Stitch, his wife, and his not-quite mistress.

Stern gives Cressida's side as she thinks out loud. Cressida recalls her mother's reaction to her engagement: "Ay Je-ew? Cres-si-da Mag-ru-der. Ay Je-ew. Are yew absolutely out of you're my-und?" (*ST* 77). The young and thin Edward charmed the Magruders into submission, but Cressida "didn't learn about Adrienne till two weeks before they married.... She should have thought then about whatever defect had let him conceal such a thing from his fiancée" (*ST* 78). Adrienne was Edward's first wife to whom he gives alimony. Stern is not necessarily saying that Edward's status as a Jew among gentiles puts him on the defensive and excuses his subterfuge, but he's not saying it doesn't. He's just not saying. The reader fends for himself. Nina loses her dog and considers it a cosmic punishment for sex with Mr. Sensitive.

Chapter eight is a Stitch stream of consciousness with important clues about what will come later. He receives a letter from S. Walter Sloterman who has a Guggenheim grant and wishes Stitch to answer a few questions. This propels Stern, through Stitch, to consider some of Stern's persistent bêtes noires: the nature of celebrity, the rush of both the legitimate seekers of knowledge and the gossip mongers to ask questions of celebrities (Edward is one of the latter), the *Golk*-media that wants to kiss and tell what Stitch (and other celebrities) tells them. Stitch particularly hates, yet, indulges "the apology-seekers. Why not? He had enough to apologize to the end of time for, and if he was not apologizing for what they thought he was apologizing for — not having committed the sins they'd assigned him — let the apology fit their pinched shoe.... And let their tears rain forgiveness.... They ate up gloom. *Zeitgeist.* Open your insides for swine, then weep they're eating you.... Know thyself. How that perverted them" (*ST* 84–5). This fragment of diatribe intimates what will become a major theme of Stern's 1978 novel *Natural Shocks*, where Stern examines in detail the celebrity-media dichotomy.

Sloterman arrives. He is straightforward, asks four simple questions related only to Stitch's sculpture. Stitch answers simply and the interview is over. Sloterman, a gentleman, then surprises Stitch with a birthday cake "with TS in pink sugar" (*ST* 86). The cake is French, a Stitch favorite that Sloterman carried from Toulouse to Venice. This is grace and sincere charm from a man who only wanted facts not gossip and was showing his appreciation. Stitch invites him to come again and S. Walter Sloterman will do so, just as he will visit his cousin Edward who knows him as "Walli."

Walli visits Edward. Cressida suggests that Walli might find a job for Edward in the foundation Walli is an important figure in. This would suit Edward; it would give him a chance to do research and write, satisfying his intellectual cravings, and it would suit Cressida, as she would get rid of him without a divorce, as he would go back to the states. (Edward, of course, envies Walli's publications, as he is, no doubt in his view, smarter than Walli.) Walli asks if Edward has met any one notable and Edward names Stitch. Edward "turned red when Walli said he'd just been lucky enough to have a few minutes with him about business, but how he envied their [the Gunthers] opportunity to really know him…. Holy God, thought Edward. One never knows. The little bugger'll probably end up marrying the grand Duchess of Luxembourg" (*ST* 91). Not quite. Walli leaves, promising to intercede on Edward's behalf. One notes that Walli is modest, while Edward is not. The former is more secure the latter insecure.

In Chapter nine, the reader learns that Nina's New Year's Eve behavior was motivated by the panic of having run out of money to the point of near total indigence. Her drunken episode was, in part, based on the shame of knowing she would need to barter sex with Edward to get money to live. The alternative was returning to her family and hearing "I told you so"—which to her is much worse than this act of prostitution. She sees Stitch for lunch, the first meeting since his attack on Edward. "In his black cape and great-brimmed black fedora, he looked like a pensioned Dracula" (*ST* 95). The allusion to blood sucking is intentional. He asks Nina about Edward. "'What do you have to do with this lopsided Rhino?' She answers, 'Huh?'" (*ST* 97), pretending not to know he refers to Edward. "She felt an answer extracted against her wish. "'Do? He's a friend. I don't have a great many. He's a decent fellow.' Though she hadn't been thinking this lately. The answer was protection against that soft malice with which Stitch had amused himself on Christmas. If she'd been doubtful, the present characterization settled it" (*ST* 98). It's settled for readers as well, as Stitch confirms that his apology to Edward was narcissistic acting. Stitch wants to see Nina again and needs to know if he went too far in his behavior. Nina does not let Stitch off, which is to her credit; yet, she tempers her answer, as she may need the old fake's esteem as much as she may need Edward's money. She wonders if Stitch is jealous of Edward because the old roué wants her sexually as well. He does, but he wants her more in nostalgia for a muse than for a tangible sexual need that he likely cannot act on physically. He tells her he wants to sculpt her head as a way of appealing to her ego so she might continue seeing him, and give him someone to talk to. "If she showed up every day, while he made at least the motions of slapping clay on an armature, he would talk to her. She was worth more than the interviewers. Even the Slotermans" (*ST* 101).

She is worth more, and after Nina and "Eddy" make up (her move because she needs the money) the two have a Sternian set piece on the nature of art and artists, motivated by Edward's solo visit to Stitch's island the day before:

It came to Edward, walking beside Nina … that he did, spasmodically, love her, yes, though as escape, open door to hopes [artistic, intellectual] he hadn't earned. And something else came: the pressure to tell her what he'd seen on the island embodied his own fault, not mindlessness, but the lethal haste of passion, hunger, ambition. Admirable as Stitch's breadth was, a marvel and wonder of work and sympathy, maybe it was what the old man had said himself, "Scattered notes." Scattered by uncontrolled desire. Beautiful, artful, but flotsam.

The greatest men exhausted what they touched, but Stitch fingered, hinted, compared, abandoned. His island was beautiful wreckage. Really great men were mad for what they treated, could not get enough of it, pored over it, smothered the world with its qualities. Their only control was their need to offer it. One felt the power of their love; so personal, it penetrated even the alien. Yes. The greatest were not anonymous, communal. Their love churned their own stuff into constellations, creatures. And what counted after the greatest spurt of nature, conception — that packaged history of matter — was the interweaving of the creature with speech, gesture, song, knowledge, with what had been. You could look at life large or small. Artists had to look at it large, too large to be lovingly recorded except in detail. Which is where Stitch failed. Stitch's great gifts, his technical skill, sense of form and mimic power made his work stunning, a marvel, but he was not among the greatest, and anyone who followed him, lacking his marvelous energy, eye, strength, curiosity, and tenacity, would create monsters. Stitch's life, as well as his island, marked the generality of his passion. He was always leaving things out, abandoning them, as he had his children. Maybe that was why, in his daughter's presence, he had lashed out Christmas Day [*ST* 110].

Is this Edward's truth or his rationalization? Or perhaps it is his impetus for a discussion so that "Nina would take the imprint of his insight." (So that she should recognize his intellectual worthiness.) Edward wishes to save her from Stitch. He tells her of his thoughts. What follows becomes an argument for whether art is particular or universal.

"But no," said Nina. "No one respects what's been more than yours t., but Edward, *mon cher fils*, that reeks of graves…. There's too much stuff in the universe. One must hint, skim, move around, suggest. A highlight here, a detail there. One must pay tribute to the over-all, not wallow in the singular. I'm with Stitch. Suggest, renew, compare, diversify, and cheer what's in front of your face. Depth analysis is for birdbrains. One must select, refine, bore tunnels into great light. Like this garbage canal." They were on the Ponte del Dose, another scheme of garbage floating for inspection. "You overlook it and what do you see?" Ahead, the sun touched silver veins in the Grand Canal. "The main stream beyond the garbaged vertical, that's what. The cross on the 'T' which makes more than another 'I.'"

"Apply my analogy," said Edward … his eyes gripping her in debater's passion. Didn't she want to be saved? "You gonna throw children into this abstract hash machine too?"

"They're there now. Personality's washed out of the world. There's no room for it.... There's not enough elbowroom for the singular. I'm not saying it's good, but let's face it, that's the way of things. The human condition will obtain, but in other ways, other modes, according to the Great Scheme."

"But, Nina! ... You're bundling singularity away. You're stuffing particulars into ovens, baking them all under one crust."

"No. Wrong. The crust isn't common. Every cook makes it different. Despite similarity of ingredients, the things which count don't change. If the consumer's subtle enough, he can distinguish a cook in one bite.... The idea's to get the mass of what counts and a mite of clearly seen detail. Stitch is on to that. But he's a pioneer, and full of tics, so his work's imperfect. I don't mean mine'll be perfect, but I mean he's still got a foot in the School of Singularity. Look at his own heads and his girlfriends' cropping up out there on the island. They're unassimilated to the over-all as far as I can see. But his general procedure is marvelous, and he can set one off. Eddy, it isn't just the artificial world, the world of *tekne*. It's the whole world. Look at your own troubles. Look at mine. Where do they come from? Leaks in the general. Maldistribution of goods. Attempts to be what we aren't. Overprizing our singularity. Egoism. Imperceptivity in situations solved long ago. Failure to adapt. The bloodline runs from the world to art's expression of it. Like this filth-ridden canal into the great one out there...."

"You're making a fatal error," he told her. "You must be wrong. You're violating life. You're a Utopian, a Platonist. Artists must be more human, not less. And human is failing. They all fail. Look at old Stitch, stuck in that tiny place, freezing his miserable bones; one of seven or eight days in his life spent in the pokey. That's not failure of the general. That's a thrust of the particular too big to be held by the — by the general arteries. Artists don't mirror the times. They create new time out of the powerful digestion of what's around them" [*ST* 111–13].

This is a statement rather than a conclusion. One can't be sure if this is what Stern believes. One *can* be certain that Stern has thought about the role of art for this set piece and wishes for readers to do the same.

Edward punctuates their arousing dialogue with a passionate hug, which is coincidentally seen by Cressida who is out for a walk. When "Eddy" returns home, Cressida, enraged, throws him out. The moments-before heights of artistic musing bottom out with acrimonious harping between Edward and Cressida, Edward and Nina, Stitch and everyone, the world in general. The contrast of the magnificent and the mundane in both life and in individuals is a Stern fixation.

In a 2001 review of his friend Saul Bellow's biography by James Atlas, Stern notes that once, some years back, while having lunch with Bellow, he marveled that the quite normal man across from him wolfing down his food was also the genius novelist. In some way, the outer life of Bellow as the doer of utilitarian human functions and Bellow's artistic inner life were coexistent but not quite fathomable parallel dimensions. When Stern met his hero, Auden, for the first time in the mid–1960s, he noticed the same gap between the art that signified genius and the man who did not seem to be the genius who created the art.

Stitch is a great artist but not a great man — not even a good man. Where is the line that measures one from the other? How is it defined, and does this line move to conform to the shifting eye levels of different observers in different times? Stern is a man who happens to be an artist. Which image does he see in the mirror — man or artist? He sees the man. The artist image is a mystery even to him.

The mystery of artistic creation as well as a paean to women become the subject of chapter 14, when Nina writes her epic poem. This chapter follows one where Edward grapples with an essay. One sees Stern's skill in his evocation of Edward's writing as being facile but ultimately derivative. He is as Stitch described him: "A secondhand dealer. Not knowledge but opinion." Stitch also said Nina had music in her, and she feels it now:

> Her life had to play a role, certainly. What she had seen, noted, what had counted for her? But whatever went in would be placed in her map of the transient, the immutable, and the reborn. Aquinas' blueprint was no longer useful. Nor was Troy, nor any history. Her palette would include epic writers' strategies, mutation from Ovid, the voyage from Homer, the home-away-from-home cosmos of Hesiod, the meeting of gods and men from Gilgamesh to Joyce, none would dominate. As for actors, they'd be arranged in series, Aeneas, the pious, swindling founder, Augustus, the ironic commissioner, Vergil, the lyric scribe broken by state service, Dante, the noble pupil, Milton, Camoens, and the Beowulfer, the stuffy, ambitious imitators. And the prophets, scholars, heroes, loud and soft, Francis L. [Nina's father] next to Carolus Magnus, Stitch beside Arjuna. And the muckers, two-for-oners, parasites, finaglers, Civitas, Savaronolas, Foglemans and Fuggers....
>
> Nina began. Not with the little purgatorial boat which hadn't made it out of the harbor New Year's Eve, but with her sisters, human, divine and mixed, the givers of songs and children, the consolers, continuers, the makers of homes to which heroes returned, the vessels of civility, transmitters of cultures, the mothers of the gods.
>
> Nymphs swam in the trees, branched in green waters; old women and forsaken wives wove and knitted; girls like rosy balls of fruit tempted gods and men.
>
> Music ran through Nina. Time dissolved in it, words formed in it.... Nina wrote as if played by a giant.... So it went for four days. She lived on the inner music, did not leave the apartment ... ate but crackers, staling bread,

the rotting cheese, did not go downstairs once, slept but twelve hours in the four days.

On the fifth day the music stopped; the giant had finished [*ST* 150–52].

Nina brings her epic to Stitch and she reads to him: "Her work was a horse beneath her. She knew its pace, its power. Exhibition, not performance. There it was, what she knew, thought, felt. The convocation of the great, the incarnations, a live transmission, the large scene broken into the new music. Sappho, Christine de Pian, Louise de Lyons, the Countess of Die, Anne of Byzantium, Jane of England, Colette of France, Emily of Amherst, Sor Juana de Mexique, her sisters, singing with her. Conception, womb, the ripening of gentility, amenity, warmth, manners, custom, the domestication of cosmos" (*ST* 155). Nina is filled with the confidence of her power; she wants Stitch to confirm it with praise. He falls short, telling her, "your fine work is without love" (*ST* 157).

Later, "Nina tells Edward what Stitch told her," and she has the self-worth to say, "He was wrong" (*ST* 166). This is the difference between her and Edward. She believes in her ability; he's not sure of his.

Walli gets Edward a job in the U.S. Stitch matches Walli and Nina. Nina publishes her epic. Cressida won't take Edward back, and he has his previously stated revelation on the day that President Kennedy is murdered.

Stitch is a novel precipitated by a nonfiction incident with Ezra Pound. The incident, however, jump-started issues that Stern was evaluating during this period: he is a Jew and allowed himself to be aware of it, even combative about it in a sense; he is an artist who received great praise in the four years preceding *Stitch*, and now was a celebrity, which itself has lessons; he was in an unhappy marriage and the preceding factors bring more pressure to bear on the last. This rush of thought became passion, and the passion became *Stitch*. His art had traveled from a self-described cold to purposeful hot and would remain hot thereafter. *Stitch* is the transition. Even after publishing it, he did not let go of Pound. His next work would be inspired by the poetic density of Pound's *Cantos*. Stern would create prose poetry and write perhaps his finest achievement, the interrelated stories of *1968*.

CHAPTER FOUR

From Johnson to Nixon: Chicago Rapture to Chicago Riots — 1968–1973

1970: *1968, A Short Novel, an Urban Idyll, Five Stories and Two Trade Notes*

> *Yes, there was another side to the pretty world. The age boasted liberation, but millions were changed by need, could scarcely admit it, even to themselves....*
>
> *People start thinking about the way things really are, the only manufacturers who'll stay in business will be the rope — knife — and gun makers.*
>
> — Richard Stern

Richard Stern has loved Chicago since his arrival there in 1954, nearly the middle of that bland decade. He wrote "Chicago: Mostly a Love Letter" (in his collected essays) to affirm his affection. It was as close to New York City as he could want without having to live there. The blandness of the 1950s welcomed him. Things changed in the next decade. On the cultural front, the Beatles invaded America and The Pill arrived along with short skirts, a bra revolt, sex, drugs, and rock 'n' roll. The media accentuated every aspect of the flower rebellion. In the political arena, President Johnson and Congress implemented the Great Society and passed landmark civil rights legislation. The South was not pleased. Vietnam escalated and flower power butted heads with hardhat power. By 1968 Johnson was gone and Nixon led by having an "enemies list" and the paranoia to do something about it. In April, Martin Luther King was murdered; in June, Robert Kennedy too. Then August came with a riotous and ugly Democratic convention in Richard Stern's beloved Chicago.

The tumult of these cumulative public events was matched by Stern's private muddle over a marriage that no longer worked and a longing for intimacy. In 1969 he began to see 19-year-old Alane Rollings, a student. Stern was 41. His private sphere was as troubled as the public sphere of hippies vs. hardhats, blacks vs. whites, Nixon vs. his enemies, U.S. soldiers vs. the Viet Cong. These latter public displays of blood and circuses were viewed nightly in the new Roman Coliseum of television. In the privacy of living rooms, these displays engendered various emotions ranging from indifference to despair to passion, anger, and hate. These emotions—freely vented in private—were carried out into the world mostly suppressed behind gritted teeth, but not always. Some expressed a knowing and directed anger for or against a cause. Some released pent-up hate through symptomatic acts of violence, psychic or actual. Some did both. In *1968* Stern encapsulates slices of these bitter times with vignettes that describe the symptoms resulting from the inner and outer chaos. He does so without the slightest narrative didacticism, but the wounds depicted are as blunt as bludgeons and as cutting as knives.

Stern has never been an overuser of omniscient narration, preferring to be spare on commentary and long on actions and particularly dialogue that gives a picture from which the reader as witness can make an evaluation. In the stories of *1968*, Stern goes even further and his inspiration is Ezra Pound, more specifically Pound's *Cantos*.

After the meetings with Pound and the writing of *Stitch*, Stern did not have his fill of Pound—rather the opposite. He would write essays about Pound and teach the *Cantos* to his students along with Pound's writings on poetry, perhaps including this passage:

> Poetry must be as well written as prose. Its language must be a fine language, departing in no way from speech save by a heightened intensity (i.e. simplicity). There must be no book words, no periphrases, no inversions.... Objectivity and again objectivity, and expression: no hindside-beforeness, no straddled adjectives (as "addled mosses dank"), no Tennysonianness of speech; nothing—nothing that you couldn't, in some circumstances, in the stress of some emotion, actually say. Every literaryism, every book word, fritters away a scrap of the reader's patience, a scrap of his sense of your sincerity.[35]

This pronouncement evolved into the Imagist Group of poets guided by Pound's three principles:

1. Direct treatment of the "thing," whether subjective or objective.
2. To use absolutely no word that does not contribute to the presentation.

3. As regarding rhythm: to compose in the sequence of the musical phrase, not in the sequence of the metronome.[36]

Stern applied these principles to his prose, which, having headed in this direction in *Stitch*, adhered to this path with even more precision. *1968* is written in a succinct telegraphese with dense meaning and staccato rhythm (one thinks of Auden's first published poems of 1930) that is precise, exacting, and — to invert Pound's phrase — a prose as well written as poetry. Every word counts. One can hardly see how it could be edited down any further. As for the critical highlighting of lines, sentences, and paragraphs from the whole that is this critic's method, he found very little of Stern's whole that he had *not* underscored. Each story is a set piece of how Pound's poetic principles could be factored into prose. Consequently, of all of Stern's fiction, these stories are better served when interpreted with the close reading normally reserved for poetry instead of prose narration. Just as in poetry, a word or phrase may be a metaphor or symbol that connotes much more figuratively than its literal sense.

Prior to and during the writing of these stories, Stern wrote essays about Chicago, Vietnam, politics, and death by violence. One essay, "Revolutionaries and Comedians" is about Chicago-Seven-trial persona Abbie Hoffman.

> Abbie, though, is no classic revolutionary. Day by day, he sits with his more classical companions in the Dearborn Street courtroom. But he is of another tribe: Abbie is a comedian.
> Revolutionaries and comedians are cousins. Both live from dissociation and subversion. The revolutionary makes the bomb that looks like a watch, the comedian the bomb that is a watch. The revolutionary takes to the streets, the comedian to the theater. The revolution is open to all; you need tickets for the comedian. Abbie sits in the courtroom because he confused the genres. "Theater, he said, is anything you can get away with" [*FH* 63].

So is fiction. Stern witnessed and commented on the "street theater" that was the year 1968 and a key element is that tragedy and comedy were partners, the latter often a release to counter the former. This duo of "straightman and comedian" factors into *1968*.

The second factor is violence. In Stern's previous fiction the violence was in the minds of characters. For *In Any Case* the violence of war is contrasted as being the inevitable development of personal psychic violence. Prior to writing *1968*, Stern's personal acquaintance with violence concerned what he knew of World War II and the Korean conflict. Both, of course, while terrible, were not nightly television events. Moreover, in the

1960s television not only put body bags in the living room, but also showed homegrown violence of race riots and antiwar demonstrations, culminating in the shooting deaths of four unarmed students by national guardsmen at Kent State. Violence was no longer an abstraction; it was live television. For Stern, violence got even closer as he writes in his essay, "The Books in Fred Hampton's Apartment."

> A few days after the lethal predawn police raid on the Chicago apartment of the young Black Panthers, I went down with other perturbed, inquisitive history sniffers and shrine makers to see what was what.... [I] walked single file through the steamy gray rooms where nine people had passed most of the night a few days before.
>
> Violent death does not make for good housekeeping; nor do lawyers, pathologists, tourists, and guides, but it was clear that this apartment had never been an idyllic place to either live or die. The gray walls were undecorated except for slogans in red spray paint ("Dead Pigs Are Good," "All power to the People") and now, gaps made by pistol and shotgun fire. The stuff of life was piled in corners, on wall tables, in cartons of Cold Duck Sparkling Wine and Old Taylor: shirts, skirts, Panther newspapers, bottles, gauze curtains, uneaten hamburgers in wax paper, a can of Johnson's Pledge Wax, a portable phonograph, a copy of *Time* (Lieutenant Calley on the cover), folded hideaway beds, some clothes in a closet, a few pots, one with hardened spaghetti fragments, and in the back room a double bed with a Supersoft Restone Mattress which bore the horrible relief map of Hampton's blood. An ugly, characteristic nameless place ... except for one thing: a few books scattered here and there in the apartment, some open, as if reading had been interrupted and were to be resumed the next day.... To a bookish man the books changed almost everything ... [they] would mean *connection.*
>
> The books ... spoke of self-improvement, of purposive learning, of curiosity.... There were people here who wanted to know how the body and the body politic were put together. The emphases were on origins, development, form, and social interpretation. "What is there and how is it thought about?"
>
> A book man like me who feared, hated, and only partly understood the violence of hunters and of hunted felt it meant that the blood which lumped the mattress and stained the floorboards was in part the blood of the books as well as their readers. If it didn't make that fierce nest a shrine, it lifted its meanness and its anonymity [*FH* 70–72].

The crux of Stern's two essays on Hoffman and Hampton is juxtaposition: revolution with comedy, violence with purposive learning, pettiness with nobility of mind, the mundane with the magnificent, and the myriad of human emotions that arise from these inner and outer conflicts. The conflicts are catalysts for emotions that are often acted out symptomatically as subliminal responses rather than knowingly direct responses that relate the behaviors to their causes (i.e., a man harangued by his boss in the afternoon yells at his wife at night).

The catalyst for the story "Ins and Outs" is a dangerous compassion. A young black man uses a ruse of seeking money for charity to get into a randomly chosen apartment for the purpose of theft. Once inside, he does not just demand money from the Caucasian, Holleb, but viciously beats him into unconsciousness. When Holleb awakens, he sees that the "apartment, it turned out, had not been so much burgled as assaulted. The man had taken a hammer to [the] Steinway, the keys were cracked, the mahogany case pocked and splintered. Chairs had been knifed, their stuffing bled into the room. Glasses and cups had been smashed and trampled; there was a glass icefall in the dining room" (*68* 88). In this instance, theft as a "business" proposition motivated by a desperate need for money was superseded by the additional and gratuitous impulse to express rage. Before the assault, Holleb, a writer — that is, a "book man" of liberal inclinations like Stern — had "subdued his uneasiness" about letting the man in: "In these times, it was a white burgher's obligation to suppress suspicion of Negroes. Of — correcting himself — blacks" (*68* 87). The sentence is a lesson on multiple implications as contained in the words "burgher," "suppress," "suspicion," "Negroes," "correcting," "Blacks." Each is charged with an implication that can be amplified in analytical paragraphs of meaning — particularly if one has just lived through the year 1968 (just two years earlier upon publication) when the correlative darts of these words would most sharply arouse associative understanding. If one were to teach this story and ask students to derive lists of positive and negative emotions and feelings from this sentence, among the positive might be sympathy, kindness, judgment, open-mindedness, political awareness, guilt, and restitution; and among the negative, suspicion, guilt, anger, rage, fear and its exponential turn into terror.

There is no narrative explaining the emotions and feelings of predator and prey, and this reminds one of a character in Christopher Isherwood's *Down There on a Visit* (Mr. Lancaster), who explains a method that a writer might try "of looking down on all human experience with absolute objectivity." He says, "What I would do ... is to write a series of stories which do not describe an emotion, but create it. Think of it — a story in which the word 'fear' is never mentioned and the emotion of fear is never described, but which induces fear in the reader. Can you imagine how terrible that fear would be?"[37]

While Stern's intent is not to single out one emotion such as fear alone, he is striving for a nearly, if not quite, "absolute objectivity."

> It was then the fellow clouted him with his fist, and something more, brass knuckles, coins, something that flashed and caused Holleb to move enough so that he was caught not in the face but the neck. It was terrific, he couldn't breathe, couldn't call. "No," he must have tried, maybe "help," and the fellow punched him again low in the stomach. The fellow's face was near his, bunched in excitement and cruelty. It was then Holleb must have seen his teeth, heard the heavy breath, smelled and felt a hot, vinegary discharge from the leaping body. He was down, his wallet grabbed, he grabbed for the fellow's shoe, a blue suede, a hush puppy which arced out of his hand and then drove into his chest. It was all Holleb remembered of that [68 87–88].

Before this incident, May, Holleb's wife of many years, has left him. When they met she admired his brain, and he shaped her enough so that she was able to outgrow him. Until the 1960s it was rare for women to walk out on men and to do so was another sign of changing times. An era of alienation had begun. Before his wife left and his beating, Holleb the writer had written: "When do we know that something really counts? When do we know a true conclusion, how to differentiate it from a 'Fading into the sunset' conclusion? We force events to cohere for us by stuffing them into old containers, old story patterns" (68 86). That is, old routines. May became tired of the routine.

In this story the randomness of psychic violence long featured by Stern now corresponds to the randomness of physical violence. The difference in mental and physical violence is only in manner rather than degree. Both hurt.

"Ins and Outs" is the first story in a sequence and Stern opens it with an epigraph that signifies his direction for the volume: how to overcome alienation.

> *Why not the quite simple effort to touch the other,*
> *to feel the other, to explain the other to myself.*
> — F. Fanon

In addition to alienation, a theme of "Melius and Melanie" is types of betrayal — physical, emotional, romantic, intellectual, and artistic in both peace and war. A third theme is the nature of the underlying psychology behind artistic creation; a fourth is a bit of satire directed at Sartrean existentialism; the fifth is that sex and desire are the impetus driving the first four; the last theme is that all of the themes, while serious, are told with a wink and tongue in cheek that they shouldn't be taken too seriously. All of it is done in 20 pages of layered phrases and metaphor. It begins:

They were to meet at Wollman Memorial Rink in Central Park. A stupid idea, his, and in the unbalanced sentiment of reunion, agreed to by her [Melanie]. If they had even heard each other's voices over the phone, they wouldn't have gone through with it, but they had transmitted the proposals and confirmations through Tsevic; it had been Tsevic who'd spotted her in his painting, Tsevic who'd told him he must see her again, Tsevic who had put in the call to Tulsa. "You must transform your emotional *situation*." Tsevic, an intellectual straggler who compensated in ferocity for modishness, was undergoing Sartre; *situation* had nothing to do with its banal English uses; no, it stood for fixity which choice would shatter [68 92].

It stood for routine that demanded a shaking up. Orlando Milius needed shaking up. He learned from the *TLS* that his book of stories had been exposed as the work of his dead father-in-law whose Chinese translations had been updated by Milius into "mod" renditions. "Dear God, what the artist had to become in America" (*68* 96).

Milius wondered if the one perfidy conditioned the other. "Was he confusing Melanie and the *TLS*? Milius's wife, Vera, the former Serbian freedom fighter (as he was and where they met), "would spot the common treason" (*68* 94).

Meeting Melanie after 24 years, Milius thinks that "Thousands of hours had not dispersed, but only screened his feelings.... Orlando Milius, hero's name on a coward's heart, oddity cloaked in oddity, he had not looked into his feelings for thirty years. A painter, his feelings were absorbed by the techniques of appearance [as were Stitch's feelings absorbed in the technique of his sculptures]. No wonder his paintings were strange. Yet one didn't choose the strange, one fell into it. Like birth" (*68* 102).

Once again, Stern considers the perpetual conundrum of appearance and illusion. Does he also do so by the use of the name Orlando from Virginia Woolf's equally illusory gender-bending novel?

Cousin "Vuk the Bard, Tito's greatest export" arrives to give a poetry recital in Madison Square Garden. He tells Lando, "Weemens is keelink me ... but waddya hell, is communist mission is focking capitalists." Vuk, who is larger than life, a "seismograph as well as earthquake, spotted unease in Milius" who tells him of Melanie (*68* 104). Vuk approves. The two have a "reunion" with Tsevic.

Reunion?
Tsevic was putting it on the existential line. Hot coffee and cold turkey. In detail. (Serious advice could not be capsular, look at *Being and Nothingness*, look at *Saint-Genet*.) He had hardly warmed up, did not relish the entrance of Milius, let alone Vuk. That [Vuk] a Tito stooge, a ninth-rate versifier, a publicity-gorger and narcissist should preempt his platform was a bit much [68 69].

Tsevic the philosopher does not want Vuk usurping his role as principal advisor and matchmaker for Milius. The reunion doesn't happen because Vuk is mugged, "skull crushed, sure of recovery, but in a bad way. Reporters were chronicling his New York day. The feature seemed to be one Orlando C. Milius…. For most of the day Milius smoked in the blaze of contemporary publicity. Pen, mike, and camera elicited every available piece of his body, every cent of his income, every stage of his life. By noon he had watched himself on television and read about himself in early editions with the happy puzzlement of a child seeing a drop of water under a microscope. 'So this is Milius, this mass of warts, this lump of crystals, this strange being who has been given my name.' He was described as 'handsome and distinguished,' 'faded and undistinguished,' 'a youthful sixty,' 'an elderly man,' 'a famous painter,' 'an unknown poet, 'a war hero and scholar,' 'an unemployed language teacher.' He could not wait to cart his new lives over to Melanie" (68 109–09). This is another Sternian jab at a voraciously sensationalist media.

Milius and Melanie escape to Antonioni's existential noir film, *Blow-up*, and during it, while "watching the two chippies wrestle each other naked on the purple backdrop paper, Milius had an erection. And simultaneously, a tremendous idea. He would paint screenlessly. He would lay clear, intricate blocks of space events directly on canvas. No subtle schemes of indirection, only direct interrogations of matter, unambiguous shafts through surface forms…. What joy" (68 109).

Later Milius thinks how "Artists … were hypersensitive to their cycles, emotional and social, intellectual and sexual…. He himself … had an elephantine cycle: his works took years to come to anything" (68 111).

In this sequence, Stern includes a number of ideas and allusions. *Blow-up* alone, for those who know the film, raises numerous issues on existentialism, art, and media that correlate with this story. The "tremendous idea" aroused by sex has no end of ramifications for the dichotomy of sex and creativity. "Milius and Melanie" provides much literary food for thought in its Everyman's brown-bag packaging.

"East, West … Midwest" is another tale of dangerous compassion with appropriate epigraphs that warn the reader of what is to come:

> *Alas, we Mongols are brought up from childhood to*
> *Shoot arrows…. Such a habit is not easy to lay aside*
> —Chingis-Kahn , March 1223

> *A small thing, lightly killed*
> —Agamemnon, line 1326

The choice of ancient epigraphs hints that the reader should expect that little has changed over the centuries.

Mr. Bidwell is a historian-translator who writes "on the Pendulum of Revenge which had swung between East and West since the thirteenth century" (*68* 113). His specialty is the Mongol Chinghis-Kahn. He hears from Freddy Cameron—"He identified the dead voice between 'Mis' and 'ter'" (*68* 114)—who, four years earlier, was hired to type his manuscripts, during which she had a nervous breakdown that caused her to imagine seeing Bidwell as Chinghis outside her window. In the present, it is nearly Christmas, and Bidwell succumbs to the same dangerous compassion he felt for Freddy four years before. He agrees to befriend her now as he did then even though the prospect causes him to have a "boiled forehead" that he relieves by scooping snow from his window ledge (*68* 115).

This anxiety is a catalyst for Bidwell to compare the heights of technology as represented by the Apollo astronauts who "were looping the moon in Apollo Eight" and the depths of technology that has become a "pendulum of ecological revenge" with harmful and disgusting pollution. Bidwell's fear of the latter (while not actually doing much about it), is one of the "classic hang-ups of the twentieth-century burgher." The burgher/bourgeois image is reprised from "Ins and Outs" with Stern blaming the indifference of the middle class—himself included—for society's ills.

Seeking advice about Freddy, Bidwell's neighbor, a psychoanalyst, tells him, "She's having an episode. Happens frequently on Christmas. On Sundays. The routine's broken, there's nothing to intrude on the fantasy" (*68* 120). He means the fantasy that everything is normal. Holidays remind fragile psyches that there *are* irregularities and that "normal" is relative. Freddy calls Bidwell at the office. Bidwell's boss thinks it's "nookie" on the side, to which Bidwell replies, "If you had nookie like that, you'd turn monk" (*68* 125).

During this time, Bidwell's scholarly works seem to reflect on current events. "This last week, Bidwell had been writing up Ye-lu Ch'u-ts'ai's revelation to Chinghis that it would be better to regard towns as resources than as pools of infection, a great moment of generous truth in the Mongol world" (*68* 125). And no less a "generous truth" in the modern world where the metropolis itself is the burgher's principal hang-up.

When Bidwell does not get his usual Thursday phone call from Freddy Cameron, he tries to convince himself that something bad has *not* happened. He learns that at the same time of the unmade phone call, Freddy chose to go out the window of the tenth floor of the Playboy office building (a protest of an unknown nature). "The famous owner of the building couldn't be reached for comment" (*68* 127).

Bidwell thought, "What a death the poor narrow thing had constructed for herself. No campaign, no successor, no trip to the cool mountains, only an elevator ride, a smashed window, an untelephoned farewell: 'This is it. I can't ask you anymore. Let alone by phone'" (*68* 128).

Perhaps a clue to Cameron is how she signs an earlier letter written to Bidwell as "(Miss) Frederick Cameron" (*68* 123). There is no explanation of any implications of her name by Stern other than that implied by her behavior. Is she — was she — a young woman with a serious identity crisis? What does her choice of the Playboy building for the suicide imply? Stern's not saying. Portentous *implication* is the *means* to Stern's *ends*. Stern's stories in *1968* toss fast-paced images on the table as if they are tarot cards subject to psychic interpretation. Words are the tips of icebergs and the associations engendered by the words form the hidden bulk that can sink ships: "Playboy," "pendulum," "(Miss) Frederick," "Christmas." The words are data to be ruminated on by the reader. They are observed data from which inferences are to be drawn.

Bidwell sees facts in the same way, as dots that demand to be connected into "A Great Story…. This ambition went against the grain of his graduate training, but there it was, a desire to shape data into coherent stories which would serve men who counted as models and guides. All right, such stories were formed by fashion and lived by style, but they were what deepened life. Didn't Chinghis, didn't all heroes, live and die by them" (*68* 117). Stern's answer is yes. And no more so than in "The Idylls of Dugan and Strunk."

The "Idylls of Dugan and Strunk" is an angst-driven, multifaceted, blood-soaked-down-to-the-roots-capillaries-and-neurons story of modern urban life. Indeed, Stern prefaces the tale by styling it an "Urban Idyll," and within it reminds the reader, "This is an idyll," which, by definition, is "*a short poem or prose piece depicting simple scenes of pastoral, domestic, or country life.*" "Dugan and Strunk" is certainly *domestic* but Stern adds "Urban" to get the story out of the wooded past. In 40 pages the symbolic symptoms of most of the ills in the modern world are "metaphorized" in scenes that may be *short* but certainly aren't *simple*. Here, even more so than in the preceding stories, the implications construed from the raw *data* of symbolic associative words are profound. These 40 pages contain 13 scenes of three or so pages of which each could, by factoring upward the gourmet and gourmand food-for-thought quotient, develop into its own novel. Or, to fulfill the analogy, a critic's analysis would require a novel's worth of words to explain the word-by-word significance.

Auden said, "I cannot now look at anything without looking for its symbolic relation to something else."[38] This is how one should read all of

1968, particularly "Dugan and Strunk," which is the main referent of the volume around which the other stories are grounded. In "Dugan and Strunk" all of Stern's themes are present, aided and abetted by the author's flush of passion aroused by the immediately preceding events of the 1960s. To this he also adds the more insidious sense of alienation and dislocation that became America after World War II. The story is a metaphor for America's failures; a Great Society caught on the jagged edges of biases built up over many years that caused it to unravel. Stern depicts greed for greed's sake, forecasting the 1980s of the Gordon Gekko character ("Greed is good") in Oliver Stone's film *Wall Street*.

There is a pervasive shroud of moral prostitution hanging over all levels of society, and this is particularly symbolized by a woman who is an unofficial "escort" for a Gekkolike shady financier and who is available to please his clients. She is a precursor of today's more "official" escort services. She is what she is and is relatively honest compared to those engaged in other forms of moral prostitution, both males and females, who compromise their ethical lives in order to survive in the modern world. There are no answers but many hard questions; nonetheless, there are the barest hints of hope within the chaos, cries for decency that say "No more," as a character does over a particular situation that is really a universal appeal. His cry is for an entire generation that has been betrayed to corporate America after World War II.

Decency, however, is at a crossroad in the two stories that follow "Dugan and Strunk." In the first, the sense of decency is ambiguous; in the second there isn't any decency. The section title for the two stories is "Two Slight Stories of Abuse." The story titles are "Gaps," and "Gifts." Each is about a man who has needs and to what degree he will go to get satisfied. Stern names the man of the first story *William*, and the man of the second story *Williams* as if to signify that the activity of the former is not isolated but that there are many "Williams" operating in society. William in "Gaps" seduces a 16-year-old girl, but just a few days later loathes the thought of the same thing happening to his own daughter. Williams in "Gifts" is not only selfishly cruel but he is a psychotic exhibitionist who shows off the extent of his immorality for his 18-year-old son's "benefit." After the father reveals a heinous act the son "who years ago ... had overcome uneasiness at his father's confidences" decides he has now heard one too many: "The Mexican confidence, however, did him in; giving ear wasn't giving absolution" (*68* 188–89). "Gifts" and "Gaps" and all of the stories in *1968* are about the burgher's moral ambiguity at best, indifference somewhere in between, and finally, conscious cruelty. In the subject of "Gaps"—which is the conflict over the difference in perception between how a father regards his own daughter and how he sees other men's daughters—becomes the subject of Stern's next novel.

1973: *The Books in Fred Hampton's Apartment*

In 1973 Stern published his first "orderly miscellany" of essays and ephemera, *The Books in Fred Hampton's Apartment.* Fifty-three pieces ranging from sociopolitical commentary, literary criticism and book reviews, to reflections on people met, and how the writer writes. The essays are an intellectual Everyman's "grouse against life" as Eliot termed it. The Last Angry Man speaks with a humorous bite. He even explains the title in a preface:

> The original title of the miscellany was *One Person and Another.* [Stern would eventually use this title for his third miscellany in 1989.] The present title—that of a piece on page 70, was suggested by Hal Scharlatt, the editor.
>
> The title of my last book (*1968*) had been suggested by its editor, Aaron Asher. I'd been hooked by it. Bloodily. Reviewing snipers claimed that the story writer was hiding behind the newspapers. (Pinned, he cried, "Never. No." Unheard.) so I rejected Scharlatt's suggestion. I didn't want to hang my book on poor Hampton's story.
>
> But the title grew on me. I tested it on a few reliable people. They felt as I did, uncertain, but they liked its specificity and slight unexpectedness. It does reach a number of the book's organizing notions: the ways men, events, and books get formed and reported; the connections between active men and the often surprising things they know; and books themselves, energizing or lethal, beautiful or false. Then too there's much in the book about Chicago; and Hampton's story is important in this city. City power took its ugliest turn with him: from pain and wild rhetoric to bad death and mendacious concealment. (One of the hero-villains of the story, a smart, vain, dutiful, careless, assiduous, mean state's attorney, a pure Chicago strutter, clown, and bumpkin, has just won a primary decision election and thus once again dimmed city lights.) So Fred Hampton and his books do stand for much that follows.

Stern here not too subtly speaks his mind; he will again in his next novel.

1973: *Other Men's Daughters*

The title implies the psychodynamics that are featured in this novel, the contradictory nature of one's internal subjectivity. Or, to put it more colloquially, what is good for this goose may not be good for another goose, and if *I* was the other goose, I might feel very differently. More specifically, the individual psyche defines its own rules to serve the ego's subjective interpretation of situations; and, to complicate matters, the psyche will change the rules day by day, even minute by minute, to keep up with changes in a situation. As seen in Stern's early short stories, he depicts the self's psychological misperceptions and the misinterpretations that the individual construes from those misperceptions. The mental process of perception and the subjective thought derived from perception are not linear. Rather, the process is a slide show of continuous thought with pictures that are not necessarily related and only loosely controlled at best. From these pictures more associative thought is created. Just as Auden said, "I cannot now look at anything without looking for its symbolic relation to something else," nor can anyone *think* of anything without thinking of something else.

Before World War II, there were experiments in "stream of consciousness" writing intended to replicate the normal zigzag thought process, one which is antithetical to the more standard linear thought of most prewar novels, and of many novels still. (This is not to say that here Stern has written a stream-of-consciousness book per se, but more of a stream-of-life book.) After World War II, the Age of Anxiety required that literary novels keep up with the times, and the psychodynamics of internally combusted subjectivity became more prevalent. The spark-driven nature of thought thrives on external stimulus that is then transformed by internal stimulus. This has always been a feature of Stern's dialogues. Yet, what his characters say is just as often concealing as revealing. Spoken words are a reaction to unspoken thoughts and often say something different than the meaning of the thoughts that provoked the words. The evocation of these symptomatic words is Stern's strong point and in *Other Men's Daughters*, he is at his strongest.

In *Golk* and *Europe* Stern admits to a bit of a chill; *In Any Case* seeks warmth while the characters speak in the linear prose of explanatory exposition; *Stitch* is hot, spoken with a flushed passion that dominates. *Other Men's Daughters* has the *truest* dialogue; words that any intellectual Everyman could say.

The novel is about a fortyish professor who sees his marriage end when he begins a relationship with a 19-year-old student. This happened to Stern and speculation on how much is transferred cannot be avoided. Are there verbatim transcriptions of dialogue from memory or from Stern's journals? Maybe, but one does not believe they dominate. What is transferred wholesale are the emotions felt at the time and from them are dialogues that capture the original implications and tones. There is not, however, the same use of implications as is employed in *1968*. This is not the compact prose poetry of Poundian Imagism. Here, there is a well-rounded, reality-based subjectivism. The prose flows to the beat of daily speech that is the most accessible, recognizable, human, and humorous in Stern's work thus far. These are words as intellectual foreplay and the reader finds mutual identification in the details.

In the summer of 1969 Robert Merriwether is a medical doctor and physiologist who prefers to be a professor of physiology at Harvard. He is married to Sarah and has four children. He is a product of the pre–1960s who copes in the New World of sexual liberation where he dispenses The Pill to female students who have discovered their sexuality and like it. In the summer they are barely dressed and he barely contains his unspoken appreciation. His eyes do not lie. Sarah has also become liberated but not sexually; and sex, she refuses to give. Her freedom is intellectual; the newly earned right to speak her mind and dispute her husband. The denial of sex may be punishment for having given up her own chance at a career during the 1950s when it was the norm for women to do so for the sake of the husband's career. Robert is denied sex at a time when it is otherwise amply available and temptation appears in his classes every day.

Robert is aware of his rut of routine as he sits in the habituated parlor of his habituated life. In *Cymbeline* he reads that "The breach of custom is the breach of all." He wonders if this is true.

> This parlor, thicker with custom than life, holds like a microscope specimen his own breaching.... Even as he thinks, "I'm peaceful, happy, this is a beautiful moment," he is aware that in four or five hours he will walk out of earshot, down the backstairs and telephone the source of his breach, Cynthia Ryder, a young girl for whom he is almost ready to give up the thousand formulas which compose this beautiful hour [O 5–6].

The breach begins with Sarah who antagonizes Robert continually. She is the Sternian female who has allowed herself to be shaped by a man and then resents the shape she's in and rebels against it. She has looked for clues to his infidelity long before there was any basis for it.

They argue over their son Albie. Sarah says,

> "It does no good to get after Albie."
> "Get after?"
> "He sees your face harden when he sleeps late."
> "How can he see it if he's sleeping."
> "Do you want a debate or truth?"

"It's you who have the truth, Sarah. But it is true that Albie is happier horizontal than any other way."

"You may stay vertical but he sees through that."

"I stay vertical because you won't have me any other way."

The black eyes burned in her pale face. Angry she is less puffy, almost the white cameo he'd thought so beautiful. "I am no legal whore" [*O* 9].

War!

Robert takes to reading books not read since before he was married, a symbolic escape from his present back to a past more sanguine. He observes the newly liberated world of the 1960s. He saw the "foam of the street, the — what could he call them? — kids, the young, girls, boys, the hippies, freaks, heads, the beauties and transfigured uglies from all over the world in every state of dress and undress.... What is the terrific need to look special. Is it so hard to be anyone now? Why so much noise? Why were the demands on others so huge? Was it that there was so much expression in the world that one had to go further and further out to even think of oneself as a person?" (*O* 13–14) The answers are "yes" and still yes today, even more so.

Merriwether likes words, plays with them, even in teaching physiology: "he'd long ago sensed an important relationship between the practice of medicine and that of the poets and sages.... Many poets had been physicians or the children of physicians" (*O* 15). Merriwether is a physician; Stern's hero Auden was the son of a physician, and Stern is the son of a dentist.

He first meets Cynthia when, on his day as volunteer physician at the student clinic, she comes to him to get The Pill. Her visit is concurrent with Sarah and the children being at her parents' home for the summer. So the attraction begins. "He saw Miss Ryder twice before he realized it was because she wanted him to" (*O* 19). The third "coincidence" is acted on when she sees Robert walking and asks if she may join him. "'Glad to have company, Miss Ryder. I'm all alone this summer.' The small excess hung between them for a bit.... Acorn Street was eleven houses each of whose windows were part of Dr. Merriwether's inner landscape.... The houses were his scene, what was permanent for him. Walking there with a twenty-year-old beauty, the familiarity became accusation" (*O* 20–21). All words and thoughts spoken or narrated have implications that become a dialogue within a dialogue of psychological cause and effect. After some innocuous banter, she tells him how nice he is and punctuates this with a kiss on the mouth. This is a new woman who will take what she wants. Robert is pleased but uncertain that it is what it is — an invitation. He is not at all practiced in seduction as the *new man*. He is, relatively speaking, dinosaur man. But he will learn. She asks to be invited into his home;

he gives in, still wary, however. He tells her he is too old for her with some self-lying nonsense:

> "I don't think love system functions usefully after thirty. Real love comes at your age. I mean the early, parent-child structure of love is matched in the late teens or early twenties by the great transference. By the time you're my age, it's but a combination of lust and nostalgia. There's no real room for new roots."
> [She counters,] "Bertrand Russell says he only found true passion when he was ninety."
> "Was he honest?"
> "If you can lie like that at ninety, it might mean it was true at seventy" [O 29].

This kind of courting repartee will develop and deepen into a love-inspired duel of wit. She goes to get a record she wants him to hear; he runs out for wine.

> The minutes of separation deepened his sense of the uniqueness of what was happening. This primary human illusion. As if human beings were empty-headed as goldfish swimming round the commonplace, astonished at perpetual novelty. Columbuses of the Bathtub. In a way, it really was that way. The neural complex was so staggering, a statistical case could be made for the absolute uniqueness of every human feeling and event. It was not true — the Harvard poet Eliot said — that humans were most alike in their moments of passion. Everything was *more or less* like something else; but just considering the fantastic number of synapses involved, passionate moments corresponded to the greatest acts of intellection. Words might be displaced by grunts, but this did not mean the simplification of sensitivity. How much of his own system right now was alerted to Cynthia's absence. Her absence was a tremendous presence in him [O 30].

On this first time alone with Cynthia, Robert resists; the second time, she insists, and his barricade tumbles like the house of cards it is.

The psychodynamic dichotomy of presence and absence, for good or ill, hereafter shadows every page. With it comes the adrenaline rush of new love, to which is added the additional surge of the love being clandestine. There is a lot of intellectual (and physical) energy expended. Robert describes himself as the "Burgher Outlaw, gripped by passion for a girl a year older than his son" (O 41). Stern still has use for the word Burgher after 1968 to signify Robert's immersion in a pre–1960s middle-class consciousness. This word-allusion to 1968 also refers to the time frame when that work was written. It is not a coincidence that Stern's most daring and nearly experimental work coincided with his first meeting with Alane Rollings.

In "Milius and Melanie," Stern correlated sex with creativity. Same here, after Robert meets with a friend who suggests that Merriwether take up his pen again to write something important Robert considers doing so since he knew "there was lots of undigested stuff in his head, [and] he might be able to make sense of it in a book" (*O* 75). This "stuff" is not restricted to professional work alone. The passage that immediately precedes his book idea is a bout of wordplay between Robert and Cynthia signifying that the "intellection" traversing the synapses is, indeed, motivated by sexual energy.

Robert reads to Cynthia his father's account of his son's birthday, which ends thus: "Character is the tenacity with which a man fulfills what is expected of him. Endurance does not suffice; strength does not suffice; ability does not suffice. Two things count: intelligence, which knows what is expected, and will, which moves to fulfill expectation." To this Robert adds,

> "Family and duty," said Merriwether. "Do you wonder I'm such a cautious cookie?" (In three months since Cynthia had moved to Cambridge, he had never gone shopping or seen a local movie with her.)
> "That's your Merriwether *fourmisme*."
> "Concern for good form?"
> "No. Ant-ism. *La fourmi*, hoarding and hoarding against perpetual winters. I was hoping I'd convert you to *cigalisme*, Grass-hopperism. Motto: it's winter now. Live it up, and not behind shades. Accept yourself."
> "When you've lived through as many New England winters as I have, you'll change the tune" [*O* 74].

Cynthia is not afraid to push. Prior to this passage, the aforementioned Tim Hellman, who is Sarah's cousin by marriage, sees Robert with her. Hellman will not squeal but he does give Robert advice on the Sternian theme of being wary of the woman who is shaped by a man whom she then outgrows.

> "Will you let me say something, though? About young girls?"
> "A warning?"
> "In a way. I know the danger of classifying human beings, but I've known a lot of these girls. That's been my companionship. Sex and tenderness. Nothing more, not even friendship. So I have to meet many women. The last few years I've felt a terrific drive in them. They want, they want, and it's we not-quite-graybeards who give them the most the quickest. We teach them, we spend on them, we show them off, we tell them what everything means. We're their graduate school. Which means they're closer to graduation through us. And that means there can be lots of tears when Graduation day rolls around" [*O* 71].

Consequently, Robert's adrenaline is fueled with sex *and* fear, a formidable duo of intellectual and creative stimuli.

In, over, above, and around the story of Robert's romance is the concurrent depiction of university life that is Stern's fullest in all his work before or after. There are portraits of colleagues that are aptly precise:

> For years, Thomas Fischer's apartment on Ellery Street was little more than a storage bin for his few possessions. His real home was his overnight bag. *Chelonia cambridgiensis*, he called himself, the Cambridge turtle. Childless, abandoned by his second wife after a year of marriage, he made a virtue of solitude. "There's a certain wastage in solitude, but as Einstein said, if it's frightening at the beginning it becomes delicious. Of course, Einstein didn't live alone."
>
> Fischer's life was his work, the first half in biochemistry, the second in scientific policy. In his twenties, he'd synthesized a pituitary hormone, and received a Nobel for it. When he was forty, he joined the National Science Foundation. The politics of science replaced the chemistry of macro-molecular synthesis at his center. In 1965, he formed an independent, international group of scientists whose aim was to designate crucial research areas. "It's like Well's Open Conspiracy. The hope is to set policies which these ballot-Punchinellos will execute. Who are they to speak for the national, let alone world deeds? Tinkerers, liars, showmen, posturing crooks." But Fischer knew how to manipulate the tinkerers. "You do their work, then congratulate them for it."
>
> In 1966, he resigned his Harvard professorship and lived on a small subsidy from the Rockefeller Foundation. His chief expense was air travel; he wore the same clothes year to year, ate little, drank inexpensive wine, and stayed in small rooms which bore the marks of permanent transience: the opened suitcase, empty refrigerator, a pile of 24-hour-service laundry. His Cambridge and Washington rooms were somewhat homier. He owned the books, the television sets, the beds; domestic leavings of his wives were in closets and cupboards.
>
> Fischer was solid, red-faced, blue-eyed, handsome. Dr. Merriweather — who had been his only real friend for years — had seen him tender, grim, furious. He had a feared wit, he had grown conscious of other people's fear of — or delight in — it, his earlier directness was now frequently a performance of what had been "natural." As he became surer of his own powers and other people's lesser ones, he indulged himself more and them less. He interrupted his friends when thoughts or jokes occurred to him; in front of them he seldom bothered to control his contempt or fury. Capable of extraordinary courtesy, responsive to fine work in ten or twelve areas of science, he could also be one of the finest listeners and critics. Still, even here he had blind spots. He was excessively strict about scientific genres. He disapproved of Merriwether's recent dipsologic models for certain cancers. "It's fanciful, trivial. You're wasting yourself, Robert. Leave cancer to virologists and geneticists. You've got plenty of important work in your own bailiwick."

His own research has applied crystallography to hormone synthesis in what was then a totally new way, but Fischer was not one to see himself as a model. In rare moments of self-examination, he swung from modesty to manic conceit. Continuous work pushed aside self-doubt, increased self-absorption, narrowed his tolerance for innovation. Since most new work was unimportant, Fischer's self-righteousness increased; but the increase was more in density and narrow fierceness than in strength. His few friends moved away from his tyranny; regretfully, for they acknowledged his bravery, intelligence and basic dignity. They had the option of telling him to stop his egoistic poaching or stop seeing him [O 78].

The description of Fischer continues, and completes a thorough understanding of the man's personality and predilections. The reader's insight into Fischer is important as it will be to Fischer that Robert confides, and this is exactly because Fischer doesn't talk to anyone else. The mutually convincing and psychologically intricate give-and-take between them works off the detailed character portrait of Fischer. What Robert says and how Fischer responds is shaded by what the reader has learned of Fischer's persona. These dialogues with someone of Robert's age also point out the differences between Robert's generation and Cynthia's.

Robert takes Cynthia (secretly) to Nice for a conference. There, another academic, a bitter eccentric, precipitates an ugly incident spurred by professional jealousy. He becomes news and Robert is interviewed for *Newsweek*. The subsequent report is brief but mentions "the Harvard physiologist, Robert Merriwether [and] his pretty, young assistant, Cynthia Ryder." The first public repercussion comes when her father reads this. This sets up in chapter eight a set piece of generational conflict, father-daughter conflict, regional North-South conflict (Ryder is from North Carolina), father-supposed lecher conflict, within which Stern enunciates the uneasy transition of his era into the 1960s era.

Previously, it has been established that Mr. Ryder has given his daughters everything except demonstrative emotional approval, which fostered a competition between them. There is a sideways implication that Robert is to Cynthia a father figure who does give approval. Mr. Ryder is a North Carolina lawyer, a sports enthusiast and hunter ("Cynthia said there were guns all over the house" [O 111]). This provokes fear in Robert who is not a competitive person and dreads confrontation with Ryder who is accustomed by his avocation to arguing.

Another Ryder daughter, Lisa, tells her father that he is out of his depth in this situation and that "The Pill's changed everything daddy. You have got to get used to it" (O 112). Lisa considers her father a righteous bully. "And the worst was she loved him" (O 113). Mr. Ryder arrives in Nice to see Cynthia and meet Robert. He imagines Robert will be a "sag-bel-lied, lecherous graybeard" (*O* 115). Cynthia argues he isn't. Ryder says she has gone against all his teachings. She asserts that Robert is "the dearest, finest man. Not unlike you. In many ways. It's probably how I found him" (*O* 116). This is a flattery he rejects. "Don't spread this jam on this stale bread, Cynthia." To which Cynthia thinks, "The nausea of authority, the old claw, the male threat in the male throat, affection quantified to death" (*O* 117). This silent rebuttal is not just daughter to father but the old war between men and women that the new woman refutes.

Mr. Ryder meets Robert and sees he is "no grandpa lecher" (*O* 118). He asks for Robert's intentions. Robert declares his sincerity, which includes ending his marriage and the unhappy choice of having to hurt his children. They discuss Cynthia's fragility and depressions, both of which she counters with a clever intellect and forwardness when she is more on the manic tilt of her manic-depression, this being the term of the era before today's less aggressive and more mollifying term, bipolar. Ryder and Robert find that, while they may never be good friends, they can come to agreement regarding Cynthia. Ryder seems to understand that perhaps his often troubled daughter might even benefit from Robert as a second father figure. Ryder leaves Cynthia with Robert, evidence that he will let the matter stand. What also stands is Robert's promise to deal with his marriage. Easier said than done.

Robert returns home to his family and finds dealing with them becomes a tortuous, guilt-ridden, and doubt-ridden undertaking. Albie sees him first.

> "What was summer like Alb?"
> "Ten thousand two-by-fours." He'd worked with a master carpenter in Williamstown.
> "No fun?"
> "I met a girl. We put up her father's garage."
> "Are you good friends?"
> "We haven't slept together."
> Dr. Merriweather didn't like this. He had never talked to his children about this sort of thing. Even when it came up indirectly, theoretically, it overburdened domestic discretion [*O* 131].

This passage juxtaposed with Robert's first meeting with Mr. Ryder under-scores the conflict signified by the book's title: one regards one's own chil-dren very differently than another's child if the other's child is also one's lover. The father and son's discussion continues and Robert now sounds more like Mr. Ryder than Mr. Ryder's daughter's boyfriend. Robert learns that Albie also saw *Newsweek* and that this is now the news in Cambridge. Father and son talk about what may be coming. This is heartfelt, adult, complicated; each makes points and the other counterpoints, and then — surprise, lest it veer towards melodrama — Albie shifts the subject to himself and dismisses his father's emotional outpouring. "Dr. Merriwether was rather annoyed to get shoved off center stage. Albie, however, had had as much of his father's confession as he could take" (*O* 135).

The direction of the confession might have included the word "divorce," common today but still a rarity and thus a more drastic step in 1969 than now when one in two marriages ends before death does part. In 1969 there was still an associative stigma that made the step of divorce extreme and one to be avoided.

Just as *Stitch* had a chapter sympathetic to Edward' s wife Cressida, there is one for Sarah but with more of an edge as concerns her midlife rebellion. Sarah represents or, more aptly, resents the new woman that she isn't. Sarah imagines the career that might have been if she hadn't taken a back seat to Robert's career. She refuses Robert sex and claims a lack of interest in him, but not just a lack of interest. She has also seen *Newsweek*. After Robert's return from Nice, bickering escalates. She throws him out of their bedroom and he moves into an extra bedroom. Their discourse, for the most part, is reduced to "grunts" (*O* 144). Both regret the effect on the children but not enough to have a truce. He wishes not to involve the children and still hides Cynthia, literally, so no reports will get back to them. He puts Cynthia in an apartment while he remains in his home. This is not easy for Robert's fragile lover. "Cynthia feels the high cost of her love for Merriwether. She spends hours and hours alone in her little apartment" (*O* 151). She also feels the need to hide just as much as Robert seems to want her to.

Cynthia does not take this solitude well and now Robert's war has two fronts, with the Cynthia front more volatile than the Sarah front. Cynthia shelters herself in the manic-depressive's compulsive-obsessive tendency to self-insulate with "routines, rituals" (*O* 151). In these routines, she sometimes insulates herself even from Robert. For his part, "The fear of losing her sometimes overcame him" (*O* 154). Yet, despite his fear he maintains the comfortable habit of home and family with girlfriend on the side.

Stern evokes this two-front war with psychodynamic dialogues that are cause and effect actions and reactions derived from inner turmoil. The word dances are clever exercises in wit, anger, sarcasm, and humor. The duels sound to a reader like FBI wiretaps transcribed verbatim. The words are reactions to emotions and feelings and their full weight takes in these emotions and feelings.

Sarah sees a lawyer and sues for divorce. Robert's have-his-cake-and-eat-it-too fence-sitting is going to be history. He goes to see Sarah's lawyer; "On Merriwether's trip to Boston the next morning, everything was dense of significance. There was a power failure on the MTA, he had to get off at Boyleston, a stop early. Hating to be late — and hating what made him hate it — he rushed through crowds, huffing, charging. He passed DeVane's where he'd had his grandmother's diamond set for Sarah's engagement ring" (*O* 166). The lawyer is smooth and Robert naively listens to the smooth talk. Guilty, he wishes to seem amenable and cooperative. He forgets whom the lawyer works for.

A colleague, in another precise portrait, reminds him of that very fact and Robert confronts Sarah about the document he just signed. She assures him it is not what he imagines. Then he cries, torn with the fear of leaving his past for an uncertain future. Sarah is not affected; she will not let him have his double life.

Thanksgiving comes with the absence of the two eldest children, Albie and Priscilla, who are away at school and use school as an excuse they'd not used for previous years. Robert realizes that his two younger children are pawns in the middle of Sarah's resentment, and he resents her words directed towards them that subtly underscore the cold war existing at their holiday table. "He discovered he could hate her.... He wanted her hurt. She was driving him from everything he loved, she'd sent him into the sexual desert — Sarah was Sahara, he'd never thought of it before. When he found water, she pounced, her chance to revenge herself. For what? His tyranny. The whole culture of tyranny. Merriwether felt the hatred leaking out of the rhetoric, but he felt weak with it, shriveled up, the room was airless, he opened the window, then the storm window, and took in the cold air. Monsters. They were both monsters. Inside them both was every animal in the zoo.... How could he have thought for a minute they could live together? The one relief of it all would be freedom from her. This was what divorce was about" (*O* 189).

Divorce is also about the effects on children. Robert wonders, "Would the children feel the breeze of subtle pariahdom? This wasn't Beverly Hills where almost every child had step- and double step-parents. All right, maybe it would save his children from unthinking ease. Though contemporary life was fuller of stories about The Children of Broken Homes" (*O* 195). Today the term "broken home" is an etymological relic only mentioned in fiction or studies of previous generations. Then it was a stigmatic appellation harmful to children and parents alike. Parental guilt and shame were more extreme. When Sarah and Robert tell the two younger children that they will separate, the scenes are painfully real. Robert, on the edge of a shame-induced crash, writes announcing-our-divorce letters to friends and relatives, a compulsive and purgative act of expiatory confession.

Christmas comes with all of the children present for the last act of *la famille* Merriwether as an entity. "Merriwether did his annual reading from the notebook of the children's sayings he'd kept for twenty years" (*O* 202). Stern's "Journal" in his second essay collection *Invention of the Real* contains just such sayings. The divorce comes through but Robert still lives in his "family" home. He wants to stay until the end of the spring semester. He clings. Sarah orders him to be out by March 20th. He finds an apartment of his own, as he does not believe his habits and Cynthia's are cohabitable. This is not easy for Cynthia who needs much approval and validation.

The final section of the book concerns the first steps toward Robert's future. Robert reads the *Bhagavad-Gita* to help him find a center he can live in while he faces his brave new world. He reads there "'Freedom from activity is never achieved by abstaining from activity.' That's the ticket.... Merriwether and the *Gita* against molecular junk." (*O* 235). He thinks of himself as "The haphazard survivor" (*O* 243). On this note the book ends.

Stern's novel is a testimony to the New World that followed the transition from the pre–1960s to the post–1960s. Hewn from the tree of life — Stern's life — it records the early years of the modern era's prevalent motif: the last days of an outworn marriage, the affair that breaks it, the divorce and its aftermath. Philip Roth, another recorder of the era's angst sums up *Other Men's Daughters*.

> There's much to admire in this book — the precision, the tact, the humane feeling, the tremendous charm — but what stands out particularly is the intelligent Harvard physiology professor who is (truly) its hero. A blend of restraint, decorum, rampant courtliness and atrophied eroticism, he is a perfect target for the wise and witty Cambridge student-beauty of the Sixties, coutured in jeans and armed with The Pill. And she is his text in the physiology of love. In all it is as if Chekhov had written Lolita: the eye and the heart telling the story of the genitals, and telling it very gently. The theme is Leaving Home, departing the familiar and the cherished for erotic renewal; Stern's accomplishment here, as in all of his work, is to locate precisely the comedy and the pains of a particular contemporary phenomenon without exaggeration, animus, or operatic ideology.[39]

CHAPTER FIVE

From Midnight to the Millennium — 1978–

1978: *Natural Shocks*

Fred Wursup is a journalist free-falling from the glory of a muck-raking nonfiction best seller. He is complacent and needs a new kick in the pants and finds it with a crisscross quest through sex, death, and the modern cultural compulsion of a ubiquitous, celebrity-driven media.

With Fred, Stern enters a new phase in his life and art. He wrote *Natural Shocks* after his 50th birthday in 1978. There are certain realities about entering the sixth decade that Everyman considers. A person is just past middle age so that the "middle-age-crazy" generated from midlife crisis is no longer an expedient excuse for clinging to immaturity. Stern became an early elder statesman of sorts as he was coming off his most successful novel, *Other Men's Daughters*. He was now a cumulatively avuncular Stern with his 24 years at the University of Chicago, his critically praised writing career, and his words of wisdom as an in-demand essayist writing "think-pieces" in which he could vent his spleen and get people to listen.

Stern writes of Wursup, "After a long professional life of asking people questions, now he was questioned. Why not? He turned out to have as much guff, vanity, curious opinion and nerve as anyone else. He knew how to seem modest, how to beat a fluent retreat (and then another, and another). He was becoming one of the most-interviewed 'seldom-interviewed' celebrities in America. A verbal Houdini: "It would take me a month to answer that, Gracie." "You put it better than I, John" (*NS* 48).

Stern here pokes fun at himself and his own opinion pieces. One Stern essay was "Inside Narcissus," originally formed as a Princeton lecture in

1976 and then augmented for publication two years late in the *Yale Review*. Stern here focuses on the intrusive eye of shock media and says he wrote the essay in a bit of an adrenaline rush muddle for which he blames the concurrent writing of his latest novel. He makes clear that the novel was more than an exercise and that the same rush of emotion carried along his essay. "In 1976 I was worn down either by writing or suffering *Natural Shocks*" (*IR* 177). "Inside Narcissus" is an early and profound nonfiction extrapolation of how Stern's intimations about an intrusive media that he set forth in *Golk* had become a ubiquitous reality.

> A modern life which is productive or peculiar is a kind of license to explain itself. And who isn't delighted by such an explanation? Poets, politicians, muggers or musicians who won't supply their inside stories look as if they're trying to put something over on us. Magic is O.K. For kids, but the rest of us need truth; and not just the cover truths distributed to the naïve, but the truths behind the truths.
>
> Every fundamental particle appears to contain more fundamental ones, so every inside story has its story. In the Age of Openness, this story is what we require. For us, the hidden is sinister, perhaps criminal. (Real criminals serve up their careers along with all the other self-sellers.).
>
> The wonderful result is that we know more about thousands of remark-able people — a few remarkable because they've been remarked — than peo-ple in epochs of discretion knew about their neighbors, their kings, and, in a way, themselves.
>
> For it is the case that knowledge of others promotes self-knowledge. It is a democratic and technological glory that millions of human beings are more sensitive to their specialness than all the pharaohs and poets of darker ages. Democracy and mass media require a sense of individuality in their participants. A collective "you" is broadcast, but in reception it is singular. (Individuals, not collectives, buy detergents.) And technology has democratized the apparatus of commemoration: Instamatics [and now home videos] harvest billions of smiles, tape recorders as many babbles. These fill parochial annals. Official files are stuffed with equivalent infor-mation. Pollsters sample opinions, archives store the whorls of billions of pinkies.
>
> So scrupulously observed, sifted, recorded, who could resist caring for himself? Who could help becoming a narcissist [*IR* 179–80]?

Who can? There is, in the crush of self-scrutiny, the equal urge for a sala-cious scrutiny of others. One wishes to know one's self juxtaposed with other selves and, if so, the others might as well be celebrities from which one may glean, however specious the ephemeral and self-indulgently sub-conscious connection, a reflected aura that substantiates the silent observer's

own much less public persona. The uncelebrated's compulsive identification with the celebrated is an attempt at the vicarious erasure of
anonymity: *I am known by whom I know or imagine I know.*

The public's need to know about the famous at whatever cost to the
celebrity's personal privacy is a key to *Natural Shocks.* Around this theme
are woven the once sacredly private human rituals of sex and death, which
in the modern media frenzy are private no more. (Was there ever a more
public death and mourning in the 1990s than Princess Diana's.) Fred Wursup will confront the issues of media and privacy while violating the latter. He spies on his ex-wife in her apartment from his apartment, the
configuration of geographical happenstance allowing him to do so.

Wursup is 44 and one can conjecture that the Stern of 50 is looking
back at himself for inspiration in writing this novel. Stern's advancing role
of commentator informs his "looking back" with a shift in his prose technique. While there is considerable *gravitas* in *Natural Shocks*, the narration and dialogue view these depths with a cynical reality that becomes a
very sharp, caustic, and satiric wit. Stern the commentator is also, and
more so than ever before, Stern the humorist. Here is a rapid-fire prose
of frequent one-liners that highlight the serious themes by seeing the
human comedy in what fools these mortals be as they go about their so-
called serious business. The humor is never unkind to the important issues
of sex, death, and celebrity, but rather the laughs are directed at how people deal with these issues, which, in their implications, can overwhelm a
person who is unable to laugh at them. The jokes are deflections to ward
off *too* much introspection. Nonetheless, some of the one-liners emerge as
quotable bon mots and even aphorisms of Mandarin incisiveness.

On an editor named Schilp: "Schilp had a basso boom ... the Mussolini of telephones" (*NS* 24), and, "He was born to oversee the conver-
sion of The Everyday into The Sensational" (*NS* 49).

On Wursup's ex-wife Susannah's view of men with delayed adolescence: "her green eyes glittered with an amused tolerance far more telling
than voiced disapproval. 'The toys of morons' was what he read in them....
When he bought an old Mercedes, the distaste was so skillful a torture of
silent looks he took a bath on a trade-in for a Chevy. When, marriage
coming apart, he bought a Porsche, she understood. (She was a fine interpreter of the symbols of revulsion)" (*NS* 13–15).

On Wursup: "Farsightedness bored Wursup. When people tell you to
watch the stars, keep your hand on your wallet" (*NS* 22).

On how Fred explains to an interviewer that his articles emerge from
"the bottle of skepticism I carry around.": "Every story gets the treatment,
you know what I mean.... Every positive is negatived, every assertion

turned inside out. Give or take a little. You don't go far wrong exaggerating the mendacity of public men" (*NS* 49).

On death: "...life's soaked with it. Until you deal with it, there's no culture. Every *polis* has a *necropolis*" (*NS* 31).

On how to write about death as per editor Schilp: "That's the kicker. Do it right, there's nothing more diverting. One way or another. The blues send people through the ceiling. *Last* quartets, *last* plays, *last* words. Irresistible.... What's death? What's dying? How to croak? Croaking right, croaking wrong?" (*NS* 25–26).

Wursup on avoiding the topic of death: "didn't eyes have lids for such protection" (*NS* 29).

Wursup on his lover's love for cosmetics: "You're the General Motors of your own appearance" (*NS* 30).

On TV: "These were the years television was altering not only entertainment but business, politics, and social life" (*NS* 37).

On reporting: "The essence of the best journalism is the revelation of hypocrisy. Every man covered his tracks" (*NS* 55–6).

On the public and media: "People adored trivia [and] the media traded on this passion for trivia. And a great career could be smashed for a few moments' amusement" (*NS* 114).

Fred on the celebrity's dilemma: "Attention's pressure to repeat. Celebrity's the vengeance of the unfamous. They turn the famous into stage settings. It's a way of paralyzing them" (*NS* 17).

Or, "In the old days, the Napoleons and Walpoles looked like giants because so few people were inspected and written about. Now, with film and cheap printing, there were thousands of celebrities. Kissinger and Nixon weren't much bigger than Marlon Brando or the Beatles" (*NS* 180).

Or, "In a celebrity-heavy world, anonymity was sometimes despair" (*NS* 19).

On Fred's mood changes: "All these currents hot and cold, running out of a person's arctic and tropic gulfs" (*NS* 216).

On intuitive knowledge: "The unsaid mastered the said" (*NS* 184).

On the small offices of *Chouinard's News Letter* where Susannah works: "It's one of those glassed-in ant farms" (*NS* 36). "There were twenty or thirty small nations which had less efficient intelligence than *Chouinard's*" (*NS* 40).

Also at *Chouinard's* Susannah begins a relationship with her longtime boss whose wife died some months before. Fred finds out with his binoculars.

Fred also finds out that being a celebrity is different from interviewing them. He gets very angry when he, as interviewee, doesn't like what the abovementioned interviewer subsequently says about him: "Like a con man or great photographer, [Fred] blends into scenery" (*NS* 49). The interviewer did to Fred what Fred said he did to his own interviewees. Stern then has Fred learn that Hamish Blick, a Wursup interviewee of six years before, has killed himself. A flashback of the interview follows (a Sternian set piece) and Blick is a reclusive, pathetic, albeit successful filmmaker who blames his extreme solitude on both parental neglect and his childhood awareness of his own homeliness. Fred writes this out in painful detail, including stabs at Blick's appearance, and upon publication Blick writes a sad rebuttal letter to the editor. Fred is ashamed, and, now writing about death in his present, confronts his role in Blick's suicide. Indeed, when Fred was given his death-and-dying writing assignment he had thought how he had never really been touched by death. This changes— Blick first, more to come.

Stern's juxtaposition of Wursup's anger over how he was portrayed with his memory of how he portrayed Blick is one of a number of juxtapositions in the novel. These "acts of "placing side by side" are deliberate. Sex, death, and man's rush for recognition are intertwined as related reflections altered by a spinning mirror in their content but not necessarily in their significance. Death is feared as the end; sex and the "little deaths" of orgasms seek to refute death's approach; self-recognition and the public recognition of celebrities are counters to anonymity, which is a form of living death that reminds one of actual death; hence, any sense of anonymity must also be avoided. These are predominantly unconscious thought processes even for intellectuals and artists who, in fact, are the worst offenders because they think *too* much. As smart as Wursup is, he does not correlate his anger over how he is depicted in an article to his regret of the way he treated Blick in an article. Blick, while protecting his solitude did not also wish this solitude to be anonymous. He sought recognition by making movies that would outlast him. An honored film removes anonymity and even cheats death, by keeping its maker's name alive, if not his body. Books do the same and Fred intuitively feels the same way about his writing—and now he is to write about death. As he researches his assignment, he ponders his topic via Stern's narration.

> Freud claimed death fear fused anxiety about mother loss with anxiety about castration "projected upon the powers of destiny." Freud himself was said to have one of the worst cases of death terror, *Todangst*. In fact, the most vital people were the greatest death-fearers and death dodgers: Goethe, Tolstoy, Dr. Johnson were divisional champs. They were examples of what Wursup called his Koufax Theorem. The famous pitcher has said his terrible arm pain derived from the same calcium deposit which gave him his extra

throwing power. So death torture gripped the libido of the world's most living livers; they exposed themselves to it again and again. The hope was to inoculate themselves [*NS* 29].

They can't, though. Even the horizontal "little deaths" of sex only distract one from death-fear but cannot remove it. In this passage Stern juxtaposes a sports metaphor with "death torture." This juxtaposition also alludes to the athlete as celebrity and to the nature of sports fanaticism (fans), who, by joining in communal adulation attach themselves to fame and give themselves a collective self-recognition that temporarily erases individual anonymity. Stern's weave of themes and ideas in *Natural Shocks* is second only to that in *1968* in metaphorical complexity.

Fred's immersion in death texts does have an effect on him as noted by his lover, Dr. Sisley Dyce "Sookie" Gumpert, Ph.D, Geophysics, who tells him, "You can't take much more Freddy. Every night a funeral. When are you going to wind up" (*NS* 29). Not anytime soon as he and the novel have just begun.

Sookie is a scientist, and through her Stern lets science have its say: Fred tells her, "Death sits on life. It dominates economy: social security, debt, conservation, pollution, the Pentagon. Half the world's stories circle it. One way or another millions are in the death business." She answers, "I'm not…. Death is nothing in my work. Life's just a little carbon zone dangled between ice ages. No technology's going to touch that. Death's a local sample of the Great Ice. I care about what it leaves behind. A Chunk of coal, a little gas, calcium. Take a long view. Relax. Life's a haphazard coagulation of inorganic soup" (*NS* 31). If only it was that simple.

Another running juxtaposition is that of Abby Schlosserberg's rise as a reporter at *Chouinard's* with Fred's re-evaluation of himself as reporter. Abby wants to get where Fred is. She is rich (her wealthy parents died in a car crash), and she funds the sinking newsletter to keep it afloat. In exchange, Abby wants to spice up the staid financial publication with some Golklike investigative articles. She does; they work. "More and more, Abby thirsted to know what public events and personalities concealed" (*NS* 56). The staid staff of the once staid newsletter is not sure they want the excitement. The *Chouinard* "gang is very nervous about her. But it's the gossip era and she is a master…." (*NS* 173). Abby becomes the "in" networker of nefarious information, doing what brought Fred fame by "exaggerating the mendacity of public men."

In addition to the Blick and Abby juxtapositions, there are many subplots and characters, all of which serve as contrasts to Wursup and as different perspectives on the themes of sex, death, media, and celebrity.

Francesca Buell is a 23-year-old terminal cancer patient who agrees to be a subject of Fred's study; her friends and her father also come into Fred's orbit.

One friend, Tina, is a poet, allowing Stern another look at his long-running—and evolving—discussion of art.

Will Eddy is Fred's book editor; they've been friends since college. Before Fred's divorce, Will had a two-year affair with Susannah.

At *Chouinard's* Susannah's friendship with Kevin, the newsletter's owner, becomes intimate after Kevin's wife dies.

Fred's agent, Tania, is a bulldog, a comedienne, and Fred's occasional reliever of sexual tension.

Jim Doyle is another college friend and a political operative about to be pulled into a personal scandal initiated by Abby's column. Doyle hopes a counter article by Fred will get him out of it. Through Doyle and others, Stern also takes his shots at the skullduggery of business and politics.

Fred's father is with Mona who replaced Fred's mother after senility put her in a home. Poppa is a bad poet but he compulsively expresses himself to seek approval and validate his existence.

Doyle goes to Rome to see Henry Knoblauch, a Hitler survivor and more recent survivor of a stroke and two heart attacks, all of which have increased his sex drive as a compulsive refutation of his aging and dying. One coupling becomes a surprisingly ironic tragedy.

His son Benny, a flaky genius, will turn out to be a friend of Francesca. He is an example of the circularity of the book's—and the world's—business. Everything seems to be related in ways that cannot always be understood.

Francesca's father, Tommy, is an over-achieving self-made millionaire and self-educated philosopher who resists his daughter's dying, seeing it as some kind of failure on his part. "…a terrible reversal was occurring, the younger was breaking up while the older was still intact" (*NS* 163). These "minor" characters are concisely drawn in deft portraits that personalize each so that the importance of their interactions have a strong reader identification even if their stage time is short. All the characters are satellites sending back information on the main themes: sex, death, media, celebrity. Fred Wursup is the catalyst. He is the big stone who makes a big splash into a large thematic pond with ever-widening circles of intricate ramifications.

Of the satellite characters, Sookie Gumpert has the largest supporting role. She makes a star-turn entrance:

> Lanky, awkward, sharp and charming, Sookie was one of those double beauties who looked gorgeous either unmade-up or as the creation of the dust

and syrup of five hundred plant and animal bladders. Her long head sprouted a snub, Renoir nose that told the air, "Come to me." She had a fashion model's emphatic cheeks, which she rouged with a hundred shades of blood; huge, dense, violet eyes which were outlined, italicized, sparkled, veiled; a Dover cliff of a forehead was topped by a mass of red-gold hair, which, two or three times a week, she metal-tortured into Versailles shrubbery.

In the morning, she was even more delectable. Subtle power streamed from her sleep-undone beauty; there were delicacies of color in her cheeks. This beauty was infinitely more appealing to Wursup than the manufactured beauty which could be lifted up and left in a museum. For Sookie, though, that made-up beauty was not just necessary mask but escape from an old conviction of ugliness instilled by a thousand sisterly digs and a girlhood of unfavorable comparison to the models in *Mademoiselle*, *Glamour* and *Vogue* [NS 29–30].

Sookie is the home base that Fred's long rope is tethered to no matter how far he wanders off. She is also a source for many of the novel's humorous gibes at Fred and the world.

Natural Shocks, as the title infers, is full of randomness, reversals, and revelations. The previously mentioned double suicide of Fred's father and companion is one of many, but one does not wish to give the others away as they are better left as the surprises they are. A hint to Stern's juxtaposing of events and ideas comes from a description of Francesca's father. "[He] was in one of those fine states in which everything heard and scene recalls something else" (*NS* 149). This is the modus operandi for the novel and the reader needs to be just as alert as the writer was in making the internal correlations. Are there morals at the end of this fable? Stern gives none but he does quote Plato: "Though human affairs aren't worthy of great seriousness, it is still necessary to be serious. Man is God's toy. And that is the best part of him" (*NS* 259–60).

Death is life; life goes on. The unsaid masters the said.

1980: *Packages*

Stern's third collection of short stories, *Packages*, although published in 1980, can be considered to have been written more or less concurrently with *Natural Shocks*. The facile prose and rapid humor — even in the stories with serious themes— are here shared with the novel. Age 50 seems to figure in the new and more effusive representation of the writer's personality. The first two stories are in the first person and seem to be the newly avuncular Stern writing about himself. "Wissler Remembers" is an aging teacher's fond recollections of his students that he has been teaching for 30 years, even the ones who annoyed him.

> Miss Fennig. Mr. Quincy. Mr. Parcannis. Miss Vibsayana. Except for your colors, your noses, your inflections, your wristwatches, I can tell little about your status. (You are from a warrior caste in Bengal, Miss Vibsayana. You wrote it in a paper. Miss Glennie, you were the brilliant, solitary black girl in the Harrisburg parochial school. You gave me hints of it in office hours.) But I know you inside out; would like to give you all A's. (Won't.) All that part is clear, though Mr. Laroche won't know that the extra paragraph he tacked on his paper lowered his grade from B plus to B; nor Mrs. Linsky that if she'd not spoken so beautifully about Stavrogin, she would not have passed [P 20].

"Mail" is the author's bemused but also fond account of letters from admirers of his work. "Still, it's still nice to get nice letters. Out of the unblue blue where people we're not thinking about are thinking about us" (P 25).

Stern is now the wise storyteller gathering an audience around his tribal fire to explain, to amuse, to give advice or solace. He is very comfortable in this role, as the just-past-middle-aged bearer of worldly experience — but he is never pretentious or remotely condescending. In public readings, Stern relishes his role as performer of his work, acting out the scenes, changing voices, making faces, pausing for dramatic or comedic effect. As he ages, he gets funnier and funnier as an arbiter and interpreter of the human comedy. Yet, he never strays far from the seriousness that his humor pretends not to take too seriously.

The story "Packages" has already been revealed as a revelatory testament to a mother's death, just as "Troubles" enunciated the domestic warfare of a young married couple.

"An Ideal Address" is about Winnie, a woman who is everyone else's stable rock but one those others neglect to realize could sometimes use a bit of anchoring herself. She knew that just once in a while she needed "a stillness in others so her own motion would count" (P 47).

"Lesson for a Day" is about a sexual fantasist who imagines much more than will ever become real. "Double Charley" deals with two long-time like-named friends and song-writing partners where one discovers a rather belated betrayal by the other that is both revelation and reversal.

"Riordan's Fiftieth" turns that birthday on its head as Riordan faces his 50th with nothing but contempt from his wife and kids. Riordan is a bus driver, and as such he is a rare blue collar protagonist for Stern. In this story, one sees similarities to another famous Chicago writer of the previous generation, James T. Farrell, best known for his Studs Lonigan trilogy.

"The Girl Who Loves Shubert" concerns two men with a 30-year acquaintance. Yntema and Scharf didn't like each other, but whenever Scharf came to New York — about once a year — they had lunch. Scharf is a king of routine, Yntema the reverse. In this regard opposites attract and they fascinate each other with their differences. On this visit, Yntema has a story that tops all others.

"In a recital for the Pope," Edward Gunther and Nina Callahan are revisited in Venice.

"Dr. Cahn's Visit" faces the hard acceptance by his children of an aging father's diminished awareness of his world.

This third collection of short stories affirmed Stern as one of the genre's most profound practitioners. In 1989 *Noble Rot* collected his stories and added a few new ones. As a compilation of 40 years, critics recognized that *Noble Rot* signified a remarkable achievement of quality and growth as an artist.

1986: *A Father's Words*

In Chapter Two of the above work, Stern said this in 1985 during the writing of *A Father's Words*:

> The point is that the core of the book was never Firetuck, Riemer, and the Farce Movement. The heart of it was — is — a transfiguration and projection of the author's relationships to two wives and four children. The miscalculations, waste pages, skewered drafts, the four thousand pages in the archives of failure have more to do with failure to see that than with the misdirections of dictation.
>
> I think I've finished now with family novels. I've hurt everyone I can hurt. Not — as far as I know — trying to hurt, but there it is, and I paid for it with the thousands of pages, the thousands of hours wasted, the typed excursions to Africa and Tulsa, the hearts and pockets of invention I'll never use. I was punished for failing to see my subject. I must get another. No amanuensis or word processor can do that for me... [*PB* 180].

A Father's Words is, indeed, essentially about the "transfiguration and projection of the author's relationships to two wives and four children." This is what emerged from his self-described muddle of a much longer book that didn't work.

The dynamic of parents with adult children is a difficult one — even if they get along. Parents find it very hard *not* to regard their adult children as if they hadn't grown up, and adult children find it even harder to have their parents see them this way. The conflict comes down to the parents' urge to continue nurturing (or meddling in their children's view), and the children's desire for independence (or rebellion in their parents' view). Here is how the dust jacket copy describes what a reader will find between the covers of *A Father's Words*:

> Cy [Riemer] is both a seeker of truth and a master of evasion. So preoccupied is he with looking for truth — and making sure he stays in control of relationships with the people he needs and loves— that he fails to notice certain crucial things about himself and those closest to him. Shrewd enough to know that something is missing in his relationship with his youthful girlfriend, Emma, he refuses to recognize that the main source of her depression is his refusal to marry her and give her a family of her own. Cy also senses that his children resent him, but he evades the criticisms of his daughter Livy, who berates him for looking for truth in books and museums instead of within himself. Above all he wants happiness for Jack, a brilliant ne'er-do-well whom Cy see as a distorted image of himself. Jack shamefacedly but cheerfully evades his father's unceasing attempts to hint and nag him into making more of himself. Unable to accept his family on their terms, and insistent on playing relationships (and life) *his* way, Cy constantly deludes himself, even as he seeks, relentlessly, to understand the truth about life. Gradually, however, both life and his children demonstrate the impossibility of keeping them within his control and propel him into a growing awareness of himself, his children, and the woman he loves.

This is the plan that the author likely intended — at least from his point of view. Stern's son, however, as also recorded earlier, disagreed. "I realized how little you understood me after I read that book." Stern countered, "Well, it's not just you." Yet, Stern has admitted that it was close enough. "I think I've finished now with family novels. I've hurt everyone I can hurt." This time, perhaps, Stern came too close.

Stitch and *Other Men's Daughters* were to some degree autobiographical, the latter more than the former, but both were written *after* the time period of actual events, even if only to or three years after. *A Father's Words* seems to have been written concurrently with the father-child difficulties described and is not so much a recollection with reflection as a recording of actual emotions in real time.

Stern has here written a parable of current events in order to teach — but to whom is the subject of the lesson directed. Was Stern aiming at his children or himself? It would seem that Stern wasn't sure and was trying to see if in this instance his writing could be a more conscious form of self-therapy. If so, that is an unsteady fence to balance on and sometimes the balance is precarious.

A Father's Words reminds one of how Christopher Isherwood felt about his 1954 novel *The World in the Evening*. In Isherwood's diaries of the previous three years he frequently bemoaned the struggle he had with the novel's writing just as Stern did concerning *A Father's Words*. Isherwood later became one of his own novel's severest critics. *The World in the Evening* has very good sections and others that are not so good.

A Father's Words is not quite so uneven but there are parts that are less surefooted than one expects from Stern who is otherwise very sure. Early in the novel, Stern as Cy, even discusses the uncertainty that comes from personal writing however it is disguised to be otherwise.

> Because we have authors in the family, our dirty linen worried me. I write about science. Agnes [ex-wife and children's author] used to write about unhappy anteaters and ambitious hedgehogs. Jenny and Ben do write about families, but in a grand — literary and scientific — way, not a gossipy revealing, and personal one. Still their books disturb me.
>
> Jenny's is a doctoral dissertation, entitled *The Wobbling Nucleus: The Family in Literature from Medea to Finnegan's Wake*. Judging from Medea, I feared the worst. *Medea* is not about your average happy family. I'd always thought Jenny a gentle person, somewhat remote, a stray from a softer part of the universe, a Cordelia of loyalty. Why such a thesis then? "Oh," she said, "it has to do with rocking the family boat. It's the rocking that saves it." Of course, no one rocked the boat more than Cordelia [*FW* 16–17].

Stern here alludes to *King Lear*, that other family drama about a father and his children. Stern may have believed that he needed to do some "rocking" of his own and thought his novel could be the wind on the family water. Cy continues,

> Ben's book is something else: "The first fetal history of mankind." Its title is *The Need to Hurt*. His notion is that the human condition is determined in the womb. Things have been decided long before the Oedipus complex. Ben shows pictures of a half-inch fetus writhing in a smoker's womb. "There is hell," he says. "The fetus, not the child, is man's father." He says all world leaders should be given fetal IQ's. "Why should the world have to reenact their placental troubles?" (What went on in Agnes's womb when she was having him?)
>
> A family, even one as well behaved as ours, is an emotional hot spot. Its members have to be instantly alert to each other's feelings. This may be especially important in a well-behaved family, where character is formed, not only as a defense against one's own violent needs, but against rival siblings. (Isn't Livy's aggressiveness the shell of the youngest child's need to perpetuate her cushioned infancy? And isn't Jenny's softness the crust which holds down the oldest child's rage at displacement.)

I asked Agnes what she thought about these antifamily books our children wrote.

She said, "You should be complimented your children study families" [*FW* 17].

This is a well-placed sarcastic shot at her ex-husband telling him that perhaps he would have done better to do his own studying earlier.

Stern's apologia-confession has here a bit of tongue in cheek. *He* is the writer in the family and he here pokes fun at himself. In addition to tongue in cheek, there is, though Stern would be loath to admit any overt sentiment, also some "catch-in-throat" emotions. Stern seems to want to send a message — but to whom — himself, his children? As recently as 2001, in a *New York Times* article entitled, "The Deliberate Calculation of Autumnal Accounting Endangers Happiness," Stern indicates that even for a much more recent work, he was capable of message-sending as well as a tad of self-flagellation.

> I know that I myself have prolonged certain painful situations because writing about them became more important than eliminating the pain. Very recently, to my relief and happiness, I did force a change in what had been a very painful separation. Along with the consequent relief and happiness, I also realized that the steam had gone out of the fiction I'd been writing.... The happiness didn't lessen, but it was accompanied by an odd hollowness and anxiety. What was I going to do about the novel on which I'd been working for two years? In it, my protagonist, not a writer, but a retired lawyer, deliberates –as I did — about clinging to pain. In a book of Emily Dickinson's given to him –and this is invention — by the loved one from whom he was separated, he finds his situation expressed in these remarkable lines:
>
> > *Rehearsal to Ourselves*
> > *Of a Withdrawn Delight*
> > *Affords a Bliss like Murder*
> > *Omnipotent. Acute.*
> >
> > *We will not drop the Dirk*
> > *Because we love the Wound*
> > *The Dirk commemorates Itself*
> > *Reminds us that We died.*

A Bliss like Murder ... Because We Love the Wound. Astonishing insights, he thinks, and he wonders about the spectral Amherst spinster as well as about his own internal savagery.

How many like my protagonist and myself not only adjust to the resentment and hatred of those who, they think, have wronged them but flourish in it? Yet of this many, it is only the writer whose love of the wound involves a professional opportunity and makes dropping his dirk a difficult decision.[40]

For *A Father's Words*, the dirk was not dropped.

It cannot be easy for a writer, or anyone else, to hold a weapon (a pen) in one hand and also rub his wound with it, opening it again to bleed anew. The result may be a vision somewhat askew or blurred from achieving the emotional distance of Wordsworth's recollections in tranquility. When Stern as Cy narrates in the first person, these are the strongest — and longest — sections in the book, with an avuncular Riemer holding court to perambulate about his inner and outer worlds, which he does to very humorous effect. Stern thinks out loud and the reader tags along on a tour of his and the world's issues. Some parts that are not quite as strong are, surprisingly for Stern, dialogues with his children. His proximity to the actuality of father-and-grown-children mis- or noncommunication might have impeded a certain amount of reality in favor of a didacticism meant for Stern and his children to learn from. The conversations seem a bit "directed" toward messages that make a point, rather than being the usual Stern dialogue that just "is" and gives the reader room for independent interpretation. The latter is parable; the former is, however unintended, subtle propaganda, but propaganda nonetheless. Still, this does not mean the dialogue is "bad," and it may be that one would only notice when reading previous Stern books closely and in comparison, and each right after the other.

The principal father-child conflict is between Cy and his son Jack. While written circa 1984–5, Jack can now be recognized in more current twenty-something terms such as "Generation X," or "slacker." His kin have been featured in numerous 1990s books and films as the vague, directionless products of the MTV era, an era that diffuses youthful thought with the flashy light and bright colors that are the modern media. For this generation it is just too easy to sit back and allow one's self to be hypnotized by the nonstop images that make one think of the brainwashing in Kubrick's filming of Anthony Burgess's *A Clockwork Orange*. Cy cannot understand how Jack can be so different from himself and, like many parents, he considers Jack's "failure" also his own. "All I know is I can't tolerate the way he acts and looks. After all, he's mine. I helped shape him. His life's a rebuke to mine" (*FW* 24). Meanwhile, Jack may be hypnotized, but he is not inert. "If Livy's the Riemer who lets out the most steam, Jack's the one who lets you know how much he's steaming. He's the family's self-dramatist, the family thermometer, the child who registers what's right and wrong with our lives" (*FW* 20). Failure is a relative term that sometimes requires patience before it sorts itself out. Jack certainly needs to get his act together but Cy's persistent efforts to nag him have the opposite effect, as they just inspire more rebellion. Cy knows this; yet, he also knows that "Knowing isn't understanding" (*FW* 12). Daughter Livy complains that her father is self-absorbed in knowing facts while not understanding himself. He answers, "Who can tell where the clues are Livy?" (*FW* 15). He's right; however, she is not necessarily wrong. A compulsive knower may look everywhere and not stop long enough anywhere to derive understanding. Stern does not let Cy off the hook in the blame game, nor does Cy let himself off. In a continuation of his speech rebutting Jack, he says, "And since I know his laziness and hypocrisy are mine, too, it makes it worse. The difference is *I* try to squeeze that stuff out of me. I don't think Jack tries." To which Emma answers, "You don't know that" (*FW* 24). And he doesn't. His talks with Jack always have little digs:

"Are you working Jack?"
"I'm writing an essay."
"Fine. On what?"
"Truth. Illusion. True illusions. Illusory truths."
"You should know a lot about that" (*FW* 39).

Yet, Jack is not blameless. Jack's younger brother, Ben, says of him, "I can't stand his falsity, his con, his laziness, his boasts of a higher calling. He acts as if only he knows how to live" (*FW* 42).

The father-children theme runs through the novel while there are three subthemes: Cy's relationship with Emma; media, the need for attention, and the post–1960s boom in pornography; and the American seduction by the stock market that started in the 1980s and thrives still.

Cy thinks how, "Emma has a strange sympathy for the children, even though she feels excluded from what she calls 'the Riemersphere.' She doesn't like them to criticize me or me them. Odd" (*FW* 22). This is only "odd" to Cy. Emma is young enough to be one of Cy's children and she is, perhaps, more acutely aware of the Cy who self-abstracts himself away from a true understanding of his children and of herself. She would like marriage and children; he resists. Emma becomes a foil for Cy's father-children dichotomy of parallel lives that cannot quite intersect.

Jack, however, does have a good idea when Cy's newsletter is in the red and may have to fold. He suggests that for the first time Cy run ads, and Jack offers to manage that part of the enterprise. Jack's plan is to run *personals* in this scientific periodical. It works. Then Cy sees an ad for Robusto Films, which is clearly for pornography. He flips. "'You know about it? I can't believe it. Jack, that's betrayal. Patricide. I'm ashamed of you. I know you think I lead a rodent's life, but it's my life, and it stands

for something. It's not up to you to— do me in.' 'That's too strong, dad'"
(*FW* 55). The ad is toned down, but runs— successfully. It turns out Jack's
new girlfriend is Robusto's daughter, Maria, and she is definitely proud of
the family business:

> "It's so simple. Why should people in need conceal it? Why shouldn't
> everybody be in each other's arms? You're so busy with all this," patting a
> stack of letters as she would have a chihuahua, "You don't know how starved
> human beings are, how full of bad time they are. That's why they're sick and
> dangerous. Assassins— there are studies— spend nine-tenths of their time
> fantasizing and masturbating in front of the TV set. Daddy's films could do
> a lot for them. I know they're not much for you and me"—*that* she didn't
> know at all—"but at least they have a sort of reality, and they can call the
> telephone numbers and there will be real people on the other end. Maybe
> not your type or mine but real voices, real bodies. Instead of confusing
> what's inside and outside their head and blasting the confusion away with
> a gun. They can see real people and talk to real people. It's not so different
> from the knights with the Grail, or the saints with their God" [*FW* 58–59].

This seems a bit of a stretch, but then again, maybe not. Cy reconsiders.

> The ads.
> I liked to think they were off in a corner, in a place sprayed for bugs then
> forgot about…. Nothing sexual surprised me anymore. If the pope answered
> Queen Elizabeth, I wouldn't blink…. I'd started checking the ads myself. At
> first, it was amazement at the solemn cleverness of the advertisers: "Systems
> analyst seeks unsystematic diversion." …Some of the answers came back to
> our "boxes," which were an alphabetized box of letters…. My job was to
> remove the outer envelope and put the address of the advertiser on the sealed
> envelope inside…. One day, addressing an envelope, I realized it contained
> a picture…. I turned it over, the flap was loose on one end…. I went to the
> kitchen, boiled some water, held the envelope over the steam until it loos-
> ened. Inside was a letter and in the letter was a polaroid of a naked woman,
> short-haired, snub-nosed, with strong breasts lifted by her pose. She
> stretched back on a lounge in the middle of a grassy lawn….
> I looked at the picture for fifteen minutes: excited, amused at my excite-
> ment, then excited some more. And fearful— even here, alone…. I went
> through other letters, feeling for pictures. There was one. More excitement.
> I steamed open the envelope and drew out a snapshot of a man pointing to
> his erection. Nonetheless, I became the steady voyeur of my advertisers and
> their pen-pals. Part of my routine: Monday, laundry; Wednesday, bank busi-
> ness; Friday, peeping. In six months I saw fifty or sixty women, half of them
> more or less naked. Many photos I wanted to keep…. No, I restricted myself
> to the steam, the contemplation, the resealing, and maintenance of an inter-
> nal portrait gallery [*FW* 66–69].

Carried over from *Natural Shocks* are the issues of privacy and sex, here combined in an odd way. Cy invades the privacy of women who have given up their privacy to a stranger who placed a personal ad. Cy is as remote to them as the ad writer; yet, something is askew in the equation. Sex — via voyeurism and pornography — is an extension of the invasions of privacy or, conversely, the desire for exhibitionism that has introduced "reality" television into American culture; in 2001–2, the most popular shows included *Survivor I & II, Temptation Island, The Mole, Big Brother,* and *Making the Band.* The inspiration for these programs, as with much of 1980s and 1990s culture, comes from MTV and its show *The Real World,* which puts seven or eight twenty-somethings like Jack into one home and "records" their natural selves. (How natural is open to speculation. Golk lives.)

Cy's voyeurism is juxtaposed with a flashback to his domineering mother. One understands that the sins of the mother are visited on the son and the grandchildren.

After this interlude, sex and money are juxtaposed as Cy's father dies and leaves him a relative windfall. The changes money brings are a revelation:

> Before I became an heir, I'd been in various anterooms of money. Comfortable, knowing it wasn't very far away, yet delighted that I needed very little of it, and that I could think — did think — I didn't give a damn about it....
>
> There is money ethics and money esthetics. There is a monetary pennant race, there are monetary wars.... In the romance of money, dollars chased each other, chased yen, chased gold, chased guesses.... What should I do with my dough...? I did give a damn about it. I altered my habits. I bought better cigars and paid eight dollars for wine instead of three.... I didn't stew over sales and bargains, though it still gave me a thrill to save a buck.... The chief pleasure was accumulation.... When I used the phone, I'd find myself thinking, "I own some of you, Ma Bell.... I understood how one could be a Republican...."
>
> It won't let you enjoy it. It just doesn't sit there. It's got a life of its own.... It gets up and tells you what to do.... I hate it. I'm afraid of it. But I'm afraid to give it up [*FW* 86–89].

Cy finds an investment counselor and goes into the stock market. He becomes a player and has to follow what he plays. He reads; he studies. He wants to become — even though the number wasn't quite what it used to be — a millionaire. "One in every four or five hundred Americans is a millionaire.... I wanted to be one too. An absurd ambition, like say, wanting be the best-dressed obstetrician in Albany or the sexual prince of Tucson, but there it was.... It got so that if stocks were up, then so was I. When they were down, it was gloom and doomsville" (*FW* 96).

After a while, the money is more hindrance than help as he explains the difficulty of having it to daughter Livy. (She is a police officer and Cy considers if this is another rebuff of him.)

> I know it sounds silly, your clients should have such trouble. But it's made my little world spin around. There were all those years just getting by. We always did, and I liked that, but now there's — what can I say — this superfluity. It makes you feel full one day and empty the next. You have the pleasure of getting something, and then you feel guilty. At least I do. I suppose that means I shoved all my dirt under the rug. I was such a high-minded cuss. I tried to raise all of you that way too. Like some Hindu or Platonist. You know, wealth stinks, material things are for the birds, and so on. I still believe it. All these dollars are like little mirrors. "Self. Self, self." That's all they say. Or *dough.* Uncooked gunk that sits in your stomach and gives you a bellyache [*FW* 100].

This bit of confession closes the "money" section of the novel. The rest is taken up with Cy and his children, especially Jack, who marries Maria Robusto and joins the porn empire. Cy chooses not to take Emma to the wedding. This does not go over very well with her. More friction. The wedding and surrounding events give Stern good reason to have Cy converse with Emma and all of his children with a certain amount of angst-in, angst-out bloodletting. Cy sounds like Jay in "Troubles" when he says to Emma, "As far as I'm concerned, analysis destroys relationships" (*FW* 120).

Cy puts together a book of his essays, *Off My Chest*, and finds no takers but one, a university press. He later finds out that Maria donated money so they'd publish it. Thus, porn, money, and academia are incestuously joined.

Jennie confronts Dad about his treatment of Jack — that Cy gives money to all the kids but him — why? Cy's answer recalls Higgins in "Assessment of an Amateur." "Because he admits, sometimes he boasts of being a moocher — which is a soft word for thief — of being a dissembler, meaning liar. Of standing back and being amused by the world — i.e., being a bum. He makes a structure out of his weakness and claims it makes him a character, someone special. I can't support that. What is he? What has he? Life, health, an unhappy bride, peanut butter, and for all I know, drink and drugs" (*FW* 144).

Jennie challenges her father's accounting. "You pulled yourself together and wrote *Off My Chest*. But suppose Jack wrote a better book, he's got the talent for it. *I think you'd cut him down.* I think you don't want him to rival you" (*FW* 141). Is this true? There is something of a "surprise" ending and the reader can decide.

A *Father's Words* has much to offer while not being among Stern's best. Nonetheless, it is another step in the education of an intellectual Everyman and as such is another link in Stern's chain. He said *A Father's Words* would be his last "family" novel and so far it has been.

1989: *Noble Rot, Stories 1949–1988*

Stern's work of collected short fiction includes the stories from *Teeth, 1968, Packages*, and four new stories including "Zhoof."

In "Zhoof" Stern finally has his bar mitzvah, albeit metaphorically. He has said the story is based on a true incident. The Stern surrogate is Powdermaker (who was born Pulvermacher but by his father changed the name in America). He is fiftyish, traveling through Germany and has never been too aware of his Jewishness. (In Chicago, it hadn't mattered much.) The American traveler — who, unknown to all he meets, speaks German, French, and Italian as well as English — bumps into a German man his age. The man tells Powdermaker in German, "First you burn us, then you ruin us." Powdermaker says nothing but thinks: "That he should say this to me, whose cousins could have been beaten to death by his uncles…" (*NR* 297). Still, Powdermaker thinks he has been insulted for being an American. At a restaurant, after he is asked by another stranger for a cigarette and says he doesn't smoke, Powdermaker is called "Filthy Yankee Liar." That night he can't sleep.

In Nuremburg, Powdermaker thinks of Hitler, Goerring, Hess, and how they came to be. On a train in a nonsmoking dining car where Powdermaker is sitting, a middle-aged couple enter, sit, then see the American and get up to leave.

> On their way back to the smoker's section, the couple passed him. The waiter followed, asking if anything was wrong. The woman said something which Powdermaker didn't hear, some sort of explanation. Still he felt nothing wrong, just faintly amused surprise. But it was enough to alert him, so that he heard the husband say, *"Zhoof."*
>
> In a second, Powdermaker had spelled this out, *"jouf"*; and in another, decided it was the harsh, pejorative version of *"juif."*
>
> He'd never heard or read the word, but he knew with certainty that the man had called him, Powdermaker, the equivalent of "kike." If there was any doubt, it disappeared when the wife said, "Shhh," and something else, and the husband responded, *"Mais il parle italien aussi."*

...Powdermaker felt as if his head had been sliced like a grapefruit and put on a plate. Everything cold in the universe poured into his decapitated trunk. His heart thumped, his hands shook the wineglass, perspiration rolled from his forehead and cheeks to the white tablecloth. He felt himself flushing, felt what he almost never felt, pure rage.... "No," he thought, "I can't dodge this." ...something had happened to the husband: he could not physically bear being close to Powdermaker. He'd dragged his wife away and given her the one-word explanation, *"Zhoof."* When she'd tried to quiet him and said, "At least speak Italian," The man said, "He also speaks Italian." (He'd heard Powdermaker talking [in Italian]..." [*NR* 301].

Son and grandson of assimilated German-Jewish burghers, his slogans were theirs: let sleeping dogs lie; don't cry over spilt milk. His father changed the name from Pulvermacher.... Young Arthur stayed out of school one day of two for Rosh Hashanah and Yom Kippur, but he was not bar mitzvahed. "Such nonsense isn't for us, why spend such money?" [*NR* 302].

...Powdermaker had spent his life posing.... Now, thanks to a twisted fellow, he'd been forced into that part of himself that he'd covered over, one it was necessary to recognize.... Only that way did you earn the right to be on the same earth with the Cézannes, the deepeners and sweeteners of life. As for haters, they existed oddly enough, to rouse the drugged souls of the world's Powdermakers [*NR* 304].

As the train pulled into Brussels ... the couple stood behind Powdermaker. When he got off, he looked behind. The woman looked at him, flushed, almost pleading. He gave her a small nod, a sympathetic nod. She understood [*NR* 305].

So did Stern, and through parable, so do his readers. The education continues.

1992: *Shares and Other Fictions*

> As I say, this Joycean sophistication came late and influenced only a few of my stories and books (Shares *and the forthcoming* Pacific Tremors).
>
> — Richard Stern

At age 64, Stern left behind familial intricacies and moved on to try something different. (At 73, he is no less inventive and curious, and retains an interest in everything.) The short novel in ten parts, *Shares*, is something of a return to the sparer and dryer Stern of the early short stories and the novels *Golk* and *Europe*. One may even see a bit of neoclassicism in comparison with the episodic stories of *The Canterbury Tales* and the *Decameron*. In the first few chapters, there is even a sense of midwestern small-town bucolic pastoral and a stripped simplicity of storytelling as fable and parable. (The first chapter is titled, "A Share of Nowheresville.") The reader learns quickly that these fables are tricks of insidious under- statement that amble along at a leisurely pace while dripping casual venom. The prose is not quite surreal and not quite as stream of consciousness as Stern asserts in the above quote, but one does sense that the thought process leading to this narrative may have been.

This author was reminded of Thornton Wilder's last two novels, *The Eighth Day* and *Theophilus North*. (While best known in the U. S. mainly for *Our Town* with his other work undeservedly neglected, Wilder is a deity in Europe and Russia with the latter voting *The Eighth Day* the great- est novel of the 20th century.) *The Eighth Day* starts in a small town and puts forth a pleasantly bucolic introduction that belies the coming dark complexity. *North* shares *Shares'* episodic nature, which Wilder said was inspired by Schliemann's uncovering of the nine cities of Troy that for *North* became the exposing of the nine cities of Newport (Rhode Island). One can see similar chapter titles from *North* to *Shares*. There is also the Wilder-written screenplay for Alfred Hitchcock's 1942 classic film *Shadow of a Doubt*. Hitchcock wanted to depict small-town America as a place that hides terrible secrets. Wilder does the same in his 1953 one-act play, *Rivers Under the Earth*, the title referring to the dark currents underlying "normal" conversation.

Wilder and Stern uncover the differences between the American dream and the American dreamer. The dream is more myth than reality, while the dreamer wishes it were more reality than myth and still hopes for a salvation that isn't there. Then, rather than admit that that hope may only be illusion, the dreamer obfuscates truth to match the surface sheen of an American scene that is often just a transparent bubble that can be burst at the slightest provocation.

While *1968, Other Men's Daughters, Packages,* and *Natural Shocks* can be considered influenced by the debris of the Nixon-Watergate era (*A Father's Words* is transitional), *Shares* takes aim at the Reagan years. Dur- ing the 1980s, Reagan said it was morning in America. Another cultural icon of the period was Bruce Springsteen who, in an angry response to Rea- gan using his name at a campaign stop in 1984, said it was "Midnight in America." Springsteen's 1984 album *Born in the U.S.A.* was a hard-bitten depiction of the country's dark side under Reaganomics. In *Shares*, Stern's political operative Robert Share remembers the presidents he's worked for:

> The presidents he'd know all interested him. The most complicated one
> was not of a piece with himself. When he should've been happy, he wasn't,
> and vice versa. In time the country came down on him [Nixon]. Share had

gotten out early, just after Schultz. In his years of public life he'd never felt so tired. "Robert's exhausted," the president said, and let him go.

This president [Reagan] was the simplest, the strangest, and the luckiest. He'd never seen such a lucky fellow. A voice, a presence, a joke barrel, he had the shine of celebrity, a variety of grand smiles. He looked like a pushover, was almost Italian in his hatred of making a bad impression, yet had the wit to make himself the butt of stories. Lazy, a poseur, full of obvious contradiction, the man went against the grain of everything he preached and no one spotted it. The only one he cared about was his wife. Tight as a drum, lazy as a lion, capable of winking at everything he spouted. It was unfair to dismiss him as an actor. (Shakespeare was an actor.) He showed his movies at the White House. Share had seen the most famous one: the father of his girlfriend is a sadistic surgeon who amputates the boy's legs. He showed that one over and over. The sadistic father, the crippled son. Wasn't his father a drunk and an outsider — a Catholic in Waspland who felt isolated and took up for minorities and was saved from disintegration by doing local political work for Franklin Roosevelt? The boy sent fifty dollars a month home when he was putting himself through school. Not bad. Aeneas carrying Anchises out of Troy. Then whom does he marry but a surgeon's stepdaughter, herself a deserted child who'd been disowned by — as she later disowned — her father?

The man was not stupid. There was some theatrical gallantry there too, and God knows, persistence and physical confidence. He'd been spotted by California money men who'd turned his tax delinquency into million-dollar LA holdings. They thought they'd ride him into the White House, and, in a way, they did; but you don't really ride these fellows. Once they've been in the world spotlight for a month, they become uncontrollable.

The national curse: news hunger. There had to be something interesting every day. Only personality could carry that cross. Since what was interesting there was its ups and downs, conflict and scandal, the government was swiss-cheesed to death.

He [Reagan] had been lucky so far. So far, no tail had been pinned on him [*SH* 132–33].

Stern's view of the Reagan era sets up the sense of how the public's shallow preference for "personality" over substance allows actors to "act" presidential (or in some other role) and pull the wool over the public's eyes.

Shares is about two brothers and how their tails do not quite get pinned either. George Share is from Willsville (Nowheresville), Illinois. "Now Willsville is the only place within a couple of hundred miles where the world's best old films can be seen, where there is a complete file of the *New York Review of Books*, a twenty year file of *Hudson and Partisan Reviews*, *Art News*, *Paris Match* and *Der Spiegel*. All this can be found in the Share Complex — six rooms of George Share's nine-room house. Here there are books recommended by *The New York Times*, the *Times Literary*

Supplement, and those George finds in European and American book-stores" (*SH* 111–12). George is Willsville's culture maven, spreading the profits of his shoe store to the locals in the form of the accumulated materials he houses and in his "discussion-recital room dominated by a Baldwin Grand piano…" (SH 112). He's been written up in the news as *"The Shoe Store Plato"* (*SH* 112). George even has a Fellowship program where he escorts young people for his annual seven weeks a year in Europe. What a guy! Except that the young people are always young women that "he'd met in the Share Film Club, the Share Library, the Share Museum, or one of the other institutions he'd formed in order to meet them" (*SH* 114). Luckily for George (bribes may have helped), "All but one of the Companions, Alicia Venerdy, had left Willsville" (134). He almost got into trouble once, but Alicia, one of the first fellows, defends him against the town's whispers. She marries Mr. Venerdy, has a daughter, and 20 years later June Bug becomes the next Share Fellow. Alicia doesn't resist the idea.

Robert Share is George's older brother. He is known for his unemotional stolidity. His daughter Obie writes him angry letters about his working for a U.S. government that does terrible things. To start with he was in Vietnam, bombing the enemy. In the present, he visits "The Wall," the Vietnam Memorial, but feels little of the emotional impact common to other visitors. He still works for the government and this prevents his emotional involvement in policies that kill. Obie has never gotten over her father's tacit involvement with the government's deadly policies; but really, she has never gotten over a childhood slight, and the memory of it is heightened when her eight-year-old son Wyn also endures an inadvertent slight. This prompted the latest letter, and the cause and effect is apparent.

Robert's son Reg shows up in later chapters and he is angry as hell with his father with a terrible seething vitriol that is frightening for its sudden intrusion into the ambling pace. Why? Dad was just too busy to ever make time for him. His career came first.

George's "career" also comes first and he takes June Bug to Venice: "An odd town, Venice has always drawn oddities to itself. Feel displaced, unwanted, unappreciated, come to Venice. Too contemptuous, indolent or poor to wash, shave or dress in one of the ninety more or less acceptable modes of the day, come to Venice. Want your nullity glamorized, your vacuity filled, your stupidity mistaken for wit, your silence for sagacity, come to *la serenissima.* Bums, thieves, con men, frauds, every kind of poseur and viper, they're all in this beautiful, watery zoo" (*SH* 143). George fits right in. He and June Bug meet some very strange characters to back up the above description — refugees from anonymity who have nothing to offer except their own desperation to get attention somehow.

Shares is not easy — it challenges by throwing together chapters that may not seem related until one considers that the narratives underscore ideas that are related by cause and effect. There are the actions and reactions of parents and children with the behaviors of the latter influenced by the former. There is the chase for approval and recognition with results that can lead to tragedy. There are the causes of governments and their effects on people, domestic and foreign. *Shares'* main issue of cause and effect is that the burghers are blind to the causes and effects and by omission allow them to continue. Stern's tone in *Shares* will be replicated by future representations in American films from 1997 to 2001 that uncover the hidden misery to be found in "Nowheresville, U.S.A." These include *American Beauty, Tumbleweeds, Happiness, Wonder Boys,* and *The Contender.*

1995: *A Sistermony*

Stern made up a word to connote his relationship with his sister Ruth when she was dying of cancer. This nonfiction memoir drawn from Stern's journals won the Heartland Prize for best nonfiction book. In it there are Stern's ruminations during the remaining days that touch on both living and dying. Included are photos of Stern with friends and family. For anyone who has endured the slow dying of a loved one, the book will be an understanding companion of mutual commiseration. No analysis is required.

EPILOGUE

Aún Aprendo
(Always Learning)

2001 (or 2002): *Pacific Tremors* (novel) and *What Is What Was* (essays)

In the previous chapter, it was noted that Stern entered an avuncular uncle stage in 1978 at age 50. In the 1990s it would be fair to say "elder statesman among men of letters" was a suitable title for him and still is in the next century. He has been described by Hungarian Professor Sorin Antohi [whom Stern met at Stanford where both where visiting fellows] as a "courtly gentleman" who seems more suited to an earlier time of civility, gentility, and solicitousness for those with whom he comes in contact.

If one peruses the latter part of the bibliography that follows, one sees that many segments of his novel *Pacific Tremors* have appeared in distinguished journals such as the *Antioch* and *Yale Reviews*. Stern worked on it for five years from 1995, but would interrupt himself to plunge into different fiction and essays that seemed to be more urgent and *had* to be written about. During the academic year of 1999-2000 Stern was a fellow at the Center for Advanced Studies in the Behavioral Sciences at Stanford and says in his preface to *Pacific Tremors*, "Much of this book was [written there] and is gratefully, affectionately and nostalgically dedicated to the Genial fellows of that year...."

Then he remembers an old friend: "I also wish to acknowledge my dear friend from Chapel Hill days [the poet] Edgar Bowers who introduced me to California in 1964 and who died in San Francisco on Feb. 4, 2000 in his 76th year."

In his role as fellow, Stern was required to address his fellow fellows with a paper or a viable substitute. In April 2000, he chose to read a chapter from *Pacific Tremors*, which is about California and movies — the great fantasy-world of American life — and how all of this light and sound show really comes down to people — naked when they are born and more so when they die. He read from the chapter "Audit."

> Spear did not think of himself as an avaricious man. Lord knows he could be generous, easily to his granddaughter, Jennifer, and, under pressure of his super-ego, even to causes. It was just that after the death of his wife and the consequent, though still baffling, estrangement from Amelia, Jennifer's mother, money became a sort of companion to him, or, sometimes, more child than his child. The nurture and growth of his modest fortune brought both tension and ease, and, though he knew this was absurd, if not shameful and vulgar, pride.
>
> Every morning, a minute or two after waking, he pressed the memory buttons on the bedside phone, which summoned the electronic voices which reported the status of his brokerage accounts and mutual funds. Now and then, a glitch in the reporting system filled him with anxiety and fury until he reached a live voice which assured him that, no, there had been no overnight embezzlement of his holdings.
>
> When, in August, 1991, a letter from the Treasury Department informed him that he was subject to tax audit, he felt a terror unlike anything he'd known since Vanessa's death. Why, after all the placid, solitary years in his Malibu Canyon cabin, had he been singled out?
>
> The letter was personalized to the extent of specifying the year the IRS was auditing — 1989 — and the area of its concern, his Contributions and Business Expenses. It also indicated the place and time of the audit — the Federal Building on Los Angeles Street — and the auditor's sinisterly comic name, G. Whipp.

Spear will, indeed, be "Whipped" in a humorous account of Everyman's nightmare audit.

Aun Aprendo was a favorite expression of Aldous Huxley who believed "always learning" was man's first purpose and that sharing his knowledge was the second. This applies to Richard Stern. Stern's art was his education and it challenged him to be new and different with every effort. What he's learned, he's shared. And often he has been ahead of the curve in anticipating cultural currents that have become subjects for later writers to expand on. He has recorded the temper of his times, and in the future, readers will better understand these times by reading him.

Richard Stern:
An Interview

Izzo: In *Golk, Natural Shocks,* and "Inside Narcissus" in particular (and other fiction, essays in general), there is a prescient forecasting of the trend toward invasive and celebrity driven media, which for the public is often a vicarious counter to the fear of anonymity or a living death that reminds one of actual death, which one does not want to be reminded of. Put these works in a current perspective and how do you evaluate current trends such as "reality" TV, i.e. "Survivor"?

Stern: As population increases and individuals feel themselves statistically categorized and pigeonholed more and more, their hunger for individuality, the uncategorizable, grows. Watching people whom they regard as behavioral extremists or as normal people pushed to behavioral extremes, they are eased by both risk and security, others' risk, their security. Each excess extends the boundaries of extremity and looks like freedom, a larger possibility for everyone. That so much is the junky sexual and violent static of the ages matters little to people still raised — even by hippies — along standard, if not Victorian, lines. One job of writers is to both display and to analyze such behavior and sentiment in ways that amuse and deepen, supplying the mental freedom, power and delight which have truly extended boundaries.

Izzo: Your answer resonates particularly in this study's readings of *Natural Shocks* and *Shares.* Of the latter, you give one of the most concise descriptions — from one side of a perspective — of President Reagan. He seems the logical "joke" on a celebrity-driven public. What motivated this description and the writing of *Shares* overall?

Stern: Anything that's not part of the central narrative is usually part of the day's flow. I'm sure that's the case with the Reagan bit — I don't remember it at all, which is indicative. If there's a motif about celebrity-madness, that's part of the flow — though it is part of the Stern palette and may well get on canvasses in different strokes and colors.

I do remember that I did want to see the novella (*Veni, Vide, Wendt* from *1968*) back in print. Then I had other stories and when I found out how to do *Shares*, which had been a full-length and pretty ordinary novel in "pieces," it looked then as if I had a pretty decent and varied narrative grab-bag. The main character of *Shares* was an ex-shoe man I'd met in Venice where he'd settled. As a soldier in World War II, this midwestern high school grad had fallen in love with Europe and decided to save enough to live there, and did after decades of hard work selling shoes. He'd mis-calculated the rate of inflation so pieced out his income by renting out rooms to visiting scholars, writers, intellectuals. (He lived with an Italian woman who was a professional translator.) He died of cancer a few years ago. I enjoyed seeing him in his nice apartment on the grand canal sur-rounded by piles of the TLS and other intellectual paraphernalia.

Izzo: In 1960–61 you blame an "impoverished Jewishness" for your resistance to writing in a manner that might have labeled you a Jewish writer. You also back off at that time and move towards at least a modified recognition of being in that group. Where does the story "Wanderers" fit into this transition? Ezra Pound? Do you see your sense of Jewishness as having evolved from that time?

Stern: No one likes his individuality threatened and thus possibly ignored by category. My experience as a Jew differed more from that of many writers I knew (Bellow, Malamud, P. Roth, Mailer) and knew about (Salinger, Henry Roth) than theirs, I thought, did from each other. (Mine was somewhat closer to Salinger's: we grew up in similar neighborhoods, both went to boys' "groups" — of one of his stories, title forgotten, about a counselor who tells a frightening story which relates to his love life.) Any-way, since I wasn't bar mitzvah-ed (I learned from my sister the year of her death that my grandfather had died and it wasn't necessary or worth the money), and was only allowed to stay home one of two days for the two big holy days, and since my Sunday school experience was short and trivial (I memorized only two Hebrew phrases for all the hours), and since I, like almost all my relatives, had secular contempt — or, a least, worldly disregard — for rituals and most religious "foolishness," the label Jewish Writer didn't seem adequate to me. The story "Wanderers" and, much later, "Zhoof," testify to a lifelong interest in the matter. I did respond fairly fully to the famous Commentary questionnaire to the younger Jewish intellectuals and writers. (I remember [Philip] Roth waiting till he'd read mine and others before answering his, and I thought that canny of him.) In *The Dortmunds* [a work in progress], I am now writing more fully about my own experience as an American Jew of German and Hungarian descent, and throughout my work there is at least slight attention to that part of my many Jewish characters. (See the piece/speech in *The Books in Fred Hampton's Apartment* given to the Chicago Synagogue about my "discovery" that the characters in *Golk* were probably Jews.) Because of my Jewishness, I took an especial interest in anti–Semitism. I've read much about Hitler (again, see "Zhoof," which, incidentally, is based on an actual experience), and Pound was particularly interesting to me because of that. I've written too much about that to repeat here. (The essay in *What Is What Was?* [Stern's forthcoming fifth essay collection] will be the fullest explanation: it's a slight expansion of the one published in *Sewanee Review* about three years ago.)

Izzo: In discussing "Zhoof," I say that, metaphorically, you finally had your bar mitzvah. Speaking of Pound you have said that teaching his *Cantos* impacted your dramatic shift in technique for *1968*, which this study calls a dense prose poetry of word-by-word significance. What were you aiming for?

Stern: I believe that the rapid, shifty, packed prose and the sophisticated intellectual attitude it expresses relate to my experience with Pound (including a course I gave in his work the year I returned to Chicago from Rome, Venice, Cambridge). *Stitch* is another — earlier, in some ways, better in others — work which registers the influence of Pound's *Cantos* — as well as Pound himself — on my prose. (The poem, "Venetians," [in *The Invention of the Real*] is another Poundian product.)

Izzo: Natural Shocks is another shift in writing style with its rapid-fire one-liners. Do you recall how this came about? Was it conscious?

Stern: I think it was a "natural" development of my prose and the thinking behind it. For Pound, poetry, *Dichtung* out of *dichten* (condense), should say much in little, and I wanted prose to do that as well. Stendhal was more influential than Pound here, but I've looked at college papers (one on Aristotle) which I wrote at 17, and the prose there too is concise, quite clear, and "packed," so this goes pretty deep in me.

Izzo: This study uses the term "set pieces" to describe segments in which you seem to posit ideas or arguments and then use narrative or dialogue (or both) to play them out. Among them are the Five Stages of Golks, the discussion of the novel between Baggish and Juliette, in *Europe*, the story "The Counterfactual Proposition," the dialogue about art with Edward and Nina in *Stitch,* and the Flashback to Hamish Blick in *Natural Shocks.* Were you intending to make cases for certain ideas or did the writing process lead to ideas that then provoked you to develop the ideas as cases?

Stern: Very good question, very difficult, probably impossible for me, to answer. I know that I want as varied a mental texture in these short books and stories as possible, which doesn't mean departing from the essential key structure. So after one sort of scene, you have a different sort. I think the writer feels this more than thinks it out. I do remember thinking that *Europe* looked and felt so "light" and "casually formed," that if I commented on its structure from within — and comically — I would be supplying the "weight" it needed. Still I worried about those exchanges, though less so after [Saul] Bellow said they were his favorite part of the book. (The book, though, was probably his least favorite of mine.)

Izzo: Does Bellow have a favorite Stern book? Or Philip Roth for that matter? Or any other contemporary authors that come to mind? How about Richard Stern? Does he have a hierarchy of his work?

Stern: I do think certain work is less meaty (say, *Europe* or certain stories) but I like to think that each work, almost each little review, was thought about and worked over pretty well. There are a few "inspired sections." (The last pages of *Stitch,* the last paragraphs of "The Illegibility of This World," in *Shares and Other Fictions,* some of *In Any Case.*) But I don't like to single them out. I prefer not to talk of the Bellow-Roth favorites: Bellow was hot on *Golk* because it was new to him; he loved "Packages," story and book, and with *Noble Rot* went out of his way to say he thought I had cornered part of the market in short fiction. Roth is very fond of certain stories, one is "The Girl Who loved Shubert," and he always calls the real-life model for Yntema by that name, and he liked all of *1968.*

Izzo: "Packed" is the word you use for your prose. Auden, one of your earliest literary influences, also "packed" his poems, particularly those from the years 1930 up to his first *Collected Poems* of 1944. (Your essay "With Auden" is quoted in this study so readers know the basis of this question.) Reaction?

Stern: Auden's swiftness, phraseological brilliance and ability to make the complex icily clear and quick probably got into my writing soul, but I've never thought of him as an influence — though as you see from the essay, he was very important to me at age 19.

Izzo: In looking at your fiction (and essays) in a single block read over months rather than as they came out over 40 years, this study identified themes that prevail. I have defined them in Sternian terms and given examples from your work. Now, I will — with no advance notice — throw the words out like flash cards for you to respond to, and the answers need not be solely in context of your art:

Stern: Routine: routine is ordinary happiness; departure from routine can bring sublimity or terror.
   Randomization: art is the trust that 'things will come to you' and that anything can be grist for your mill.
   Reversals: the stuff of narrative and pace — Aristotle — dramatic power.
   Revelations: they must earn the surprise that is the emotional frosting (or layer of ice cream in the chocolate cake).
   Redemption: a marvelous human pattern, and although I just read that humans have only 300 genes not shared by a mouse, it is one thing so profoundly and originally human, that the separation from the genomic egalitarianism via those 300 genes make one admire and wonder at again the fantastic economy of creation.

Izzo: Auden is a mutual hero of ours; Aldous Huxley is also on my list. Huxley loved to borrow a phrase from the painter Goya who, when asked how he could still be so innovative in his eighties, answered *Aun Aprendo* (always learning). This became Huxley's modus operandi for all his endeavors. I was thinking of Huxley and *aun aprendo* when I began this book and chose the title accordingly: *The Writings of Richard Stern: The Education of an Intellectual Everyman.* You still have no end of fascination with the human comedy; yet, there is a child-in-the-adult fascination that you bring to all of this triumph and folly. Where have you been? Where are you going?

Stern: On the brink of 73, I still feel childlike about learning, and learning is one of the wondrous gifts the universe has given us. As to Huxley, I adored *Point Counter Point,* which I read at 15 — it opened up the world of "culture" in a great way, but when I started seriously writing in my early twenties, Huxley was one of the people (Forster, a better, novelist, was another) whom I did *not* want to be like. I thought he [Huxley] depended too much on knowledge. I wanted my creations to be somehow able to sustain themselves in their own planetary systems. I may well have been and continue to be unfair to Huxley. I did read and reread many of his essays a few years ago (Nick, my youngest son, gave me a book of them for a birthday) and I did like them very much. He was a wonderful essayist;

the learning there was at home. It unleashed his own high intelligence. In the novels, the characters "unleashed" were "leashed"—like Spandrell [in *Point Counter Point*]—too closely to the positions they more or less represented—or contradicted. Recently, I reread what had been—at 19 and 21—a favorite book, Mann's *Magic Mountain*. I was very disappointed to find this Huxleyan defect so conspicuous there as well. (Though Mann's a much greater writer.) There are a few Huxley stories—ones in Italy, I recall, ["Little Mexican,"] which are "freer," and stronger. He would have been great to know. The scenes in Robert Craft's writings on Stravinsky between Huxley and Stravinsky (like those between Auden and Stravinsky), point to peaks of cultured civility.

Notes

1. "The Guilty Vicarage," *The Dyer's Hand.* New York: Random House, 1962, p. 158.
2. "Musée des Beaux Arts," *Collected Poems.* New York: Random House, p. 146.
3. *Nathaniel Hawthorne: A Biography.* New York: Oxford UP, 1980, p. 7.
4. *The Power of Blackness.* New York: Vintage Books, 1958, p. 47.
5. "Poets, Poetry, and Taste," *The English Auden.* New York: Random House, 1977, p. 359.
6. "Psychology and Criticism," *The English Auden.* New York: Random House, 1977, p. 357.
7. *Shares.* Harrison, N.Y.: Delphinium Books, 1992, Dust Jacket.
8. "The Individual Life of Man," *The Human Situation.* New York: Harper's, 1977, p. 108.
9. "Preface," *A Certain World.* New York: Viking, 1970, pp. vii–viii.
10. "Tragedy and the Whole Truth," *Music at Night.* London: Chatto & Windus, 1931, p. 12.
11. Ibid. pp. 14–15.
12. "Poets, Poetry, and Taste," *The English Auden.* New York: Random House, 1977, 329.
13. *Lions and Shadows.* London: Hogarth Press, 1938, pp. 173–74.
14. "Knowledge and Understanding," *Tomorrow and Tomorrow and Tomorrow.* New York: Harper's, 1956, p. 33.
15. *Richard Stern.* New York: Twayne's United States Authors Series, 1993, p. 43.
16. "Squares and Oblongs," *Poets at Work.* New York: Harcourt, Brace, 1948, pp. 166–71.
17. Waggoner, Hyatt, *The Presence of Hawthorne.* Baton Rouge: Louisiana State UP, 1979, p. 106.
18. Wilder, Thornton, *The Eighth Day.* New York: Harper's, 1967, p. 435.
19. "Dyer's Hand," *Anchor Review.* New York: Doubleday Anchor Books, 1957, p. 266.
20. When Branch Rickey, the man who brought Jackie Robinson to the Brooklyn Dodgers in 1947 and integrated major-league baseball, was told that he had been "lucky" in that Robinson turned out to be such a good choice, he responded, "luck is the residue of design."

21. "Great Pain from Gain," Sacramento Bee, June 4 2000, p. A2.

22. "Interview with W. H. Auden," *Writers at Work: Paris Review Interviews, Fourth Series.* New York: Viking, 1976, p. 245.

23. Schiffer, James. *Richard Stern.* New York: Twayne's United States Authors Series, 1993, p. 157.

24. Ibid. p. 157.

25. Dust Jacket, *Golk.* London: MacGibbon & Kee, 1960.

26. "Writing," *The Dyer's Hand.* New York: Random House, 1962, p. 19.

27. Schiffer, James. *Richard Stern.* New York: Twayne's United States Authors Series, 1993, p. 157.

28. *A Single Man.* New York: Simon and Schuster, 1964, p. 160.

29. AE. *A Song and Its Fountains.* London: MacMillan, 1932, pp. 8–9.

30. Ibid. p. 9.

31. Ibid. p. 19.

32. "Sermons in Cats," *Music at Night.* London: Chatto & Windus, 1931, pp. 267–68.

33. "Introduction," *Texts and Pretexts.* London: Chatto & Windus, 1932, p. 4.

34. "Review of *Open House*" (Roethke), *Saturday Review of Literature*, April 5, 1941, p. 30.

35. As quoted in Ellmann, Richard, and Robert O'Clair, eds. *The Norton Anthology of Modern Poetry.* Second Edition. New York: Norton, 1973, p. 376.

36. As quoted in Ibid. p. 377.

37. *Down There On a Visit.* New York: Simon and Schuster, 1962, p. 39.

38. *The Prolific and the Devourer*, Hopewell, N.J.: Ecco Press, 1993, p. 10.

39. Dust jacket, *Other Men's Daughters.* New York: Dutton, 1973.

40. "An Old Writer Looks at Himself," *New York Times.*

Richard Stern Bibliography

1948

Two poems, *Factotum*. Spring 1948.

1953

SHORT STORIES

"The Sorrows of Captain Schreiber," *Western Review*. Summer. Vol. 17, Iowa City: State University of Iowa: 260–271; reprinted, *Prize Stories of 1954: The O. Henry Collection*. Doubleday: NY 1955.

"Cooley's Version," *Kenyon Review* 16.2 (Spring 1954): 257–267. Ed. Gambier, O. Kenyon College

ARTICLE REVIEW

"Pound as Translator." Rev. of *The Spirit of Romance*, by Ezra Pound. *Accent* Autumn, ed. by Daniel Curley, George Scouffas and Charles Shattuck. Urbana, University of Illinois Press: 265–267.

REVIEW

"A Critique of Rilke." Rev. of *Rainer Moria Rilke: A Study of His Later Poetry*, by Hans Holthusen. *Poetry* 82.6 (September 1953) ed. H. Monroe, Chicago.

1955

SHORT STORIES

"Good Morrow, Swine," *Accent* (Spring 1955): 108–110. ed. by Daniel Curley, George Scouffas and Charles Shattuck. Urbana: University of Illinois Press;

to be reprinted in *Anthology of World Literature*, eds. Kenner, H. and others
(John Wiley and Co.).
"After the Illuminations," *Western Review* Vol. 19, Spring, Iowa City: State Uni-
versity of Iowa: 167–181.

POETRY

Translations from Baudelaire and Rimbaud in *Reading Modern Poetry*, eds. Engle
and Carrier. Chicago: Scott, Foresman and Co.

1956

SHORT STORY

"Arrangements at the Gulf," *Epoch* (Fall), Epoch Associates, Cornell University,
Ithaca; reprinted in *Midland*. Random House. 1958.

POETRY

"Eunuch, Spectator and Pupil," *Chicago Review* (Winter), University of Chicago;
reprinted *Chicago Review Anthology*. Ed. Ray, David. University of Chicago Press.

ARTICLE

"Proust and Joyce Underway: Jean Santeuil and Stephen Hero," *Kenyon Review*
(Summer), 486–96.

REVIEWS

"Picaresque Extra Cuvée." Rev. of *Confessions of Felix Krull: Confidence Men*, by
Thomas Mann. *Western Review* (Spring) 1956: 251–253.
"The Poetry of Donald Hall," *Chicago Review* (Spring).

1957

EDITED

American Poetry of the Fifties, *Western Review Vol. 21*, Spring 1957, pp. 164–238.

ARTICLES AND REVIEWS

"PNIN and the Dust Jacket." Rev. of *PNIN,* by Vladimir Nabokov. *Prairie Schooner*
31.2 (Summer): 161–164.
"A Note on Aldo Palazzeschi." *Western Review Vol. 22* (Autumn 1957): 61.

Rev. of *The Fugitives* by John Bradbury. *Modern Philology* (November 1958): 142–144.

"The Poetry of Edgar Bowers." *Chicago Review* 2.3 (Autumn 1957): 69–75.

TRANSLATION

"...est" from Palazzeschi's "...issima," with Noce, *Western Review* (Fall).

1958

SHORT STORIES

"Nine Letters, Twenty Days," *Western Review* (Fall).

"Toujours l'audace," *Gent* (September) rewritten without author's consent by editor.

REVIEW

"A Perverse Fiction." Rev. of *By love possessed*, by James Gould Cozzens. *Kenyon Review 20.1* (Winter) 1958: 140–144.

TRANSLATION

From Mallarmé and Appollinaire in *Anthology of French Poetry from Nerval to Valery*, ed. Flores. Anchor Books.

1959

SHORT STORY

"The Assessment of an Amateur," *Kenyon Review* 21.2 (Spring): 250–259; reprinted *Town*. London, 1964; (Longwood Foundation Award); tr. Spanish *(Los Papeles de Majorca)*.

ARTICLES AND REVIEWS

"Dr. Zhivago as a Novel." Rev. of *Doctor Zhivago*, by Boris Pasternak. *Kenyon Review* 21.1 (Winter 1959): 154–160; reprinted *The Technique of Composition*, 5th ed. Rhinehart. NY. 1960.

"Lillian Hellman on her Plays," *Contact* 3 (1959): 113–119.

"A Poet's Self-Portrait." Rev. of *Life Studies*, by Robert Lowell. *Commentary* (Sep 1959): 272–274.

"Henderson's Bellow." Rev. of *Henderson The Rain King*, by Saul Bellow. *Kenyon Review 21.4* (Autumn): 655–661.

"Hip, Hell and the Navigator," *Western Review*, 23.2; reprinted in Mailer, *Advertisements for Myself*.

1960

NOVEL

Golk. New York: Criterion Books; New York: Meridian (1961); London: Macgibbon and Kee; Penguin Books (1963); Rome: Bompiani; Copenhagen: Wangels Forlag (in Book Club edition) Nominee Pulitzer Prize.

SHORT STORIES

"Two Talking," *Big Table* 5 (Spring).
"Gardiner's Legacy," *Noble Savage* 11.

REVIEW

"*A Ballad of Love* by Prokosch." Rev. of *A ballad of love,* by Frederic Prokosch. *New York Times* (Oct. 30, 1960).

1961

NOVEL

Europe, or Up and Down with Schreiber and Baggish, New York: McGraw-Hill; London: Macgibbon and Kee; Penguin Books (1966).

TRANSLATIONS

From Rilke and Montale in *December* (Winter).
"La Giugliottina a Vapore of Giusti," *Noble Savage* 111.

ARTICLES AND REVIEWS

"This Same Pain, This Same Pleasure: An Interview with Ralph Ellison," *December*, (Winter); reprinted *Shadow and Act*, Ellison and in anthologies.
Reviews of Heller, *Catch-22*, *New York Times*; Mauriac, *The Frontenacs* and Brooks, *From the Shadow of the Mountain*, *Chicago Sun-Times*.

SYMPOSIUM CONTRIBUTION

"Jewishness and the Younger Intellectuals," *Commentary*, (April), 356–8.

1962

NOVEL

In Any Case. New York: McGraw Hill and McGraw Hill Paperbacks; Macgibbon and Kee and (1971) Penguin Books: London Friends of Literature Award; Nominee National Book Award.

ARTICLES AND REVIEWS

"A Valentine for Chicago," *Harpers* (Feb.) ; reprinted *Chicago Sun-Times*; reprinted in part in *Chicago*, edited Wade and Mayer. University of Chicago Press.
Reviews of Gilbert Highet's *Anatomy of Satire, Sat. Review of Literature* (Sep.).
Of Emmet John Hughes', *Ordeal of Power, Times*, London (Sept.).
Article-review on John Updike, *Spectator*, London (Sept. 27).

SHORT STORIES

"Teeth," in *Partisan Review* (Fall); *Encounter* (Jan. '64); tr. in French, *Preuves* (Oct. '63).
"A Counterfactual Proposition," *Transatlantic Review* No. 14 (Autumn 1963): 128–134.

1964

COLLECTION

Teeth, Dying and Other Matters. New York: Harper and Row; Macgibbon and Kee; includes play *The Gamesman's Island* and article on Kennedy and Nixon.

SHORT STORIES

"Orvieto Dominos, Bolsena Eels," *Harpers* (June); tr. for *La Revue Du Poche*, 1966.
"Wanderers." *Partisan Review* No. 17 (Summer): 122–133; reprinted *Transatlantic Review*.

ARTICLES AND REVIEWS

A. Miller and J.G. Cozzens for *Encyclopedia Britannica*.

1965

NOVEL

Stitch, New York: Harper and Row; London: Hodder and Stoughton; Pan Books, 1966.
One of Year's 10 best books: American Library Association.

ARTICLES

"Faulkner at Home Abroad." *Books Abroad* 39: 4 (1965): 408–411.
"Flannery O'Connor: A Remembrance and Some Letters," *Shenandoah* 6.2, (Winter 1965): 5–10. Letters reprinted in Flannery O'Connor's *The Habit of Being*, ed. S. Fitzgerald.

Poems

"Venetians," *College English* 26.7 (1965): 566–567.
"Gus's Guidecca," *Caravella*, Venice and NY; reprinted in *Anon*. 1970.

Translations

From Char and Jaccottet in *Contemporary French Poetry*, ed. Aspel and Justice. University of Michigan.
From Catalan poems of Joan Brossa with Pilar Rotella in *Chicago Review* 17.4 (Spring).
From German of H. Böll, with Stefan Schultz, *Chicago Review* (Spring).

1966

Edited

Honey and Wax, the Powers and Pleasures of Narrative. Chicago: University of Chicago Press; Phoenix Books (1969).

Articles and Reviews

"Report from the MLA," *New York Review of Books*, Feb. 17.
Review of Capote's *In Cold Blood, Chicago Daily News*.

1967

Statement

"The Artist-in-Residence: Fact or Fancy." *Arts in Society* 13.4 (Summer 1966): 488.
Autobiographical sketch for *World Authors.*
Interview of Richard Stern by Robert Raeder, *Chicago Review* Vol. 18, No. 3–4 (Spring-Summer 1966):170–175.

Articles

"Yarmolinsky and the Cannibal," *The Nation*, Dec. 12.
Editorials for *Nation*, "Dec. 2" (reprinted *Minneapolis Tribune* and *University of Chicago Magazine*); on McCarthy and Press; on Mao, Malraux and Students; on Chicago Convention Aftermath; on Clark and Daley

Reviews

"Farming the Tundra." Rev. of *Division Street: America*, by Studs Terkel. *Nation* Jan. or Feb.; of Pound/Joyce; Reck's *Pound*; of *Couples* and Rogers' *Pursuit of Happiness* for *Chicago Sun-Times* and *Book Week*.

Symposium

Remarks in *The Arts and the Public*. Ed. Miller and Herring. University of Chicago Press.

1968; 1969

Articles

"Events, Happenings, Credibility, Fictions." *Yale Review* (Summer 1968): 577–585; reprinted in *American Literature Anthology 111*, (1970) ed. Plimpton, New York: Viking. National Humanities Award in Criticism.
"Borges on Borges," *American Scholar* (Summer 1969) (translated in Latin America, 1978).
"On Johnson's Library," *Encounter* (March 1969).

Short Story

"Milius and Melanie," *Hudson Review* 21.3 (Autumn 1968): 487–504.

Play Scenes

From *Dossier: Earth, Twenty-Four Blackouts from the Middle Electric Age* (commissioned by Lincoln Center Repertory Theater in '66, written Summer '66) in *Chicago Today*.

Poems

"Marleniad," and "Song for Instant Knights," in Chicago *Maroon* (Feb. and March '68).
National Institute for Arts and Letters Award (for fiction), 1968; Award, National Foundation on Arts and Humanities, 1969; Rockefeller Award for Fiction, 1967.

1970

Book: Novella and Stories

1968, A Short Novel, An Urban Idyll, Five Stories and Two Trade Notes. New York: Holt, Rhinehart and Winston; London: Gollancz,1971; story tr. In *Les Lettres Nouvelles*, 1971.

Poems

In *American Scholar* (Fall, 1970); "Sestina at Trenta-Due," *Transatlantic Review* vol. *37–38* (Autumn-Winter 1970–71): 126–128.

ARTICLES-REVIEWS

"The Books in Fred Hampton's Apartment," *Nation*, Dec. '69.
"A Memory of Forster." *Nation* 29 June 1970: 795–796.
"Mies and the Closing of the Bauhaus." *Nation* 22 Sep 1969: 290.
Of I. Gold's *Sick Friends. New York Times*, (Oct. '69).

NOVELLA

"Veni, Vidi. Wendt," *Paris Review* 49 (1970):82–151.
Reviews of books on Mailer, Eliot's *Waste Land* ms., Malamud's *The Tenants* and
    sports book, *Chicago Daily News, Book World.*

1972

POEM

"Above the Snow," in *The Carleton Miscellany* 7.1 (Fall/Winter 1971–72): 78.
Reviews of Edel's *James* in *Encounter* (and *Chicago Daily News*); of Morris's *Inti-
    mate Behavior,* Choron's *Suicide,* Litwak and Wilner's *College Days in Earth-
    quake Country,* and Kenner's *The Pound Era* in *Chicago Daily News*; of
    Malraux, *Fallen Oaks*; of Wyndham Lewis, *Drawings and Paintings.*

IMAGINARY INTERVIEW

"Aurelia Frequenza Reveals the Heart and Mind of the Man of Destiny," *Paris
    Review* 66 (1976): 117–122.

1973

Reviews in *Chicago Daily News* of the following books:
Cochrane, *Florence In The Forgotten Centuries.*
Braudel, *The Mediterranean* etc. Vol. 1.
Mailer, *Marilyn.*
Brandon, *The Retreat of American Power.*
Langer, *Mind.* 11.
A Supplement to the *OED.*
(Interviews with and articles about Stern in various publications, in connection
    with lectures in Asia and Europe, summer of 1973, and with publication of
    Fred Hampton and *Other Men's Daughters*).
Guggenheim Fellowship: 1973–4

1973; 1974

The Books in Fred Hampton's Apartment. New York: E.P. Dutton; London: Hamish
    Hamilton, 1974.

Various reviews (of *Hesse* in *Chicago Tribune*; of Nadia Mandelstam in *Chicago Tribune*; poems in *Encounter,* and "A Writers Thoughts about Time" and "Anniversary Poem" *Quarry* No. 4 [1974]: 62–66).

Article on Pound in *Paideuma,* I. 2, Orono, Maine (partly reprinted in *University of Chicago Magazine*) reprinted and translated into Italian by Alfredo Rizzardi; *Pound*, Rizzoli.

NOVEL

Other Men's Daughters. New York: Dutton; London: Hamish Hamilton; (translations: Dutch, Swedish, Japanese, Spanish, Portuguese, French).

One of year's six best works of fiction: *Time.*

Translation of parts of 1968 into Hindustani in *Quadambini*; and parts reprinted in English in India.

Stories reprinted in anthologies.

1975

Poems in *Exempla, Eine Tübinger Literatureitschrift.*

Review of Paul Fussell, *The Great War* in *Panorama* (*Chicago Daily News*).

Two stories translated into German and printed in *Austrian Pen* publication and read on Austrian radio.

Recipe in *John Keat's Cookbook,* University of Iowa Press.

Exchange with "Aristides" in *American Scholar.*

Review of Kundera's *Laughable Loves* (*Chicago Daily News*).

Review of V.S. Pritchett's *The Camberwell Beauty* (*Chicago Tribune*).

1976

Poem in *Critical Inquiry.*

Interview in *Chicago Review.*

Story in *Harper's* — "Ideal Address."

Essay (Princeton Faber Lecture) "Inside Narcissus," *Yale Review,* 1978.

Self-portrait for Burt Britton's collection (Random House).

Story — "Dying" in Mark Harris's anthology.

Rev. of *Come the Sweet By and By* by Eleanor Lerman. *Chicago Review* 27.4 Spring 1976.

1977

"Interview with Richard Stern," Larry Rima, *Chicago Review* 28.3 (Spring 1977): 145–148.

Reviews

"*Maxwell Street, Survival in a Bazaar. I. Berkow.*" *New York Times*, Nov. 18, 1977.
"*Lazarus.* A Malraux," *Chicago Tribune*, Sept. 18, 1977.

Articles

"Bellow's Gift," *New York Times Magazine*, Nov. 1976 on Bellow, in *Chicago Sun-Times* and on radio, television, and in foreign papers.
Reprinting of translation in Junkins, *Contemporary World Poetry*.

1978

Novel

Natural Shocks. New York: Coward McCann and Geoghegen; London: Sidgewick and Jackson; Swedish translation; French translation (1991).
Winner Carl Sandburg Award in Fiction.

Story

"Troubles," *Tri-Quarterly 42* (Spring 1978): 191–202 (Illinois Arts Council Award).

Essay

"Inside Narcissus," *Yale Review*, Winter (or Spring) 1978.

Review

"Rev. of *RN: The Memoirs of Richard Nixon*," *Chicago Magazine*, Aug 1978: 166.

1979

Interviews in numerous periodicals in Latin America, March 1979.
Speaker, USA Day at International Book Fair, Buenos Aires, March 14, 1979.
"Dr. Cahn's Visit," *Atlantic Monthly*, October, 1979. Tr. Into Russian for *America*, included in *Best American Stories of 1980* and in *100 Years of The Atlantic Monthly*.
Review of Mary Robison's *Days, Chicago Magazine*, August.
Review of Henry Kissinger's *White House Days, Chicago Sun-Times*, November.

1980

Book of Stories

Packages. New York: Coward McCann and Geoghegen; London: Sidgewick and Jackson.

STORIES

"Wissler Remembers," *Atlantic Monthly* (reprinted *Best American Stories of 1981*).
"Mail," *Encounter*, June 1980.
"Riordan's Fiftieth," *Chicago*.
"Lesson for the Day," *Commentary*.

JOURNAL EXCERPTS

Tri-Quarterly.

INTERVIEWS

"A Conversation with Richard Stern." Elliot Anderson and Milton Rosenberg. *Chicago Review*. Winter 1980.
"A Conversation with Richard Stern," G. Murray and M. Tapp. *Story Quarterly 10*. Winter 1980: 154–163. (Another interview with Ms. Tapp in review whose name isn't remembered here.)

ARTICLES

"Missingeria," *Georgia Review* 34.2 (Spring 1980): 422–428.
"On Donald Justice's Poetry," *Book World* (Tribune) March 9.
Reviews of Mailer's *The Executioner's Song* in *Chicago*; of Barry Hannah's *Ray* in *Book World*, November.

STORY-COMMENTARY

"Prose-Thumbing," *Shenandoah* 31.2 (Winter 1980): 99–101.

1981

Reissue of *In Any Case* as *The Chaleur Network*. London: Sidgewick and Jackson; New York: Second Chance Press.

ARTICLES

"The Invention of the Real." *Georgia Review* 35.1 (Spring 1981): 17–38.
"Roth Unbound." *Saturday Review* (June 1981): 28–29.
"American and African Winters." Printed in English and French (in Togo, Morocco and other African nations).
"Extracts from a Journal." *Tri-Quarterly* 50 (Winter 1981): 261–273.

STORY

"Packages," *Barat Review* (reprinted from book).
Translations of "Gifts" into Spanish; of "Wissler Remembers" into German.
Articles on Richard Stern: *Revista Chilena De La Literatura*; *New Statesman*.

Feb 5–Mar 31. Lectures in Rabat, Marrakech (Morocco), Freetown, Sierra Leone, Lomé, Togo; Cotenu, Benin; Libreville, Gabon; Lusaka, Zambia; Nairobi, Kenya; Butare, Rwanda. Lecture on "Reflections of the Inside-Outsider," reprinted widely in French (translation, F. Meltzer) and English. Many interviews.

1982

BOOK

The Invention of the Real. Athens: University of Georgia Press, 1982.

ARTICLE

"Reflections on Hunos, Historians, and Story-Tellers" *Shenandoah* 32.4 (1981): 55–68. Given as the Gottschalk Memorial Lecture, University of Illinois.

Letter on Current Problems in *Tri-Quarterly* symposium.

Review of Jacobo Timerman, *The Longest War, Chicago Tribune*.

Participated in conference in Rome and Venice on Italian and American literature, June and July 1982.

1983

Reviews of Langer, *Mind III*, in *Chicago Sun-Times*; of Ian Hamilton, *Robert Lowell*, in *Chicago*.

Interviews with Richard Stern in *Chicago Sun-Times* (Coburn-Froelke).

1984

FICTION

"In the Dock." *Tri-Quarterly* 60 (Spring/Summer 1984): 177–192.

Remarks on translation in *Translation* (taken from conference in Rome, June 1982).

Tribute to C. Kulshestra, *Saul Bellow Journal* vol. 3.

Contribution to *Writer's Workshop Cookbook*, ed. Brothers.

1985

REVIEWS

Hugh Hefner's First Funeral and Other True Tales of Love and Death in Chicago, by Pat Colander, Contemporary; in *Los Angeles Times*, "The Book Review," July 14.

Darlinghissima by Janet Flanner. Ed. by Natalie Danesi Murray. Random House, *Chicago Tribune*, "Book World," October.
Racehoss: Big Emma's Boy by Albert Race Sample. *Chicago Tribune*, Spring.

ARTICLE

"Lunch with a Goddess." *Chicago* (Oct, 1985: 198–201).
"A Friendship of Thirty Years." *Saul Bellow Journal* 4.2 (Summer 1985): 4–5.

1986

NOVELS

A Father Words. New York: Arbor House, 1986.
Reprint of *Other Men's Daughters*. New York: Arbor House.
Reprint of *Stitch*. New York: Arbor House.
Reprint of *Natural Shocks*. New York: Arbor House.

ORDERLY MISCELLANY

The Position of the Body. Evanston, IL: Northwestern University Press.

ARTICLES

"Chicago in Fiction" lecturer University of California Library Society.
"Country Fiddlers, City Slickers." *Formations* 2.3 (Winter, 1986): 50–54.
Tribute to Saul Bellow (on his 70th birthday) *Saul Bellow Journal*, vol. 4.
Reprint of "Lillian Hellman on Her Plays," in *Collected Interviews of Lillian Hellman* by J. Bryer (University of Mississippi).

STORIES

"Losing Color," *The Antioch Review* 44.1 (Winter 1986): 40–41.
"Removal of a Superfluity," *Stand Anthology* (Prize Winner).

REVIEWS

Rev. of *The Fatal Equilibrium* by Marshall Jevons. *Journal of Political Economy* 94.3 (June 1986): 683–84.
The Garden of Eden, by Ernest Hemingway. *Chicago Tribune*, Book World. May 1986.

INTERVIEWS

Chicago Sun-Times; Los Angeles Times; Chicago Tribune.

ARTICLE

"Penned In." *Critical Inquiry* 13.1 (Fall 1986): 1–32.

POETRY

Sequence, "Common Market," *Raccoon* (Anniversary Issue).

REVIEWS

Of *Perfume* by P. Sussman, in *Chicago*, Dec. 1986.
The Counter-Life, by P. Roth, in *Book World*, *Chicago Tribune*, Jan. 11, 1987.
Contribution to "Contemporary American Fiction" *Michigan Quarterly Review*,
    Winter 1987–88.
Japanese translation of "Chicago in Fiction," *Trends* 10/87. (Lectures in Japan:
    Tokyo; Osaka; Fukuoka; Nagoya. In China: Fudan University, Shanghai; For-
    eign StudiesUniversity, Beijing.)
"Intellectuals Then and Now," Proceeding of the *Congreso Internacional de Int-
    electuals y Aristas*, Valencia, Spain, June 15–20, 1987.

1988

ESSAYS

"American Poetry, 1957–87," *World and I*, March 1988.
"On the Reissue of *Golk*," in *Agni*, Spring 1988.
"On Feeling 'This Is the Way It Was'" *Salmagundi* No. 78–79 (Spring-Summer
    1988): 220–227.
"Penned in (Some Members of the Congress) Part II." *Critical Inquiry* (Summer
    1988): 860–891.
Reprint of "Dr. Cahn's Visit" in *Full Measure, Modern Short Stories On Aging*,
    edited by Dorothy Sennet, Graywolf Press.
Reviews of *Black Box* by Amos Oz, *Book World*, *Chicago Tribune*, May 8, 1988, and
    Whistlejacket, by John Hawkes, July 17, 1988.

SHORT STORIES

"Zhoof," *Formations*, Autumn, 1988.
"La Pourriture Noble," *Chicago Times*, Nov-Dec 1988.
"In Return," *Encounter* (July/Aug 1988): 10–14.

1989

BOOKS

Noble Rot: Stories 1949–88. New York: Grove Press, 1989.

Reprint of *Golk* with intro by Bernard Rogers. Chicago: Phoenix Books.
Portuguese translation of *Other Men's Daughters*: Editora Globo. Rio di Janeiro, 1988.
French translation of *Other Men's Daughters, Les Filles Des Autres,* Presse de la Renaissance, Paris, 1988.
Lectures, readings, seminars, in Australia. Sydney, MacQuarie, and Wollongong Universities; National Library (Canberra); New South Wales Library (Sydney); Harold Park (famous Sydney pub); Carnevale (multicultural festival), Sept. 1988.
Reprint of "Dr. Cahn's Visit," in *Intravenous Lives: Contemporary Fiction About Medicine.* New York: St Martin's Press, 1990. Ed. John Mukand: 103–108.
"When Pen Meets Sword," Op-ed page, *Los Angeles Times.* Feb. 21, 1989. (On Rushdie's *Satanic Verses.*)

1990

Review of Timothy Lewontin's *Parson's Mill. Chicago Tribune.*
Review of Rockwell Gray's *Ortega Y Gasset. Modern Philology.*
Short Stories
"In a Word, Trowbridge," *Antioch Review.*
"The Beautiful Widow and the Bakery Girl," *Literary Outakes.* Ed. Larry Dark. New York: Ballantine Books, 1992: 168–171.
"Interview of RGS by G.E. Murray." *The American Story: The Best of Story Quarterly.* Eds. Brashler, Pritchard, Williams. New York: Cane Hill Press, 1990: 215–228.
Reprint of "Noble Rot," in *Chicago Works.* The Morton Press.

ESSAYS

"Old Humanists and New," *Encounter.* October, 1990.
"Gaps 1," *Bostonia.* (April 1991).

1991

Reprint of *A Father's Words.* Chicago: Phoenix Books.
Chocs Naturels. Presse de la Renaissance. Paris.
Interview by Roger O'Flaherty, *Chicago Sun-Times.* Feb. 7, 1990.

POEM

"Who Knows," *Garnet* Vol. 100 (Virginia): 22.
"Richard Stern in Conversation about *Pound* with David Brooks," *Phoenix Review.* Canberra, Spring/Summer 1990. 47–57.

FICTION

"A Share of Nowheresville," *Chicago Tribune Magazine,* May 5, 1991.

Essays

"Afternoons with the Grand Jacques" or "Derridiary," *London Review of Books*, August 15, 1991.
"Samuel Beckett." *Salmagundi* No. 90–91 (Spring/Summer 1991): 179–190.

Op-Ed

"The Actions of an Innocent Person," *Chicago Tribune.* Oct. 15, 1991.

1992

Short Stories

"The Illegibility of This World," *Commentary* 93.2 (Feb, 1992): 42–48.
"Obie's Troubles," *Antioch Review* 49.4 (Autumn 1991): 497–513.
"Del Plunko Performs," *Paris Review.* Winter 1992.
"The Degredation of Tenderness," *Bostonia.* Summer 1992.
"The Anaximander Fragment," *Forward* 31 July 1992: A9.
Reviews of Thomas Bernhard, *The Loser* (Knopf), *Franz Kafka, Representative Man,* W.S. Merwin, *The Lost Upland,* all in *Chicago Tribune, Book World.*
Review of *The Letters of Albert Schweitzer, Chicago Tribune Book World.* September 1992.

Book

Shares and Other Fictions. Harrison, NY: Delphinium Books, 1992 (distributed by Simon and Schuster).

Articles

"On Wimbledon," *Chicago Tribune.* June 27, 1992.

Op-Ed

"On Perot & the Deficit," *Los Angeles Times.* October 28, 1992.
German translation of stories, *Charleys Vermachtniss* (Residenz Verlag). 1992.

1993

Reprint of *Noble Rot: Stories 1949–88.* Chicago: Another Chicago Press.
One Person and Another. On Writers and Writing. Dallas: Baskerville Publishers Ltd.

ESSAYS

"Chicago. Mostly a Love Letter." *Swissair Gazette* (March): 16–20.
"Words About Hugh," in *There Is Always More in the Head,* ed. Caroll Terell. Orono, Maine: North Height Press.
"Tennis, Anyone?" *Commentary* vol. 95, no. 4 (April 1993): 48–50.
"Dipping Into Fifty Years. A Few Memories of Donald Justice," in *Donald Justice,* ed. William Logan and Dana Gioia.
"Janet Lewis." *The Virginia Quarterly Review* 69.3 (1993): 532–543.
Review of Jane Jacobs, *Systems of Survival, Chicago Tribune.*
Review of Austin Wright, *Tony and Susan, Chicago Sun-Times Book Week.*
Review of C. Moorehead, *Bertrand Russell, A Life. ChicagoTribune.*
Review of Henry James, *2 Volumes of Travel Writings, Chicago Tribune.*

BOOK ON STERN

Schiffer, James. *Richard Stern.* New York: Twayne. Includes an interview.

INTERVIEWS

South Carolina Quarterly 25.2 (Spring 1993): 83. (by J. Schiffer).
Book Press (Buffalo). Spring '93 (by Mark Schechner).
Chicago Maroon. Sept. 15, 1993 (by Ben Howe).

1994

Review of Henry Roth, *Mercy of a Small Stream, Chicago Tribune.* February 6, 1994.
Review of John Updike, *Brazil, New Republic.* February 1994.
Review of *The Correspondence of Walter Benjamin.* Edited by T. Adorno and G. Schloem, *Books Chicago Tribune.* July 17, 1994.

INTERVIEW

In *Bulgarian Studies in Literature,* Sofia (by Prof. Milena Kirova).

LIBRETTO

Golk. Composer: John Eaton for 1996 production.
Reprint (unauthorized adaptation) of "Tennis, Anyone?" in *Racquet,* June 15.
Michael Collins, "Richard Stern," *Contemporary Biography.* June 1994.

1995

BOOK

A Sistermony. New York: Donald I. Fine Inc. Heartland Prize, Nonfiction, 1995.

SHORT STORY

"Almonds," *Tri-Quarterly*. June 1995.

ESSAYS

"Ralph Ellison," *Antioch Review*, Spring 1995. (Reprinted in *Callaloo*, Spring 1995.)
"On Paul, Life, and the Workshop," in *An Absolute Vision*, edited by Huahling Engle (forthcoming).
"Warriors of the Open." *The New Leader* Oct. 9–23, 1995: 10–11.
"A Few Works from One Who's Written a Few Too Many," in *Words To Live By*, edited by K. and L. Katz, Two Rivers Press (forthcoming).
"The Poetry Club: Janet Lewis." *An Unsentimental Education*. Ed. Molly McQuade. Chicago: University of Chicago Press, 1995.
"Studs Terkel." *Antioch Review* 53.4 (Fall 1995): 454–464.
A tribute to Regenstein Library; a eulogy for John Wallace in the *University of Chicago Chronicle*.
Speech on receiving Heartland Award for Best Nonfiction book of Year (*Sistermony*).

REVIEWS

Journals of Isaac Babel, ed. Avins (Yale University Press).
Hannah Arendt and Martin Heidegger, ed. Ettinger (Yale University Press).
Edward Hopper by Gail Levin (Knopf).
(All in *Book Week, Chicago Tribune*.)

POEM

"The Hole," *Poetry* Vol. CLXVII No. 6 (March, 1996): 331.

1996

The following pieces of fiction were in revised version part of *Pacific Tremors*. Those starred (*) were not included in the final version of the novel:

"Down Under," *Antioch Review* 54.1 (Winter 1996): 40–45.*
"Oscar and Hypatia," *Marlboro Review* No. 1 (Winter/Spring 1996): 91–103*
"From Marcia to Hypatia," "Melanie and Spear," *Southwest Review* 81.2 (Spring 1996): 175–189.
"In and Out of the Pacific," *Iowa Review*.

1997 (or 1998)

"To Work," *Agni*.
"Audit," *Paris Review* No. 140 (1997): 175–192.

"California: An Anthology." *Tri-Quarterly.*
"Sylvan and Agnes," *On The Make* 1 (1997): 87–96.*
"Keneret: After Surgery." *The Antioch Review* 56.4 (Fall 1998): 438–447.
"Downsized," *Antioch Review* 55.4 (1997): 426–449.
The following appeared in Summer 1999:
"Wool," *Yale Review* 87.3 (July 1999): 130–141.

ESSAYS

"Remembering Pound," *Sewanee Review* No. 1 (Winter 1998): 132–139.
"A Few Things American Fiction Says." *Southwest Review* 82.2 (1997): 243–254.

INTERVIEW

Business Japan.

REPRINT

A Sistermony, Primus (Penguin) paperback.

REVIEWS

House Arrest, by Mary Morris.
The Other Life, by Paul Theroux.
The Insult, by Rupert Thompson.
A Few Things, essays by David Foster Wallace.
The Collected Stories of Bernard Malamud, by Malamud.
The Man on the Flying Trapeze, The Life and Times of W.C. Fields, by Simon Louvish.
(All in *Book Week, Chicago Tribune.*)
Aria: "From Van Meegeren to Van Blederen," *Republic of Letters.*
Reprints: "Borges on Borges," in anthology edited by Richard Burgin.

1999/2000

"Packages," in *Smokestacks and X.*
"The Illegibility of This World," in anthology *The Workshop*. Ed. Tom Grimes.
New York: Hyperion, 1999: 103–119.
"Grandpa." *Southwest Review* 84.3 (1999): 423–439.

POEM

"To Go with an Old Necklace." *Poetry* (July 2000): 209.

INTERVIEW

James Atlas, "The Art of Richard Stern," in *Chicago Review* (Fall-Winter 1999).

Essay

"Where the Chips Fall." *Republic of Letters* No. 8 (Winter 2000): 2–3.
"With Auden," *Antioch Review* 58.4 (Fall 2000): 389–397. To be reprinted in Auden anthology edited by David Izzo.
On "Edward Levi," *Edward Levi*, University of Chicago Law School.

Reviews

Memoirs by Norman Podhoretz and Thomas Sowell. *Book Week*, August 2000.
Quarrels and Quandaries, by Cynthia Ozick. *Book Week*, September 2000.
The Golden Age, by Gore Vidal, *Book Week*, September 2000.
From September 1999 to June 2000: Fellow at Center for Advanced Studies in the Behavioral Sciences (Stanford, California) and circulated — among other responses to seminar papers — "On the Social Sciences" and "On Technology and Education," to be included (see below) in orderly miscellany. Various biographical and critical accounts of self and work in such reference books as *Contemporary Authors and Encyclopedia Britannica*.

Novel

Pacific Tremors, published in September 2001 by Triquarterly Books, Northwestern University Press.

Essays

What Is What Was? Feb. 11, 2001.
Golk, the opera was performed again in December 2000 (three performances).
Working on novel(s) under provisional title(s) *Dortmund* and *Goldman*.
"An Old Writer Looks at Himself," *New York Times* (in "Writers on Writing" series: Feb. 12, 2001).

Index